CW01498997

Contents

Personality and Environment

Personality and Environment

Assessment of Human Adaptation

Edited by

P. J. HETTEMA
Tilburg University

JOHN WILEY & SONS
Chichester · New York · Brisbane · Toronto · Singapore

Other Wiley Editorial Offices

John Wiley & Sons, Inc., 605 Third Avenue,
New York, NY 10158–0012, USA

Jacaranda Wiley Ltd, G.P.O. Box 859, Brisbane,
Queensland 4001, Australia

John Wiley & Sons (Canada) Ltd, 22 Worcester Road,
Rexdale, Ontario M9W 1L1, Canada

John Wiley & Sons (SEA) Pte Ltd, 37 Jalan Pemimpin 05-04,
Block B, Union Industrial Building, Singapore 2057

Library of Congress Cataloging-in-Publication Data:

Personality and environment: assessment of human adaptation/edited
by P. J. Hettema.
    p. cm.
    Includes bibliographical references.
    ISBN 0 471 92406 7
    1. Personality and situation. 2. Adaptability (Psychology)
I. Hettema, P. J.
BF698.9.S55P46 1989
155.2'4—dc20   89-38259
                                                                                               CIP

British Library Cataloguing in Publication Data:

Personality and environment: assessment of human
    adaptation
    1. Environmental psychology
    I. Hettema, P. J. (P Joop)
    155.9

    ISBN 0 471 92406 7

Typeset by Mathematical Composition Setters Ltd
7 Ivy Street, Salisbury, Wiltshire SP1 2AY
Printed and bound in Great Britain by Courier International Ltd, Tiptree, Essex

Appendices

List of contributors

DR. G. L. VAN HECK
Tilburg University
Dept. of Psychology
P.O. Box 90153
5000 LE Tilburg Netherlands

DRS. D. P. M. HOL
Tilburg University
Dept. of Psychology
P.O. Box 90153
5000 LE Tilburg Netherlands

DR. A. J. J. M. VINGERHOETS
Free University
Faculty of Medicine
Dept. Medical Psychology
P.O. Box 7161
1007 MC Amsterdam
The Netherlands

DRS. G. M. VAN DER MOLEN
University of Limburg
School of Medicine
Dept. Medical Psychology
P.O. Box 616
6200 MD Maastricht
The Netherlands

MR. C. BRANDT
Scorpius 36
5175 XN Loon op Zand
The Netherlands

PROF. DR. D. T. KENRICK
Arizona State University
Dept. of Psychology
Tempe, AZ 85287
USA

DRS. A. J. R. VAN DE VIJVER
Tilburg University
Dept. of Psychology
P.O. Box 90153
5000 LE Tilburg Netherlands

PROF. DR. P. J. HETTEMA
Tilburg University
Dept. of Psychology
P.O. Box 90153
5000 LE Tilburg Netherlands

Introduction

This book deals with the adaptation of individuals to everyday situations. It gives a comprehensive report of a research program designed to study cognitive, physiological as well as behavioral aspects of adaptation.

The history of the book goes back to the late 1960s when a major crisis shook up personality psychology and confused many workers in the field. The person versus the situation as the primary source of behavioral variation became a major issue, dividing personality researchers into different camps like personologists, situationists and interactionists. Since its beginning, the person–situation debate has occupied theorists, methodologists and empiricists without really coming to an end.

To me, the crisis in personality constituted a challenge that could only be answered adequately by theoretical and methodological innovation, deepening our conceptions and sharpening our tools. Rather than adding one or two personality variables to the large number existing already, I developed a new personality model, emphasizing the adaptive processes, occurring at the interface between the person and the situation. The open-systems adaptation model was first presented in 1979 in a book entitled *Personality and adaptation*.

Reviews of the book were generally favorable. Qualified as 'a serious attempt to reconceptualize some of the most fundamental problems in contemporary personality theory' (Averill, 1981); '... producing a strongly formalized conception of personality, avoiding many flaws of the older personality models' (Günther, 1982); and '... a really new theory on human functioning in concrete situations' (Bonarius, 1981), the book was hoped to '... sign the beginning of a new era of vigorous theorizing in personality psychology' (Buss, 1982).

After the appearance of the book, we set out to operationalize the major concepts of the model and design tests for its fruitfulness. This endeavor rapidly turned out to be a journey into the unknown with fascinating views of human personality, but also with many pitfalls and dangers along the wayside. The present volume is the report of that journey. Its broader aim is to offer a framework for the study of human adaptation in daily-life conditions. To materialize this purpose, adaptation is studied along three major paths: conceptual, methodological and empirical.

Conceptually, the open-systems adaptation model in its present shape is explained in detail. Its position in the context of current personality theory is indicated in a joint chapter with Douglas T. Kenrick (Arizona State University) on biosocial interaction and individual adaptation. Personality and environment are conceptualized, emphasizing the relations between the two. Person–environment relations are postulated at three different levels: the cognitive level, the control level and the sensorimotor level.

Methodologically, several classical procedures needed rethinking to accommodate the open-systems adaptation model. The multilevel approach of the model is reflected in the choice of different media to represent situations and different measurement modes to study behavior. Special attention has been devoted to the issues of reliability and validity of the measures developed. As a result specific models are presented to study behavioral coherence and to predict behavior in the context of the new model.

Empirically, the development of measures of adaptation at each level is described in detail. Data are presented concerning the reliability and validity of the measures, and, finally, evidence is provided with respect to the predictive validity of the model as a whole.

Strategically, the research program was designed to develop measures and study adaptation separately at each of the three levels of the person–environment system. Over the years, the three program lines gradually converged to meet in the final study reported in this book. In view of the many uncertainties existing at the onset of the program, we have attempted to clarify some major basic issues before starting with the development of measuring instruments. Such issues include the choice of media and modes as well as the identification of environmental and behavioral elements.

The capacity of modes to yield empirical definitions has been investigated in preliminary studies for each of the three levels of the model. For the identification of environmental elements a comprehensive taxonomy of situations has been developed, defining single situations as well as connections among situations. The situation taxonomy was used subsequently as a basis for stimulus presentation via questionnaires, films and behavior settings.

A behavior taxonomy was developed to classify responses in the context of the model. Behavior has been studied with the aid of self-reports, physiological reactions and observations. Based on the results of the studies mentioned, instruments were constructed for assessment at each of the three levels separately. Those instruments include a new type of personality inventory, the

SRS-questionnaire, a situation film technique with physiological recording and standardized settings for role playing and behavior observation.

The studies outlined have been arranged in 15 chapters, systematically ordered in five parts. Part I gives a theoretical and methodological introduction. Parts II, III and IV are concerned with the study of adaptation at different levels, i.e. the cognitive-symbolic level (II), the control level (III) and the sensorimotor–operational level (IV). Part V deals with the model as a whole, integrating the findings of the earlier parts.

Obviously, a research program as reported in this volume can only be the result of a cooperative effort. The successful completion of the program is due first and foremost to the project group at Tilburg University. Senior research associate Guus L. Van Heck has made an invaluable contribution with the development of the situation taxonomy, acting as a cornerstone throughout the program. Research associate Ad J. Vingerhoets (presently at the Free University of Amsterdam) has made a major contribution in physiological measurement, and research associate Dorien P. Hol has contributed considerably with her work in behavior assessment. Major support to the program was given by research associates Fons J. van de Vijver in methodology and Margo van der Molen (now at the University of Limburg) in psychophysiology. I am especially grateful to Douglas T. Kenrick (Arizona State University) for his willingness to participate and his invaluable contribution in establishing the theoretical position of the model.

The program has profited considerably from the methodological advice and support from Bo J. van den Bogaart, Emanuel J. Bijnen, Marcel A. Croon, Peter J. Flohr, Cees van de Vleuten and Sjaak Wijnen. Special acknowledgement is due to the film crew, particularly Cor Brandt (director), Henk Breimer (producer), Michael Tomlinson (camera) and Jacques Huynk (scripts).

Critical comments to parts of the program or earlier drafts of the manuscript have been given by Han Bonarius, Lee J. Cronbach, Lewis R. Goldberg, Sarah E. Hampson, Willem K. Hofstee, Gustav Jahoda, Howard Leventhal, David Rosenhan, John B. Rijsman and Richard E. Snow. Their contributions are gratefully acknowledged.

The manuscript was prepared typographically by Marloes Ypelaar, Jannie van Baardwijk, Arda van de Velden and Francine van Remunt.

Major financial support for the research program has been obtained from two sources: grant no 58–61 from the Netherlands Organization for Scientific Research (NWO) and Tilburg University.

JOOP HETTEMA

Part I

Theoretical and methodological introduction

1

Biosocial interaction and individual adaptation

JOOP HETTEMA

and

DOUGLAS T. KENRICK

THE CRISIS IN PERSONALITY PSYCHOLOGY

The growth of science is much less regular and monotonic than we once assumed. Rather than a systematic accumulation of knowledge, science shows all the features of an organic development: accelerations and standstills, deviations and progressions, regression and crisis. A major crisis in personality psychology developed during the 1960s, when personality researchers came to realize that their empirical results failed to redeem the promises raised by carefully constructed theoretical models and sophisticated methodology. A much-cited example is the study of Kogan and Wallach (1964) who hardly found any relationship between different personality traits and the amount of risk persons are willing to take in practical decision making situations. In that study the nature of the situation turned out to be a much better predictor of behavior than the personality traits studied.

Later review articles seemed to cast serious doubt on the generality of trait measures and suggested a large (but usually unknown) influence of situation variables (Hunt, 1965; Petersen, 1965). Earlier, Endler, Hunt, and Rosenstein (1962) had studied the effects of traits, situations and response modes separately. Their results seemed to be devastating for classical personality psychology. Working with a 'Stimulus–Response' questionnaire, these authors

Personality and Environment: Assessment of Human Adaptation
Edited by P. J. Hettema. ©1989 John Wiley & Sons Ltd

tried to establish the extent to which anxiety depends on specific situations and response modes (like heart beat acceleration, respiration and nausea). A reanalysis of their data by Gleser, Cronbach, and Rajaratnam (1965) suggested that the general trait of anxiety explained only 6% of the total variance, leaving the lions' share for the effect of situations, response modes and various interactions. Later, a detailed survey of 53 different studies in this area by Sarason, Smith, and Diener (1975) argued that individual differences generally account for only small proportions (about 9%) of the total variance.

The milestone critique was Mischel's (1968) *Personality and Assessment.* Reviewing a host of empirical studies, Mischel noted that behaviors that seemed to reflect a trait in one situation were often poorly connected with behaviors reflecting the same trait in a different situation. On the basis of those results he raised serious questions about the practical utility of personality measures:

> 'In sum, the data reviewed on the utility of psychometrically measured traits, as well as psychodynamic inferences about states and traits, show that responses have not served very usefully as indirect signs of internal predispositions ... These conclusions for personality measures apply, on the whole, to diverse content areas including the prediction of college achievement, job and professional success, treatment outcomes, rehospitalization for psychiatric patients, parole violations for delinquent children, and so on. In light of these findings it is not surprising that large-scale applied efforts to predict behavior from personality inferences have been strikingly and consistently unsuccessful' (Mischel, 1968, pp. 145–146).

Mischel went on to look for the causes of the failure. Rather than attributing the problems to methodological flaws, he directed his main attack at the theoretical framework underlying classical personality assessment. He was especially critical of 'global personality dispositions': Broad behavioral dispositions that manifest themselves across time and different conditions. In Mischel's view, the case for global dispositions was very weak, since individual behavior becomes inconsistent as soon as there is even a slight change in the situation. He therefore advocated a social behaviorist approach that emphasized the study of situational determinants of behavior. Mischel's attack called forth many reactions (Alker, 1972; Block, 1977; Epstein, 1977; Hogan, De Soto and Solano, 1977; Stagner, 1976). His criticisms were taken not only as an attack on the prevailing personality paradigm, but also as an invitation to abandon the area of personality psychology altogether.

Those early criticisms of personality seem to have overrated the case in some ways. As one of us recently noted, the research generated by the person–situation debate has produced ample evidence that personality traits do exist (Kenrick and Funder, 1988). However, the data hardly suggest that the situationist attack was unjustified, and that traditional personologists are justified in ignoring the criticism. Instead, it is necessary to understand how personality traits and situational pressures interact with one another. Although the field has made some progress in understanding these 'person–environment' interactions (Endler and Magnusson, 1976a; Snyder and Ickes, 1985) there has been little progress in applying the interactionist approach to personality assessment technology, or in providing a theoretical model that will encompass environments as well as traits as they were traditionally conceived.

ATTEMPTED SOLUTIONS

In attempting to resolve the person–situation debate, investigators have taken three general paths. Some investigators have proposed more sophisticated *prediction models* to directly increase the validity of traditional personality measures. Others have *redefined traits* and emphasized different aspects of test behavior. And still others have tried to replace the *personality paradigm* with models that deemphasize traits as basic units.

Solution 1: Improving the validity of trait measurement

The first approach to solving the person–situation debate has focused on the difficulties of finding generality, consistency and stability with traditional measurement approaches. The assumption of this approach is that measurement flaws rather than the traits *per se* are responsible for the problems. For instance, a lack of generality could be due to factors inherent in the specific test procedure being used. Campbell and Fiske's (1959) classic article on multitrait multimethod matrices demonstrated how large portions of the test variance often attributed to personality traits could be due to the specific method used to measure the traits. For instance, a self-report measure of 'friendliness' could correlate more highly with another self-report of 'aggression' than with a behavioral measure of friendliness.

Artificial test variance is 'method-centered' rather than 'trait-centered'. One methodological artifact involved in almost any personality test is response style, which includes extremeness tendency, acquiescence, and social desirability. Since stylistic variance is usually not assumed to contribute to validity, prediction can be improved by using stylistic measures as *suppressors* of the unwanted variance (e.g., Dicken, 1963; Goldberg, Rorer, and Greene, 1970). However, the empirical effectiveness for suppressor variables in predicting socially relevant criteria is not impressive (cf. Wiggins, 1980).

An alternative strategy to improve validity is based on the assumption that trait inconsistency is not a general phenomenon but is restricted to a subgroup of the population. This approach assumes that traits are not necessarily expressed in overt behavior in the same way by different individuals. Frederiksen and Melville (1954), for instance, assumed that the presence of one trait could interfere with the expression of another trait. For instance, two people might be similar in academic interests, but might differ in expressing those interests because of differences in compulsiveness. The second variable, compulsiveness, is called a *moderator* variable. Once identified, it might be useful in improving prediction. Ghiselli (1960) used an empirical approach to identify a number of moderator variables. Further research showed, however, that the moderators were highly specific not only to the particular predictor used but also to the criterion that had to be predicted.

Bem and Allen (1974) studied individual variations with respect to consistency on specific traits. They asked each subject in their study to indicate how consistent he or she would be on friendliness or conscientiousness. Their results partly confirmed the hypothesis that people who said they were more consistent on a given trait would also be more predictable. Kenrick and Stringfield (1980) replicated the Bem and Allen study and extended it to a broader domain of traits by having each subject pick his or her most consistent dimensions from a list based on Cattell's 16 P.F. In addition, they added a new element by introducing 'observability' ratings in which subjects indicated whether or not each trait would be publicly visible to other people. They obtained the best predictions for consistent and highly observable subjects (see also Amelang and Borkenau, 1982; Cheek, 1982). Although this version of the moderator approach has shown some promise, there are also disadvantages (cf. Kenrick and Dantchik, 1983; Rushton, Jackson, and Paunonen, 1981). In addition to limiting predictions on a given trait to only a subset of the population, it is not embedded in a more general theoretical framework.

A third strategy to improve validity focuses on enhancing stability of trait measures by using a large number of measures of the same trait, and *aggregating* the results into one single score. Epstein (1979, 1980) demonstrated that when measures of behavior are averaged over an increasing number of events, stability coefficients increased from around 0.20 (from one day to the next) to 0.70 and higher (from one week to the next). On the basis of these findings Epstein (1979) claimed that most people's behavior can be predicted correctly much of the time. However, stability of behavior is not the same as transsituational consistency. Stability studies attempt to generalize over time, not over situations, whereas consistency studies are meant to generalize over situations, not over time. As can be explained with the aid of generalizability formulas (cf. Cronbach, Gleser, Nanda, and Rajaratnam, 1972) the two are far from identical and may produce very different results. Mischel and Peake (1982) therefore maintain that consistency of observational personality measures is generally low from one situation to the next, and they continue to debate with Epstein over the extent to which aggregate predictions are admissable evidence (Epstein, 1983).

Summarizing, different attempts to increase validity by using more sophisticated prediction models have not provided a definite solution for the crisis in personality psychology. Successful attempts to increase the over-all validity of personality measures have been reported with suppressor, moderator and aggregation strategies but a debate continues about the extent to which the moderator findings are replicable (Kenrick and Braver, 1982; Rushton, Jackson, and Paunonen, 1981; Zuckerman, Koestner, Deboy, Garcia, Marbsca and Sartoris, 1988), and whether the aggregation strategy completely solves the problems raised by critics of the classical approach to personality.

Solution 2: Redefining traits

Attempts to improve the validity of trait measures have been mainly inspired by psychometric considerations, emphasizing formal aspects of the prediction model rather than content of either predictors or criteria. Other investigators attempted to modify the classical trait conception to meet the criticisms. Theoretically, the classical trait concept hinges on stimulus equivalence as well as response equivalence. Thus, for instance, Allport (1937, p.295) has defined a trait as 'a generalized and focalized neuropsychic system (peculiar to the individual) with the capacity to render many stimuli functionally equivalent and to initiate and guide consistent (equivalent) forms of adaptive and expressive behavior'. Redefinitions of the trait model have challenged the assumptions of both stimulus and response equivalence.

Situation specificity

Already in 1949 Coutu advocated the study of 'tinsits' (tendencies-in-situations) as the object of personality researchers. The classical example of this approach to trait measurement has become the S–R questionnaire (Endler, Hunt, and Rosenstein, 1962). In the S–R questionnaire the requirement of item homogeneity is abolished and any conclusion concerning an individual's status on a particular trait is restricted to specific situations.

To facilitate more general predictions, Hettema (1967) proposed the use of a representative sample of situations from a specific domain. This procedure would allow the investigator to draw conclusions beyond single situations and to indicate precisely the degree of generality of his conclusions. Obviously this approach would require a well-defined taxonomy of situations and situation domains. Thus far, S–R questionnaires have been elaborated and tested, but validity results have been far from unequivocal (cf. Furnham and Jaspars, 1983; Knudson and Golding, 1974; Mellstrom, Zuckerman, and Cicala, 1978; Van Heck, 1981).

Studies using S–R questionnaires remind us that individual behavior is to some extent subject to constraints stemming from the specific situation. They allow for accurate estimates of the magnitude of variance components associated with traits, situations and response modes. But they have not provided us with a more profound insight in actual dynamic interactions between persons and situations, and the processes involved (cf. Magnusson, 1980; Patterson and Cobb, 1973; Raush, Barry, Hertel and Swain, 1974).

Response specificity

Two men may be equally friendly with people as part of their business, but one of them may refrain from talking to a woman who sits by him on a train if he thinks she will interpret his friendliness as an advance. The trait measurement model has traditionally been based on the assumption of a definite relationship between inner traits and external behavioral expressions. However, there are many factors that can interfere with someone's behavioral expression of a trait. For instance, if a person has a particular ability, it may or may not be expressed in behavior depending on other factors like specific reinforcement expectancies (cf. Bandura, 1986; Mischel, 1973).

Learning and cognition are important factors interfering with trait expression. Wallace (1966, 1967) has pointed out that responses have to be learned and practiced before they can be expressed in overt behavior on a regular basis. Rather than a trait conception Wallace advocated an *abilities conception of personality*, emphasizing the repertoire of skills a person has at his or her disposal at any particular moment. To retain the trait concept, several authors have proposed to use trait terms as *summary labels* to indicate divergent behaviors related to the same disposition (e.g., Alston, 1975; Buss and Craik, 1983; Mischel, 1973). According to Buss and Craik (1983), the acts subsumed under a particular disposition may be very dissimilar and empirically uncorrelated, yet still refer to the same disposition.

To be able to predict particular behaviors rather than others more or less independently of the specific situation, some authors have proposed a coherent *hierarchical organization* within the individual of specific modes of responding (Lantermann, 1980; Magnusson and Endler, 1977). This approach assumes that some individuals would have a tendency to shout while angry, whereas others would smash the furniture and break dishes. This conception allows individuals to express the same trait in different ways, and requires a looser connection between traits and behavior.

Some approaches focus on intraindividual comparison and do not hope to make comparisons across different individuals. An example is Lamiell's (1981) *idiothetic approach* in which personality is described in terms of 'what the person tends to do—not in direct contrast with what others tend to do, but in direct contrast with what that person tends *not* to do, but could do' (p. 281). The idiothetic approach allows for inconsistencies at the nomothetic level, while defining personality in terms of individualized traits or attributes.

Summarizing this section, there have been several attempts to liberalize the trait measurement model in order to account for apparent inconsistencies in individual behavior. They have led to the suggestion that the same trait may be expressed in very different ways. Up to now, however, a clear conception of the rules governing trait expression is still lacking.

Solution 3: Replacing the basic personality paradigm

Thus far we have focused our attention on the trait paradigm, assuming internal tendencies and capacities of the person as the major basis of individual behavior. A more radical proposal is to replace the trait model with models that emphasize situations as the primary source of behavioral variation. An early example of *situationism* is the ecological psychology of Barker which downplays personality variables. According to this view, 'most people at church "behave church" and most people at school "behave school"' (Barker, 1963). Overt behavior in public settings is not seen primarily as behavior of individuals but rather as behavior *en masse* (Moos, 1976). Situationists see behavior as highly dependent on the situation in which it occurs and therefore do not assume broad generalization across diverse settings (cf. Mischel, Jeffery, and Patterson, 1974). Situationists seek to identify the elements in the situation that elicit behavior, and to identify the functional relationships between situations and behaviors with the aid of behavior assessment procedures (cf. Hartmann, Roper, and Bradford, 1979).

Clearly the situationist approach downplays the inner self of the behaving individual. Among social psychologists, it reflects the influence of sociological thought on concepts like 'roles', 'norms', and 'expectations', which presuppose that behavior is tailored to a frequently changing audience instead of the inner self (cf. Kenrick and Dantchik, 1983).

The *interactionist* approach to personality explains individual behavior as a joint function of the person and the situation (cf. Endler and Magnusson, 1976b; Magnusson and Endler, 1977). This approach assumes that behavior is regulated according to the principle of reciprocal causation: not only does the situation affect behavior, but behavior also affects the situation. From the interactionist point of view, no straightforward predictions of behavior can be made from mere information about either the person or the situation alone. Both elements need to be represented, as does the relationship between the two.

Thus far, interactionism consists mainly of a number of statements of principle, instead of a well-designed theory. Current interactionism is dominated by notions derived from the social cognition tradition among social psychologists. While cognition no doubt plays an important role in mediating interactions it fails to provide an exhaustive explanation of behavior (Hettema, 1979; Kenrick, Montello and MacFarlane, 1985). We propose to reexamine the roots of person × situation interactions in order to provide a broader theoretical basis. In addition to considering cognition we will address the biological as well as the social-cultural basis of personality, thus following a tradition started by personality theorists like Freud, McDougall, Allport, and Murray.

PERSON × SITUATION INTERACTIONS FROM A BIOLOGICAL PERSPECTIVE

Biological factors can contribute to a theory of individual differences at three levels of analysis (Kenrick, Montello and MacFarlane, 1985). At the ultimate level *sociobiology* considers traits as products of genetic evolution. Mechanisms of variation and selective retention are assumed to underlie stable individual differences. Applying modern evolutionary theory to social behavior, sociobiology has attempted to relate social traits to ecological pressures that existed during evolution. Processes of natural selection are held responsible for such divergent traits as aggression, altruism, revenge, conformity, love, territory drive and xenophobia (cf. Kenrick, Dantchik and MacFarlane, 1983; Wilson, 1978).

At an intermediate level of causation *behavior genetics* has studied the heritability of important portions of behavior. DeFries and Plomin (1978) selected mice for open-field activity and managed to remove any overlap between the activity level of the high and low lines after thirty generations of selective breeding. Family, twin, and adoption studies (cf. Plomin, 1986) have supported the claim that at least some of the variance in human behavior is genetically determined. In a recent study by Rushton, Fulker, Neale, Nias, and Eysenck (1986) the heritability of altruism, empathy, nurturance, aggression and assertiveness was estimated at 56% to 72% of the phenotypic variance. Studies in this area have generally found that approximately 50% of the variance is associated with additive genetic influence. Accordingly, Goldsmith (1983) has warned that theories of personality development ignore the action of genetic factors at some risk.

At the most proximate level, genes have the capacity to control behavior through the development and functioning of *physiological mechanisms* (cf. Plomin, DeFries, and McClearn, 1980). Genes control the production of proteins, which in turn exert profound influence on behavioral structures and processes via the nervous system and the production of behaviorally relevant hormones and neurotransmitters.

Are some traits heritable whereas others are not and, if so, what is the difference between the two categories of traits? Twin studies employing self-report measures have indicated that nearly all scales used suggest comparable amounts of genetic influence (cf. Plomin, 1986). This point was noted earlier by Loehlin and Nichols (1976) after completing a study in which 850 sets of twins acted as subjects. Loehlin (1982) suggested that extraversion and neuroticism can be held largely responsible for the consistently positive heritability estimate, since those traits usually appear as second-order factors in personality questionnaires, and are definitely heritable.

These findings suggest that *temperament* is involved in the heritability of personality traits. Temperament has been connected with nervous system properties for a long time, especially by Soviet psychologists (e.g. Rubinstein, 1946; Smirnov, Leontev, Rubinstein, and Teplov, 1966). More recently, Strelau (1985) has formulated a regulation theory of temperament, in which behavioral flexibility, activity and preferred stimulation are viewed as mechanisms for regulating inputs from the environment and from internal events. Thomas and Chess (1985) proposed an explicit interactional conception of temperament. Those authors use the concept of 'goodness of fit' to indicate the balance between the properties of the environment and the individual's characteristic style of behaving. Thus, extraverts seek out stimulating social situations (Furnham, 1981) that fit with their temperamental disposition. Buss, Gomes, Higgins, and Lauterbach (1978) found clear links between standard dimensions of temperament (like neuroticism and extraversion) and the use of specific sorts of manipulation tactics. In another recent study, Van Heck, Hettema, and Leidelmeijer (1990) studied person-situation mechanisms as a function of temperament. Using different current temperament scales—The Adolescent Temperament List (Feij and Kuiper, 1984), the EASI-III (Buss and Plomin, 1975), the Strelau Temperament Inventory (Strelau, 1972, 1983) and the Temperament Traits Inventory (Gorynska and Strelau, 1979)—they identified several associations. For instance, emotional subjects were more physically and mentally active than non-emotional subjects. Fear and anger had different patterns: fearful subjects tended to have others act on their behalf, whereas angry subjects tended to exert direct control over the environment. Subjects scoring high on strength of excitation preferred physical activity and direct action, whereas subjects with high scores on strength of inhibition were not very active physically.

Findings of this type reflect *Genotype-environment interactions* (Plomin, 1986): differential effects of environments on individuals of different genotypes. Plomin, DeFries, and Loehlin (1977) proposed three different types of genotype-environment correlation. *Passive* interactions occur when a person's environment fits with the genetic predisposition because his parents (who share the same genes) also control the environment. For instance, intellectual parents provide not only genes for their child, but also a well-stocked bookshelf. *Reactive* interactions occur when the environment responds differently to people who have different genotypes. Young aggressive males are more likely to be picked out for training in aggressive sports, for instance. *Active* interactions occur when individuals seek environments to match their genotypes, as when a shy child chooses a career as a librarian.

Summarizing this section, person × situation interactions are a partial function of biological preprogramming. From a biological perspective, interactions may be fruitfully studied from a long-term perspective, emphasizing enduring characteristics of the person, but also from a short-term perspective, stressing immediate reactions to actual situations. In particular, temperament is a highly heritable aspect of personality that provides a basis for studying interactions from a biological perspective. Recent studies of temperament have suggested several different types of genotype-environment interactions. Those interactions involve different preferences for environments as well as different tactical manipulations to improve the fit between person and environment.

PERSON × SITUATION INTERACTIONS FROM A SOCIAL-LEARNING PERSPECTIVE

In addition to biological factors, the environment in which a person is raised exerts a major influence on his personality. From a learning perspective the environment is conceptualized in terms of *discriminative stimuli* and *reinforcing stimuli* that guide behavior. Learning processes contribute to personality development in a gradual and systematic way. Repetition and practice serve to establish *habits* in the learner that affect his subsequent behavior in the same environmental conditions.

Direct reinforcement has a powerful influence on behavior but people also learn a great deal without any direct rewards by *observing* the consequences of other people's diverse behaviors. Social learning has been emphasized by Rotter (1954) and Bandura (1969, 1986), as a reaction against shortcomings in earlier learning theories. S–R theories were unable to explain the acquisition of novel complex response patterns without practice. Neither did they pay much attention to cognitive functions in learning or the social context in which it occurs.

The processes described by social learning theorists leave behind products in the individual that are the basis for subsequent behavior. Mischel (1973) argued that learning experiences lead to individual differences in cognition that, in turn, guide behavior. According to Mischel, people are confronted with a flood of potential stimuli in any particular environment. These stimuli must be selected, perceived, processed and interpreted before they have any effect on behavior. Individuals can be characterized by differences in:

1. *Competencies* to construct diverse behaviors under appropriate conditions.
2. *Encoding and categorization* of situations.
3. *Outcome expectancies*.
4. *Subjective values* of such outcomes.
5. *Self-regulatory systems and plans* for guiding behavior.

Thus, behavior is seen as the end product of a sequence of cognitive transformations. Bandura's social learning approach focuses on the way that experiences lead to differences in perceived self-efficacy (cf. Bandura, 1986). These expectancies influence performance, persistence at tasks, experience of stress, and so on.

Cantor and Kihlstrom (1987) take a similar approach, focusing on *social intelligence*, defined as 'declarative and procedural expertise for working on the tasks of social life in which social goals are especially salient' (p. 71). Declarative knowledge refers to individuals' static concepts about other people, social situations, and themselves, which help them to make sense of social events. Procedural knowledge involves dynamic processes such as forming impressions of people, making attributions about the causes of events and predicting the likely events in a social situation. At a more complex level, strategies (Cantor and Kihlstrom, 1987), scripts (Schank and Abelson, 1977), and personal projects (Little, 1983) involve long-term sequences of contingency/behavior relationships. Cantor and Kihlstrom (1987, p.175) define *strategies* as 'sets of cognitive processes that link a person's goals to his or her subsequent behavior in a life task situation... The strategy involves the ways in which the person interprets the "problem" and plans a "solution" so as to be consistent with his or her prevalent goals in that "task" '.

From a social-learning perspective then, person × situation interactions primarily refer to cognitive transformations of life environments. Interactions may be based on long-term goals or on intentions emerging in a specific situation. The declarative and procedural knowledge required for the attainment of goals is summarized in behavioral strategies to guide and regulate consistent forms of goal-directed behavior.

THE BIOSOCIAL INTERACTION MODEL

By themselves the biological and social approaches to personality can only offer partial answers to the questions asked. Since personality psychology is concerned with the whole organism, solutions that focus only on temperament, only on learning, or only on cognition are not acceptable. This is especially true to the extent that biological and social factors interact in non-additive ways. Elsewhere, one of us has presented a framework for considering interactions between genes, overt behavior, cognition, and the environment, emphasizing the contributions from each perspective. According to the biosocial interactionist model (Kenrick, 1987; Kenrick, Montello, and MacFarlane, 1985), environmental events (the focus of traditional learning models), cognitive interpretations (the concern of more recent social learning models), and physiological predispositions (the mainstay of the biological model), are all necessary, but not sufficient, as explanations of individual differences.

Consider the trait of depression. A simple biological model would explain depression in physiological terms, noting that depressives have abnormally low blood flow through their brain during depressive periods, abnormal EEG patterns during sleep, and so on (Andreasen, 1984). Learning theorists have explained depression as due to learned helplessness or to reinforcement patterns in which other people reward depressive comments with attention and reassurance in the short term (Coyne, 1976; Strack and Coyne, 1983), while they avoid contact with the depressed person over the long term (Gotlib and Robinson, 1982; Strack and Coyne, 1983). More recent social learning approaches have commonly adopted an attributional model of depression which assumes that depressives take personal responsibility for negative events in their lives, and deny responsibility for positive events (Abramson, Seligman and Teasdale, 1978). Figure 1 indicates how these different sorts of processes might interact with one another.

According to the interactionist model, a person will not become depressed unless he or she has an unpleasant experience of a particular sort (like a serious argument with their spouse or a new person in their house). However, not everyone who has an argument with his or her spouse or who takes on a new housemate becomes clinically depressed. Unless a person devotes cognitive

D	=	E	x	C	x	O
DEPRESSIVE RESPONSE		**ENVIRONMENTAL EVENTS**		**COGNITIVE APPRAISAL**		**ORGANISMIC FACTORS**
(LIKELIHOOD)		PERSONAL		IMMEDIATE		GENETIC
		Repeated failures		Reminders of anything in E ←		Threshold for conservation/withdrawal response
		Fatiguing demands				
		Separation from a loved one				
		ECOLOGICAL		LONG TERM		ACUTE
		Resource availability		Expectancies for future success or failure		Physical illness
		Population density				
		Climate		Attributions about past success or failure		Norepinephrine depletion as a result of previous stress
		No. of relatives nearby				
		Social position				

Figure 1 A biosocial interactionist model of depression. Environment events, cognitive appraisal, and physiological factors interact to determine whether someone will become depressed or not. Note that a value of zero for any of the three columns means that a person will not become depressed. This implies that environment, cognition, and biology are all *necessary*, but none is *sufficient* (from Kenrick, Montello and MacFarlane, 1985)

attention to that unpleasant experience, it will not bother him or her. On the other hand, if the person mentally rehearses the argument, recalling evidence that their own faults have always broken up previous relationships, tells themselves that he or she will never be able to get along with others, and convinces themselves that their spouse is probably going to leave, then the event will be more likely to lead to depression. However, even a series of negative events that an individual accepts blame for may not lead to depression if that individual has a high physiological threshold for such a response. Antisocial individuals are very unlikely to experience depression under any circumstances, while some individuals experience depression at the drop of an unkind word. Furthermore, even individuals who are physiologically prone to depression can weather negative events if they take drugs that block norepine-phrine depletion in their bodies.

The interactionist model assumes that environmental events, cognitions, and physiological predispositions cannot be completely separated from one another. Consider the differences between males and females in psychopath-ology. Males are overrepresented in categories like sexual deviations and antisocial personality disorders, females are overrepresented in depression and phobic anxiety disorders. Some of those differences may be due directly to physiological differences between the sexes. The fact that males produce more testosterone, for instance, is probably related to their over zealous sexuality and to their low threshold for aggressive behaviors (Kenrick, 1987). However, small initial differences in predisposition may lead males and females to choose life experiences that exaggerate the differences (males are more likely to enter the military, and to play aggressive sports like wrestling, for instance).

Cognitions are also not independent of physiological differences between us. A depressed mood causes even normally non-depressed individuals to process social information in a more negative light (e.g. Forgas, Bower, and Krantz, 1984). If those negative thoughts contribute to later depression and to behaviors that lead others to treat the individual differently, what begins as a small difference between two individuals can grow over time. In short, the line between environment, cognition, and biology is not a distinct one. Changes in any one of the three can lead to changes in the other two, in the short term, and in the long run.

The evolutionary perspective

The biosocial interactionist model is based on an evolutionary perspective. It assumes that individual differences are related to different strategies for acquiring status, resources, and mates (Kenrick, 1987; Kenrick, Dantchik, and MacFarlane, 1983). Even seemingly maladaptive traits are assumed to be the products of natural selection that made them useful for enough of their bearers to be adaptive. For instance, depression may be related to a generally adaptive physiological *conservation–withdrawal response* that prompts rest and recuperation when the animal is physically or emotionally exhausted (Schmale, 1970). The extreme example of this occurs in animals that go into hibernation, and the reaction is also found in young animals that are separated from their parents (Bowlby, 1969). It would probably be adaptive to 'lay low' if the person has just put out a lot of effort that resulted only in repeated failure (Seligman, 1975). For individuals who have a particularly low physiological threshold for depression (because of other genes, early experience, or sensitization by disease), the normally adaptive response may go awry. Nevertheless, if the genes that predispose depression led to an average gain for our ancestors that had them, then they would have survived the process of natural selection.

A similar analysis has been applied to antisocial behavior (Kenrick, Dantchik, and MacFarlane, 1983). Antisocial behavior is associated with a genetic predisposition (e.g. Mednick, Gabrielli, and Hutchings, 1984), and is also related to a psychophysiological insensitivity to punishment (Hare, 1975). Although many antisocial individuals end up in jail, the genetic predisposition towards selfish exploitation of others could well have had an adaptive advantage for their ancestors. Note that a common characteristic of antisocial personalities is to have a series of exploitative sexual relationships and bigamous marriages. Since the 'bottom line' of evolution is successful reproduction, the average reproductive payoff for such selfish exploitation may have been high enough to compensate for the occasional tarring and feathering.

By considering traits in light of evolutionary theory, the biosocial perspective points to certain features of the environment that are more likely to be important, i.e. those involving potential mating possibilities and threats to one's position in the local dominance hierarchy.

The proximate–ultimate distinction

Another perspective on the interaction of biology, learning, and cognition comes from considering the proximate–ultimate distinction. As discussed above, proximate explanations deal with events as they are occurring (immediate causes), ultimate explanations deal with the underlying causes of those current events (long-term causes). Biological theories pay most attention to the ultimate explanations of our behavior. For instance, Hogan noted that the cross-cultural universalities in personality circumplexes indicate that those personality dimensions were related to survival for our ancestors (e.g. Hogan 1982). At a closer, but still relatively ultimate level, behavior geneticists examine how traits are inherited, and how personality is connected to developmental variations in morphology and physiology. Genetic explanations do not rule out the effects of the later environment. Genes only influence the way we respond to the environment, they do not construct an organism that is insensitive to outside pressures. Our genetic differences act by making some of us more sensitive to particular sights and smells, by biasing some of us to learn and remember particular events, by producing hormones that make some of us more prone to anger or anxiety, and so on (Kenrick, 1987).

Learning concepts address behavioral variations in more proximate terms. Conditioning and modeling processes address how environmental contingencies shape our responses as we are developing. However, modern learning theorists have found that learning is not independent of biological constraints. Just as there are differences between species in the things they are programmed to learn, so there are differences within our own species. Some of those differences are related to personality. For instance, Eysenck and Rachman (1965) have shown that emotional adjustment is related to heritable differences in autonomic arousal which cause neurotic individuals to condition anxiety to new situations more easily. At the opposite extreme, sociopathic prisoners are low in arousal, and do not learn to avoid punishment very well. However, if they are given a dose of epinephrine which disrupts learning in non-sociopaths, they then begin to avoid punishment in the normal fashion (Schachter and Latané, 1964). Thus, learning experiences connect back to physiological predispositions.

Cognitive approaches deal with the most proximate kinds of explanations. No matter how much a person's genes and learning history may bias them towards being outgoing and friendly, they are unlikely to smile at a friendly joke about their shoes if they misinterpret it as an insult. However, it is important to keep in mind that ongoing thoughts are not independent of either biology or learning history.

Consider the relationship between physical attractiveness and the personality trait of friendliness. In the most 'ultimate' sense, the features that people find attractive are probably related to health or genetic characteristics that were adaptive for our ancestors (Lott, 1979; Symons, 1979). Physical attractiveness is related to facial features and body type (Cunningham, 1986). These physical features are heritable: children tend to look like their parents. On a more 'proximate' level, physically attractive people will have different experiences as they are growing up. They will be treated better by teachers and classmates (Dion, 1972), and will be treated better by people they meet when they get older (Snyder, Tanke, and Berscheid, 1977). As a result of the warm reception they get from others, physically attractive people end up being more friendly (Goldman and Lewis, 1976). Those different life experiences, which can ultimately be traced to different genes, will also cause differences at the most proximate level. Physically attractive people will probably think differently about social interactions. Someone who is accustomed to being treated nicely is likely to interpret an ambiguous comment (like 'Where did you get those shoes?') differently from someone who is accustomed to being picked on. Thus physical differences between people lead to different experiences, and those different experiences lead to chronic differences in information processing. Ultimate and proximate causes thus form an unbroken chain in influencing individual differences.

THE OPEN-SYSTEMS ADAPTATION MODEL

Biological and social-learning factors make major contributions to the adaptation of individuals to their environment. Hettema's (1979) open-systems adaptation model is an attempt to conceptualize the processes involved and their effects on personality. Starting from a working definition of personality as 'a system of interacting biological and culturally determined elements, which maintains an open relation with the environment actually obtaining' (Hettema, 1979, p. 26), his major objective was to provide answers to two central questions: How do biological and social-learning factors interact to generate behavior in any given situation? and: What are the major effects of person–situation interactions on personality?

To answer those questions, Hettema adopted two central assumptions of Endler and Magnusson's (1976b) interactional psychology:

1. Personality is an active, intentional entity that has considerable impact on situations, and
2. Persons and situations reciprocally affect each other, so that persons obtain feedback on their actions from the situation in which they act (cf. also Hettema, 1982).

Contrary to previous conceptions (Endler and Magnusson, 1976b; Mischel, 1973) Hettema (1979) developed an intersubjective conception of situations, emphasizing normative aspects and treating situations as elements of the public domain. Situations can be defined with the aid of objectively discernable sensory cues and features, so that different people come to consensus on the nature of a particular situation (this does not preclude the possibility that the same situation can have different connotations for different observers).

To conceptualize person–situation interactions, personality is conceived as an adaptive open system: the situation is the system's environment. The model posits several types of relationship between person and situation: Human adaptation includes deliberate-intentional processes as well as spontaneous-autonomous processes. Person–situation interactions occur at the cognitive–symbolic level, at the control level and at the sensorimotor-operational level of psychological functioning. The three levels of the personality system are connected by couplings to allow for interlevel transactions to occur. For a more detailed explanation we use a schematic representation of the system (Figure 2).

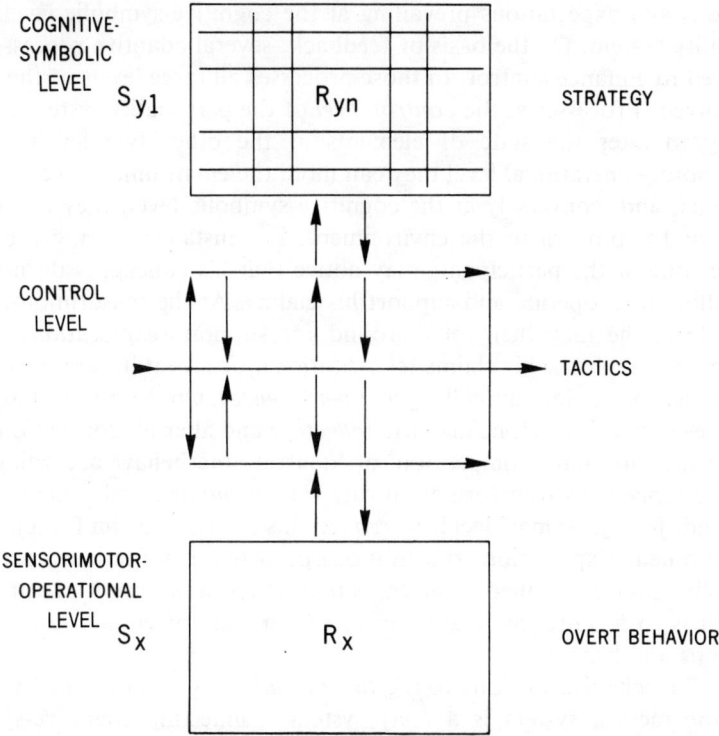

Figure 2   Strategies and tactics as determinants of overt behavior

The personality system tends to affect and transform its environment by means of behavior. At the *cognitive–symbolic level* the system represents situations, and specifies (situational) goals to be attained, as well as (behavioral) means to be used for the attainment of the goals. Major elements at this level are *situation concepts* (S_y) and *transformation rules* (R_y). For instance, individuals have conceptions of situations like classes, dates, quarrels, and so on. They also have rules to deal with those situations, like taking notes for classes, going to movies on dates, settling quarrels, and so on. Based on social learning and private experience, individuals are assumed to have preferences for particular transformation rules in specific situations. In the open-systems adaptation model, those preferences are summarized in a subsystem of personality, the *strategic system*.

Behavior specified by the strategic system may or may not be effective in transforming the environment as intended by the individual. Effectivity becomes manifest at the *sensorimotor–operational level*. If the environment responds to behavior in a lawful and predictable way, the system is in a state of control. Control is lost, if the environmental events fail to corroborate cognitions and expectations prevailing at the cognitive-symbolic level of the personality system. On the basis of feedback, several adaptive processes may be started to enhance control. In those processes all three levels of the system are involved. Processes at the *control level* of the personality system have the capacity to alter the state of elements at the other two levels. At the sensorimotor−operational level they can mold the environment to conform to cognitions, and, conversely at the cognitive-symbolic level, they can replace cognitions to conform to the environment. For instance, during a business meeting, one of the participants may notice that his colleagues do not seem very willing to cooperate and support his claims. At the sensorimotor−operational level, he may then look around for support (*exploration*), attract attention and rephrase his claims (*substitution*), or repeat his arguments with more power to convince his colleagues (*persistence*). On the other hand, at the cognitive−symbolic level, he may use *reflection* and alter his conception of the meeting situation into 'competition' or 'quarrel' and behave accordingly. He may also replace his transformation rule via *uncoupling* and generate a new plan. And, finally, he may decide to *redirect* his efforts and aim for a new goal to be attained. Exploration, substitution, persistence, reflection, uncoupling and redirection are called *state-transition (ST)-mechanisms*. Their major function is to acquire, maintain and restore a state of equilibrium between cognitions and behavior.

The ST-mechanisms belong to the *tactical subsystem* of personality. Essentially, the tactical system is a relay system, connecting cognitive-symbolic elements with sensorimotor−operational elements of the system. Its primary function is a maximize control, given the limiting conditions prevailing. However, ST-mechanisms may fail to restore control. In that case, according to the model, *disruption mechanisms* are started to minimize non-control. For instance, escape reactions may be evoked, leading to *avoidance* of the uncontrollable situation in the future. Or, alternatively, the behavior ineffectively used to transform the situation may be *extinguished*. And, finally, the *goal* set originally may be *abandoned* because it cannot be attained in this type of situation.

The strategic and tactical subsystems of personality cooperate to create optimal environmental conditions for the person, to maximize control and to minimize frictions and disturbances. Together they are a powerful coalition to enhance *individual adaptation* to environmental conditions.

ASSUMPTIONS

The open-systems adaptation model is based on 14 *assumptions* (cf. Hettema, 1979, pp. 154−159). Besides formal system characteristics, the assumptions pertain to personality processes as well as to the products of those processes.

Thus, the theory contains an explicit conception of personality functioning as well as personality development. To elucidate the assumptions we will use an example that is familiar to most of us: A state of shyness occurring in a young teacher during class.

1. System assumptions

1.1. The open-system assumption

Personality is an open system: the system comprises a number of relatively permanent subsystems, and, in addition, an environment that is altered continously.

1.2. The level assumption

The personality system functions at three different levels: the cognitive–symbolic level, the sensorimotor–operational level, and, in between, the control level.

Shyness may become manifest at different levels. At the cognitive-symbolic level, the teacher may suddenly realize that he or she does not know how to proceed and gets confused. At the sensorimotor–operational level, a sudden remark of a student may interrupt his or her ongoing stream of behavior. The teacher starts looking around for help or shows displacement behavior. At the control level a discrepancy may become manifest between the teacher's intentions and his or her actual behavior, for instance when he or she makes a mistake. As a consequence he or she may blush or show other physiological reactions.

1.3. The transaction assumption

Transactions among the three levels of the personality system occur continuously.

An interruption of behavior at the sensorimotor–operational level, e.g. by a student's remark, may cause our teacher to cognitively redefine the situation as one including students' remarks. Alternatively, the teacher may become self-conscious and think he or she does not function adequately. As a consequence his or her behavior may be disrupted or disturbed.

1.4. The input assumption

Input to the personality system may be defined either at the cognitive-symbolic level or at the sensorimotor–operational level.

For the teacher in our example there are different ways to become shy. By looking at the faces around him or her, the teacher may notice that pupils do not understand very well. In that case the system's input is located at the sensorimotor-operational level. But also one of the students may tell the teacher that his or her teaching is incomprehensible, thus providing the system with cognitive–symbolic input.

1.5. The output assumption

The system's output may also be defined at the cognitive–symbolic level or at the sensorimotor–operational level.

The teacher may simply tell the students that he or she feels shy (cognitive–symbolic output), but he or she may also demonstrate shyness by looking around helplessly or bowing his or her head (sensorimotor–operational output).

2. Process assumptions

2.1. The control assumption

Internal and external activities of the individual are governed by the principle to acquire and maintain control over the environment.

If shyness becomes manifest at the control level, the system will do the utmost to abolish that state, for instance by redefining the situation (internal activity) or by substituting new behaviors for the ones emitted before shyness occurred (external activity).

2.2. The information assumption

Individuals collect information either from personal experience or social learning to help them control the environment.

Control assumes that information in the personality system can be used to conceptualize or reconceptualize the environment, to set goals and to generate plans for action. Shyness may be the consequence of an inproper conceptualization of the situation. Thus, the number of alternative conceptualizations present in the system has a direct bearing on the question of whether control can be regained.

2.3. The transformation assumption

Directed activities can modify the environment and produce feedback to the personality system.

If shyness becomes manifest in the teacher, he or she may ask the students not to interrupt any more. Thus, in the context of the open-systems adaptation model, the teacher attempts to transform the situation to his or her benefit. The subsequent course of events will show if the teacher's action to remove the cause of shyness has been successful.

2.4. The maximizing assumption

If the equilibrium between organism and environment is disturbed, ST-mechanisms attempt to maximize control given the limiting conditions in which the disturbance occurred (short-term adaptation).

Control can be maximized in several ways. At the cognitive–symbolic level the teacher in our example may redefine the situation to include critical remarks. The teacher may alter his or her action plans by routinely building in questions about whether they are being understood. The teacher may also decide to prompt a discussion among students instead of lecturing. At the sensorimotor–operational level, the teacher may explore the class to look for problems, or rephrase sentences to further understanding, or even proceed in the same way but use more verbal emphasis to stress arguments.

2.5. The minimizing assumption

If the application of ST-mechanisms fails to restore equilibrium, disruption-mechanisms attempt to minimize loss of control (long-term adaptation).

Our teacher can henceforth attempt to decrease the probability of becoming shy by avoiding teaching situations enhancing shyness. The teacher may also suppress the kinds of behavior criticized most by the students, or distract him or herself from the original goal (providing insight to the students), and replace it with a new goal, such as creating a pleasant atmosphere in class.

Product assumptions

3.1. The differentiation assumption

The collection of new information causes progressive differentiation in the cognitive–symbolic behavior structure of the personality system.

By communication with colleagues or reading specific materials on teaching, our teacher may obtain the insight, that only very specific situations, actions or goals will provoke the occurrence of shyness and loss of control.

3.2. The experience assumption

Repeated experience with behavior in the same environment (practice) leads to integration processes, causing the cognitive symbolic behavior structure to simplify and to obtain a better fit with that environment.

With increasing experience the regulation of the teacher's behavior in class will change. Eventually, elements provoking shyness will be abolished and only effective elements will be retained.

3.3. The conditioning assumption

ST-and disruption-mechanisms tend to be coupled with the situation concepts with which they initially occurred.

Once a control reaction has proven to be effective in overcoming shyness, it will tend to become a preferred reaction in confrontations with the same kind of situation.

3.4. The generalization assumption.

Via processes of generalization ST- and disruption-mechanisms are coupled with elements of the symbolic behavioral structure, which resemble characteristics of the environment where the disruption initially occurred.

If shyness leads our teacher to minimize non-control by avoiding specific situations, by suppressing particular behaviors or by distracting him or herself from the original goals, these effects will not be restricted to the situation where they emerged but become visible in similar situations as well.

Interaction of social-learning and biological factors

How do social-learning and biological factors interact to generate behavior in a given situation? The answer to this question can be obtained from the *process assumptions* of the model. The leading principle of the processes occurring is control (assumption 2.1). As long as directed transformations are carried out producing the results intended, the system is assumed to be in a state of control (cf. Hettema, 1979, pp. 120–122). Thus, control as defined here emphasizes two separate elements; transformation and equilibrium.

Transformations are based on the information present in the system, acquired by social learning or personal experience (assumption 2.2). Whether or not behavior is effective in producing the desired results becomes evident on the basis of feedback (assumption 2.3). As we stated earlier, the major personality structure regulating directed transformation of the environment is *the strategic system*. This structure is defined at the cognitive—symbolic level of the personality system.

Equilibrium, the second element of control, is a function of the correspondence between cognitive and situational events. A loss of correspondence can be counteracted by ST-mechanisms attempting to restore equilibrium and maximize control (assumption 2.4). If correspondence cannot be obtained disruption mechanisms try to minimize non-control (assumption 2.5). Both types of mechanisms are part of the *tactical subsystem* of personality. Tactics are assumed to be largely innate mechanisms, acquired on the basis of heredity (cf. Hettema, 1979, pp. 170—171). It is assumed that some individuals have a general 'preference' to use reflection, whereas others would preferably use persistence or redirection when disequilibrium becomes manifest. If disruption-mechanisms are called for, some individuals will be more inclined to react with avoidance, whereas others tend to use extinction or distraction. Tactical preference is assumed to be connected with temperament and its major dimensions like introversion—extraversion and neuroticism. Connections of tactical mechanisms with emotion and motivation have been pointed out earlier (Hettema, 1984, 1986; Hettema and Van Heck, 1987).

Both strategy and tactics are involved in goal-directed behavior. The actual nature of the interaction between the two systems is a function of the type of relationship existing between person and situation. Three major types of person—situation relationships can be distinguished. The first type are familiar situations that are frequently met in daily life and in which goals as well as means are quite obvious. In those situations there is an optimal fit between individual and environment (cf. Pervin, 1968). The cognitive—strategic system is the major structure while directly providing goals as well as means governing behavior. The second type contains situations in which the person's goals are sometimes hard to be attained because behavior meets with frictions and resistance. In these situations tactical ST-mechanisms will offer a necessary supplement for the strategy. Social-learning factors (underlying strategies) and biological factors (underlying tactics) are both active and may be assumed to be in balance here. The third type are stressful situations in which the ST-mechanisms fail to provide control. In that case disruption-mechanisms will take over and cause the biological based tactical system to dominate the strategic system. The general conclusion to be drawn here is that the interaction between social-learning and biological factors is primarily *compensatory*. The dominance of either type of factors depends on the relationship between person and situation as a whole, i.e. the amount of control available in the system.

How do person—situation interactions contribute to personality development? The *product assumptions* of the model specify the effects of person—situation encounters on the strategic and tactical subsystems of personality.

Assumption 3.1 states that strategies are subject to progressive differentiation with regard to situation concepts as well as transformation rules. Differentiation will become manifest particularly in environments belonging to the individual's 'ecological niche'. Thus, for instance, politicians will use fine-grained discriminations in group decision making situations, as well as differentiated plans to effectively deal with those situations. Professional football players will discriminate clearly between field situations that all look the same to the layman. Accordingly, they will have several plans available to operate successfully in each of those situations. According to assumption 3.2, repeated experience with the same situation will start integration processes arranging different transformation rules in longer chains, to be emitted if specific environmental conditions are met. Transformational chains are particularly effective in molding situations so as to attain individual goals. As a result of assumptions 3.1 and 3.2 then, individual strategies will show differentiation and integration in areas representing familiar situations, whereas in other areas those effects will be less pronounced or absent.

Assumption 3.3., the conditioning assumption, establishes connections between situations and tactical mechanisms. This assumption implies that an individual will have a tendency to use a specific ST-mechanism as soon as there is a threat of losing control in a specific situation. Thus, for instance, during an exam a student may use reflection when he cannot find the right answer, whereas persistence may be his major weapon in discussions with his fellow students.

The generalization assumption (3.4) states that disruptive reactions are not restricted to the stressful situation where they emerged, but generalize to other comparable situations. For example, a person who is offended in a dating situation may henceforth avoid not only dates with that same person but other interactions with the opposite sex as well.

Summarizing, according to the open-systems adaptation model, personality development can be characterized as a complex of different processes through which the major systems of personality became fixed to situations as a function of experience with those situations. In some situations a perfect fit between personality and environment may be developed on the basis of social learning, providing the strategic system with a dominant position. In other situations, control is seldom warranted so that state transition mechanisms are given a prominent position to compensate for strategic flaws. And, finally, in stressful situations, disruption mechanisms may take over to warrant individual adaptation. As a final conclusion, in the context of the present model an individual's personality emerges as a *pattern of fixed relations with situations* met in the course of his or her life. Depending on individual experience, those relations will be dominated now by social-learning factors now by biological factors.

COMMON PRINCIPLES

Although stemming from different areas of theorizing, the biosocial interactionist model and the open-systems adaptation model use several common principles to explain individual behavior. Both models include attention to biology, learning and cognition. Accordingly, behavior is studied as a function of ongoing thought processes, physiological reactions and situation factors. For prediction purposes all three types of determinants are considered to be essential. Both models assume the three types of determinants to operate non-independently, that is in interaction with each other. Special attention is paid by both models to the time perspective, stressing proximate versus ultimate causality (Kenrick *et al.*) and short-term versus long-term adaptation (Hettema).

The differences between the two approaches are mainly differences of emphasis. While the biosocial interactionist model is primarily concerned with the analysis of general conditions for particular behaviors to occur, the open-system adaptation model focuses on dynamic person–situation interactions and their effects on personality. The dominant perspectives in the two models may thus be designated as ultimate versus proximate causality. Accordingly, while Kenrick *et al.* focus more on traits, Hettema's model is primarily concerned with states. The perspectives emphasized in both approaches may thus be conceived as complementary rather than either coinciding or mutually exclusive.

The biosocial interaction model may shed new light on the interaction between genotype and environment. While specifying the positions of innate and acquired behavioral structures in one comprehensive model, it opens up the possibility to scrutinize and systematically study their cooperation in actual behavior as well as their development during lifetime. Issues like goodness of fit (Thomas and Chess, 1985), genotype-environment correlations (Plomin, DeFries and Loehlin, 1977), and person–environment correspondence (Buss, 1985) may be studied more fruitfully from this perspective.

The open-systems adaptation model is particularly concerned with ongoing person × situation interactions. The model postulates social-learning factors and biological factors to interact with situations in different ways. Strategies are primarily concerned with the transformation of situations and provide a basis for 'between-situation interactions'. Tactics, on the other hand, are directed at maintaining and restoring the person's control over the situation, thus providing a basis for 'within-situation interactions' (cf. Magnusson, 1976, 1980).

PURPOSE OF THIS BOOK

The open-systems adaptation model gives a detailed conceptualization of the connections between strategy and tactics, allowing for predictions to be made of overt behavior in specific situations. Due to the high degree of specificity obtained in the model, more accurate predictions of behavior in person–situation studies may be expected (cf. Hettema, 1982, 1984). The studies to be reported in this book are meant to provide evidence and test this expectation. This book is concerned with the assessment of human adaptation. Its primary aim is to operationalize and test the basic concepts of the open-systems adaptation model.

The description of the model has made it clear that no classical assessment techniques can be readily adopted and applied to measure the concepts used. The model differs from the classical trait model in many respects. Its multilevel character, its biosocial interactive nature, as well as its emphasis of adaptive personality properties require more complex designs than are normally used for the development of personality tests.

First of all, the three levels of the model call for the development of special assessment techniques to adequately represent the structures and processes postulated there. The *measurement modes* (Fiske, 1971) used at the cognitive–symbolic, the control, and the sensorimotor–operational levels of the personality system will have to answer specific requirements.

For *prediction* purposes, a second major feature of the model deserves attention. While emphasizing different subsystems of personality, the *connections between subsystems* will demonstrate idiosyncrasies that have to be taken into account. For prediction, the traditional linear additive model is presumable inadequate, Instead, more complex interactive models will have to be considered.

Finally, the open-systems adaptation model assumes that the actual environment is an essential determinant of behavior and that intrapersonal characteristics are not sufficient to explain individual behavior. The proper design to reflect this aspect of the model is the $P \times S \times R$ design, taking into account persons and situations as well as behaviors. The evidence obtained with this design may demonstrate that the same person adapts in different ways to different situations. Whether or not information obtained in one situation can be generalized to other situations will depend on person characteristics as well as situation characteristics. This conception may cause problems with the classical requirements of reliability of the personality measures involved. Therefore, special attention will be paid to the development of models to test *generalizability* while taking into account different contexts of generalization.

CONCLUDING COMMENT

The person–situation debate originated from a growing concern with the effectiveness of personality measures as predictors of socially relevant criteria. The issue of the person versus the situation as the main source of behavioral variation occupied a central position. Accordingly, the basic personality paradigm was critically evaluated, and current personality measures were scrutinized with respect to their generality, consistency and stability. As a whole, the person–situation debate concerned epistemological and theoretical as well as methodological issues. Each of those issues has attracted considerable attention in attempts to resolve the criticisms raised. Subsequent solutions have defined the problem either as a prediction problem, as a measurement problem, or as a theoretical problem.

In our view, none of the earlier solutions has been completely satisfactory, particularly because each has provided only a partial answer. Methodological solutions tended to neglect the construction of a theoretical framework to account for the technical corrections proposed. Theoretical solutions, on the other hand, were confined to mere principles and did not manage to provide a methodological elaboration.

To offer a more definite solution we started from a fundamental reconsideration of person–situation interactions from a biological and social-learning point of view. This analysis yielded several major factors to be taken into account while designing personality models with the capacity to systematically interact with the environment, biologically as well as socially. Each of us has attempted independently to integrate those factors in one comprehensive personality model. Both models converge in a number of ways: differences are mainly differences of emphasis.

The open-systems adaptation model is especially concerned with personality at a proximate level of analysis. While conceptualizing dynamic person × situation interactions, the model provides a basis for the study and prediction of individual behavior in specific situations.

2
Principles of personality assessment

JOOP HETTEMA

The person–situation debate has led to several new insights, not only theoretically but also with regard to the methods used to explore personality. In the previous chapter we have seen how theoretical and methodological principles held by traditional trait theorists were challenged and modified by modern personality investigators. In general, the proposed alternatives attempt to introduce more differentiation and finesse in the rather crude models developed earlier. Innovative efforts have led to results pertaining to personality measurement and prediction as well as to the consistency of personality.

To improve the accuracy of personality measurement, the stimulus situations offered and the responses recorded are very carefully defined and have become more specific than they used to be. Instead of one single type of measurement mode, the use of different methods prevents unwarranted conclusions. Craik (1986) has analyzed the history of personality research methods and concluded that methodological pluralism currently prevails in the field. Our knowledge of persons can be derived from several sources, as, for instance, everyday conduct, imaginative productions, social impressions, life history data, general reputations, self-characterizations and behavior in standardized conditions. The inherent agenda of personality research encompasses each and every one of these sources of information about persons. A basic goal is to move further toward a scientific integration of information about persons from all of these diverse sources (cf. Craik, 1986, pp. 33–34).

In the context of the person–situation debate, Houts, Cook and Shadish (1986) have advocated a 'critical multiplist perspective' referring to the selection of options among different measures available. In their view, single

Personality and Environment: Assessment of Human Adaptation
Edited by P. J. Hettema. ©1989 John Wiley and Sons Ltd

measures will inevitably be inadequate and multiple measures preferred. But not any other measure: 'To be critical, multiplism supposes a thorough theoretical analysis' (Houts, Cook and Shadish, 1986, p. 55). Each measure selected should contain theoretically relevant components not in other measures or manipulations.

The prediction of individual behavior is no longer the exclusive domain of the linear additive model. Some of the newer models take into account the organization of processes within a single individual. Besides sheer idiographic approaches the idiothetic approach developed by Lamiell (1981) belongs in this category. Others have used combinations of nomothetic and idiographic approaches, as, for instance, Pennebaker and Epstein (1988) in their study of symptom reporting. Some models have emphasized the typical ways that individuals express traits in contrast to others, as in the moderator strategy mentioned earlier. Other models take into account the specific ways in which individuals interact with specific situations. An example of this approach is a study by Magnusson and Stattin (1978) directed at the uniqueness and stability of individual cross-situational patterns of behavior. All prediction models mentioned have in common that they take account of more information than just trait scores. Obviously, each model requires a theoretical conception specifying what individual information should be used as well as how information should be included in the prediction model.

A central issue in the person–situation debate has been the *consistency* of individual behavior over different conditions. For the traditional trait model this issue is of vital interest with respect to the reliability of trait measures, as well as, ultimately, the sheer existence of traits.

It has been the special merit of Cronbach, Gleser, Nanda and Rajaratnam (1972) to shed new light on consistency. While relaxing some of the assumptions of reliability theory, Cronbach *et al.* have liberalized the classical model and replaced it with their theory of generalizability. According to this theory many different types of 'reliability' can be distinguished, depending on the conditions over which generalizability is established. For instance, transsituational consistency of a trait may be studied simultaneously with (and independent of) stability of the same trait and yield different results. Generalizability theory has put the consistency issue in a new perspective. Several models have been developed to establish specific types of consistency, for instance by Brennan (1978), Ozer (1986) and Van Heck (1981). Depending on the trait studied, different types of consistency may be emphasized and different models can be used to establish consistency.

Summarizing then, it has become clear that the areas of personality measurement, prediction and consistency have witnessed an increase of methodological alternatives in recent decades. Current investigators have a choice among several different methods in each of these cases. Options will have to be based on theory. In our own research, our choice has been guided by two considerations. First of all, we have scrutinized the alternatives available with respect to their specific merits. And, subsequently, our choice is based on a careful consideration of the assumptions of the open-systems adaptation model.

MEASUREMENT

An assumption customarily made in personality assessment is the assumption of indifference of indicator (Cattell and Birkett, 1980), stating that the same personality dimensions can be found using different methods of data-collection, as, e.g. questionnaires, life history data, or objective tests. This assumption allows investigators to restrict their efforts to one type of data, usually questionnaires. However, recently, considerable doubt has been raised against this assumption. Particularly Fiske (1971, 1978) has stressed the differences inherent in using different modes of measurement in personality assessment.

Fiske (1978 pp. 16,19) has stated:

> 'Perhaps the most important generalization that has emerged in recent decades of research is that personality data have a high degree of specificity... Investigators place little emphasis on the setting in which each observation is made, even though the setting is typically a particular instance unrepresentative of the condition they wish to generalize about... Relying on particularistic judgements and casual syntheses, investigators make unwarranted extrapolations and unsystematic generalizations'.

Empirical evidence supporting Fiske's position on this issue can be found easily. For instance, Van Heck (1981) compared several indices of the same personality trait: anxiety. Using overt expressive behaviors, a self-report questionnaire and three psychophysiological measures collected in different situations, he computed correlations between all pairs of indices. Between observations and self-reports there was almost no relationship and the correlations between both types of indices and psychophysiological reactions were very low. Van Heck (1981, p.261) concluded that 'relationships *across modes*' between measures of the same concept are nearly absent'. More recently the same conclusion with respect to self-report and psychophysiological measures was drawn by Myrtek (1984) after an elaborate study of constitutional variables.

The specificity of response modes can be illustrated further by consistency studies (cf. Hettema, 1988a). In an earlier study, De Bonis (1977, p. 207) compared different response modes with respect to consistency across time and situations. She concluded that '...consistency across time and situations may be found in respect to one level of behavior, but not to another'. Later, I compared observer ratings and self-ratings with respect to internal consistency and obtained results indicating a clear superiority of rating scales (Hettema, 1981). On the basis of findings of this type, I raised the hypothesis that different response modes are systematically connected with different personality models (cf. Hettema, 1981). The mode of ratings appeared to be well suited to represent the trait model, whereas self-reports primarily reflected person × situation interactions. The latter conclusion was corroborated in Van Heck's (1981) study of anxiety. Van Heck primarily sees response modes as 'mirrors of individuality' indicating the sensitivity of each mode to illuminate specific aspects of personality as an integrated whole. After exploring several relationships between response modes and personality aspects Van Heck stated that: 'The domain of personality may simply be too large and heterogeneous to be studied using only one paradigm' (Van Heck, 1981, p. 280). However: 'What is clearly needed eventually is not partitioning of the field, but the establishment of theory-based links between the concepts of individuality on the one hand, and methods of data collection (modes) on the other' (p. 281).

Theories of personality should indicate precisely what type of measurement operations are required for the empirical definition of each concept used. Due to its biosocial nature the open-systems adaptation model obviously requires more than one measurement mode. The system assumptions of the model provide a basis for the choice of measurement operations because those assumptions specify different aspects of personality emphasized in the theory. The level assumption (1.2) states that personality functions at three different levels: the cognitive–symbolic, sensorimotor–operational and control levels. Each level of the personality system is specific with respect to the nature of the input for which it is sensitive as well as with respect to the output it can generate. The assumptions 1.4 and 1.5 of the theory state that the input as well as the output of the system may be defined either at the cognitive–symbolic or sensorimotor–operational levels. Obviously then, to assess personality at each of the levels separately, assessment procedures will have to be designed with specific stimulus properties as well as specific response properties. Therefore, in the present volume, special attention is paid to the media of stimulus representation and to the modes of behavioral measurement to be used.

To allow for a more systematic study of media and modes it is convenient to think in terms of a matrix in which both aspects are represented. With respect to media the several ways in which situations are represented in psychological research can be taken as a starting point. This has been done in some detail by Craik (1970, 1971). He has made a distinction into:

1. Direct presentation of situations.
2. Simulations.
3. Films, photographs, pictures and the like.
4. Verbal representation of situations.

With respect to modes Fiske (1971) has made a classical categorization into:

1. Self ratings.
2. Descriptions of direct experience.
3. Psychophysiological measures.
4. Ratings.
5. Measures of performance.
6. Observations of behavior.

The viewpoints of media and modes may be systematically combined to obtain a matrix representing different kinds of settings used to assess personality. Here we will restrict ourselves to a reduced media × modes matrix (cf. Hettema, 1982) that can be obtained without, presumably, much loss of information by reducing both classifications to three classes (Table 1). In this matrix several classical approaches to the personality assessment problem can be categorized: specific assessment methods are connected with separate cells in the matrix.

For instance, the conventional personality questionnaire, using the verbal medium of stimulus presentation and the response mode of self-reports is located in cell I. Projective measures, using pictures as stimuli, belong in cell IV. Interviews used as assessment techniques are natural situations with self-reports as a response mode, so cell VII is the proper location for that approach. The mode of psychophysiology can be used to assess state changes as a consequence of emotions, as in lie-detection. The stimulus material is of a verbal nature, so this technique belongs in cell II. If films are used as a medium, as in the study of stress, cell V is the correct place to accommodate the assessment method. Physiological measures are sometimes recorded in real-life circumstances, for instance by means of telemetry, in that case we find ourselves in cell VIII. Behavioral observation is often used as a tool for the assessment of abilities and achievement. Verbal intelligence tests should be

Table 1 Reduced media × modes matrix for personality assessment

		Mode		
		Self report	Psychophysiology	Observation
	Verbal	I Personality questionnaires	II Lie detection	III Verbal intelligence
Medium	Pictorial	IV Projective measures	V Film stress studies	VI Performance intelligence
	Natural	VII Interview	VIII Telemetry	IX Natural observation

located in cell III, whereas performance tests of intelligence belong in cell VI.
Finally, cell IX is the appropriate place to locate natural observation as an
assessment technique.

To decide on the proper cells to be chosen for the assessment of personality
in the context of the open-systems adaptation model the base is provided by
the distinction into three levels of personality functioning. As regards assessment at the *cognitive–symbolic level* the input of the system as well as the
output is defined at the cognitive–symbolic level. Therefore, the mode of
self-reports is the obvious option at this level, specifying cell I of the media ×
modes matrix as the proper cell. As regards assessment at the sensorimotor–
operational level the input as well as the output are defined at that level. This
implies the choice of natural settings as the proper medium and the choice of
observations of overt behavior as the proper mode. Thus, measurement at the
sensorimotor–operational level will take place in the context of cell IX of the
matrix.

The first thing to be considered for assessment at the control level is that
control mechanisms are put to work as a consequence of a disturbance of the
equilibrium between the cognitive and operational levels. Thus, specific
situations will have to be presented dynamically and allow for discrepancies to
be built in. Among the three types of media mentioned, films are unique in that
they provide the opportunity to display specific situations while at the same
time the course of action can be controlled in detail. With respect to the mode
of measurement we have pointed out earlier that psychophysiological
measures are the proper means to measure states within the context of the
open-system's adaptation model (Hettema, 1979, p. 183). Thus, for measurement at the control level cell V will offer the proper context. Table 2
summarizes the decisions made regarding media and modes.

Before concluding this section on measurement problems, there is one final
issue deserving attention. Thus far, we have treated the levels of the personality system as separate aspects of personality to be assessed with specific
media and modes. The issue of interlevel connections has not been discussed in
detail. The transaction assumption (1.3) states that between the levels of the
system transactions will occur on a continuous basis. Those transactions are
possible by virtue of a number of couplings designed between the levels of the

Table 2 Media and modes selected for assessment at different levels of the personality
system

	Medium	Mode	Cell
Cognitive–symbolic level	Verbal	Self report	I
Control level	Pictorial	Physiology	V
Sensorimotor–operational level	Simulation	Observation	IX

system (cf. Hettema, 1979, pp. 115–117). In the development of assessment procedures care should be taken to define elements (situations, actions) in the same way at different levels of the system. Earlier (Hettema, 1982) I have indicated this as the isomorphism requirement to be used as a major guideline throughout the studies to be reported.

PREDICTION

Behavior predictions are usually cast in prediction models specifying the relations between different conditions and behavior. A classical and generally accepted prediction model in personality psychology is:

$$R = fP, S \qquad 1$$

indicating that behavior (R) in concrete circumstances is determined by conditions in the person (P) as well as in the environment (S). If these conditions are known to the observer as well as sufficiently stable, predictions of future behavior in the same circumstances are possible. A further specification of the model can be obtained by introducing the causal chain:

$$S \rightarrow P \rightarrow R \qquad 2$$

stating that the situation S affects the person P to emit the behavior R. Further differentiation of this general model depends on the particular conception of personality held by the investigator. Two major approaches have been followed in the past, starting either from a nomothetic conception of personality or an idiographic conception.

The classical example of a nomothetic conception of personality is Cattell's trait model. In Cattell's view in a particular situation the same traits are activated regardless of the particular individual acting. This conception is reflected in the specification equation, stating that a specific response (R) in a given situation may be predicted on the basis of traits (Tr), each weighted (W) by its relevance in that situation:

$$R = W_1 Tr_1 + W_2 Tr_2 + W_3 Tr_3 + \cdots + W_n Tr_n \qquad 3$$

The nomothetic approach is based on the assumption that personality can be defined using general characteristics (traits). Contrary to the nomothetic model the idiographic approach states that personality can only be measured with personality characteristics of an individual nature. Thus, for instance, Allport (1937) emphasized the uniqueness of personality, assuming that each individual has his own unique traits underlying his behavior in a particular situation. In the prediction model uniqueness may be indicated by providing the person term with the subscript i:

$$R = fP_i, S \qquad 4$$

A different position is occupied by cognitive–phenomenological theories of personality, assuming that each person creates his own subjective situation, rather than the general situation, studied by the investigator. Theorists like Kelly and Rogers have based their work on this assumption. A prediction model along this line would include the subscript i for the situation term:

$$R = f P, S_i \qquad\qquad 5$$

Depending on the specific model, the P term might need a subscript i as well.

The cognitive–phenomenological approach emphasizes man's freedom to make his own judgements and choices when confronted with a specific environment. However, as an idiographic approach it can never obtain unequivocal predictions of behavior like those emerging from the nomothetic model.

In the open-systems adaptation model I have attempted deliberately to avoid the use of idiographic elements and to define person–situation interactions using a general language (cf. Hettema, 1979). For instance, at the cognitive–symbolic level the individual strategy is the major structure regulating behavior. The information assumption (2.2) states that individuals use general culturally-defined information to deal with the situation. Situation concepts and transformation rules represent general elements included in individual strategies to identify and transform situations. At the control level the tactical system is the main structure governing person-situation interactions. Assumption 2.4 states that ST-mechanisms serve to maximize control in case of disequilibrium. Assumption 2.5 states that disruption mechanisms attempt to minimize control loss. ST-mechanisms as well as disruption mechanisms are defined in general terms and are assumed to be operative in any single individual. Thus, like the strategic system the tactical system operates with general elements.

The personality conception emerging from the open-systems adaptation model cannot be designated as idiographic. On the other hand, single individuals are assumed to have their own individual ways of reacting to specific situations on strategic as well as on tactical grounds. Therefore, the nomothetic conception is not fit to describe the model either.

The conception of individuality applied in this approach is *idiosyncratic*, using general elements with individualized connections between elements (Hettema, 1979, pp. 161–171). It can be described with the general model:

$$R = f(P, S)_i \qquad\qquad 6$$

Predictions of behavior with this model hinge on a further conceptualization of the interactions between person and situation. As mentioned before, two major assumptions of Endler and Magnusson's (1976b) interactional psychology are adopted in the open-systems adaptation model:

1. Personality is an active, intentional entity that has considerable impact on situations;
2. Persons and situations reciprocally affect each other, so that persons obtain feedback on their actions from the situations in which they act.

The first assumption determines a unilateral relation between person and situation of the type $P \rightarrow S$. The relation is conceived as the transformation of S based on the individual's intention to maximize the utility of his environment. The major structure governing transformational behavior is the strategy. Predictions of behavior may be derived from the strategy taking into account the situation actually prevailing. They take the form of behavioral categories presumably fit to accomplish the transformation intended, with the exclusion of behavioral categories not answering that description.

The second assumption—reciprocal causation—determines a bilateral relation between person and situation of the type $P \leftrightarrow S$. This second relationship between person and situation reflects the individual's tendency to retain equilibrium while acting. The major structure governing behavior directed at equilibrium is the tactical system. Depending on the specific tactical mechanism used by the individual in that situation, different categories of behavior are expected to become visible. As we assume both the strategic and tactical systems to be active in most situations, predictions include the sets of behavior predicted by both systems.

To summarize then, in the context of the open-systems adaptation model, prediction studies are situation specific as well as person specific. Based on strategic and tactical considerations, behavior categories are established that are expected to become dominant in an individual's overt behavior in a specific situation. To test those expectations, individual behavior should be observed in concrete situations to yield a differentiated picture of the several behaviors occurring.

CONSISTENCY

Reliability of measurement is a basic requirement in personality assessment, in interactionist approaches as well as in trait theory. Classical theory defines reliability as the correlation between parallel measures. Errors of measurement are assumed to have zero means and uniform variances. They are uncorrelated and independent of true scores. In the true score model an observed score is defined as the sum of the true score and the measurement error. The correlation between parallel measures equals the ratio of true score variance to observed score variance (cf. Gulliksen, 1950; Lord and Novick, 1968).

The classical trait model postulates individual behavior to be *transsituationally consistent* and *stable* as well as *internally consistent* (cf. Ozer, 1986;

Van Heck, 1981). The three types of consistency mentioned are not the same. Behavior may be transsituationally consistent, but lack consistency in other respects, e.g. stability. For instance, a person can be in a powerful mood state, like anxiety, that becomes manifest in different situations, lingers on for a while, and vanishes eventually. Behavior may also be stable but show inconsistencies, as soon as the situation changes. For instance, phobias can be connected with very specific cues, such as snakes, but shed consistency as soon as the stimulus disappears. Behavior can also be internally consistent without showing any sign of transsituational consistency or stability. This will be the case with sudden states of panic, accompanied by cognitive disorganization, physiological arousal (increased heart rate, dry mouth, elevated blood pressure) and overt manifestations like trembling and restlessness, without recurrence. In none of the examples given can we say that the individual *is* anxious. Such a statement is meaningful only if all three types of consistency are realized.

In the context of generalizability theory (Cronbach, Gleser, Nanda, and Rajaratnam, 1972), the classical model intends to obtain generalization to the universe of persons (P), across different situations (S), across different responses (R) and across time (T) (cf. Ozer, 1986). In each type of consistency the object of measurement is P. If more than one trait is studied simultaneously, generalizability of individual *trait profiles* across S and T is postulated by the classical model. In multiple trait studies the object of measurement is P × R, instead of P (cf. Cronbach, Gleser, Nanda, and Rajaratnam, 1972, pp. 309–344). The several designs to be used in the study of consistency are presented in Figure 1.

Transsituational consistency can be studied, using design VII (Figure 1a),

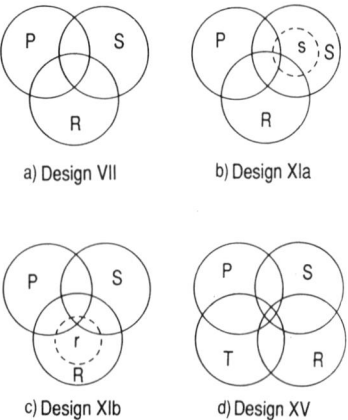

a) Design VII   b) Design XIa

c) Design XIb   d) Design XV

Figure 1   Designs used to determine generalizability

and estimated with:

$$\rho^2_{(PR)S} = \frac{\sigma^2_P + \sigma^2_{PR}}{\sigma^2_P + \sigma^2_{PR} + 1/n_S(\sigma^2_{PS} + \sigma^2_{PSR;\ error})} \qquad 7$$

in which:

ρ^2 = the generalizability coefficient;
PR = the object of measurement;
S = the facet over which generalization is intended;
σ^2 = the variance component, associated with P, PR, PS or PSR; error;
n = the number of levels of a facet.

For the study of internal consistency, variations of behavior within traits should be included in a partially nested design of the form P × S × r:R (Design XIb; Figure 1c). Internal consistency can be estimated with:

$$\rho^2_{(PR)r:R} = \frac{\sigma^2_P + \sigma^2_{PR}}{\sigma^2_P + \sigma^2_{PR} + 1/n_r\sigma^2_{Pr:R;\ error}} \qquad 8$$

in which r refers to different behavioral manifestations of the trait R.

To obtain a measure of *stability* use can be made of Design XV (Figure 1d), to yield:

$$\rho^2_{(PR)T} = \frac{\sigma^2_P + \sigma^2_{PR}}{\sigma^2_P + \sigma^2_{PR} + 1/n_T(\sigma^2_{PT} + \sigma^2_{PRT;\ error})} \qquad 9$$

The person-situation debate has directed attention to lawful variations as a function of the situation. Situationism is specially interested in intrasituational consistency, i.e. generalizability of situation effects across persons. The object of measurement studied in situationism is S, or S × R as more traits are studied in one design. The latter component reflects the intention to generalize to trait profiles as a function of discrete situations either across persons or across time. Using Design VII (Figure 1a), consistency across persons can be studied with:

$$\rho^2_{(SR)P} = \frac{\sigma^2_S + \sigma^2_{SR}}{\sigma^2_S + \sigma^2_{SR} + 1/n_P(\sigma^2_{PS} + \sigma^2_{PSR;\ error})} \qquad 10$$

Consistency across time can be estimated with:

$$\rho^2_{(SR)T} = \frac{\sigma^2_S + \sigma^2_{SR}}{\sigma^2_S + \sigma^2_{SR} + 1/n_T(\sigma^2_{ST} + \sigma^2_{SRT;\ error})} \qquad 11$$

For interactional models of personality, the classical reliability model is clearly inappropriate, since one of its assumptions, viz. the assumption of uncorrelated errors, is not warranted.

As Cronbach Gleser, Nanda and Rajaratman (1972) have pointed out, measurement error can be attributed to multiple sources, connected with different facets of the measurement operation. Slight variations in the experimental setting, in the formulation of items, in the time elapsing between test sessions, can cause correlations to occur that are erroneously included in the error term. This is especially true in interactionistic models in which, by assumption, specific connections between persons and measurement conditions are to be expected. Rather than discard them as error, they should be conceived as components of the true variance. Behavior varies as a function of several conditions, as, for instance, persons, situations and time. A major question to be answered is to what extent individual behavior is invariant as situations change and as time goes by. Meaningful statements about personality are possible only if individual behavior shows some kind of consistency.

Interactionism has directed attention to consistent forms of behavior as a function of both persons and situations. Thus, the logical object of measurement for interactionistic models is $P \times S \times R$ instead of either $P \times R$ or $S \times R$. The problem of consistency in interactionism has been treated by Magnusson and Endler (1977). In their view, consistency should be conceived of as *coherence*, defined as 'the individual's pattern of stable and changing behavior across situations of different kinds' (Magnusson and Endler, 1977, p. 7).

In interactional studies, several types of coherence are relevant as they reflect different aspects of person–situation interactions. Especially, the generalizability of $P \times S \times R$ across variations in situations (S), in responses (R) and across time (T) merits attention. These three types of coherence represent the interactionist counterparts of transsituational consistency, internal consistency and stability. They will be designated here as:

1. *Transsituational coherence.*
2. *Internal coherence.*
3. *Coherence stability.*

The first type—transsituational coherence—refers to individuals showing behavior that is specific to the situation, but is consistent across minor variations in the situation. To determine transsituational coherence, studies can be done according to the partially nested Design XIa and generalizability may be estimated using:

$$\rho^2_{(PSR)s\,:\,S} = \frac{\sigma^2_P + \sigma^2_{PS} + \sigma^2_{PR} + \sigma^2_{PSR}}{\sigma^2_P + \sigma^2_{PS} + \sigma^2_{PR} + \sigma^2_{PSR} + 1/n_s(\sigma^2_{Ps\,:\,S} + \sigma^2_{Ps\,:\,SR;\ error})} \qquad 12$$

The second type—internal coherence—refers to individuals showing situation-specific behavior but use alternative forms of behavior belonging to the same category. To determine internal coherence the partially nested Design XIb is the proper design and generalizability can be estimated with:

$$\rho^2_{(PSR)r\,:\,R} = \frac{\sigma^2_P + \sigma^2_{PS} + \sigma^2_{PR} + \sigma^2_{PSR}}{\sigma^2_P + \sigma^2_{PS} + \sigma^2_{PR} + \sigma^2_{PSR} + 1/n_r(\sigma^2_{Pr\,:\,R} + \sigma^2_{PSr\,:\,R;\ error})} \qquad 13$$

The third type—coherence stability—occurs if individuals consistently use the same behavior in a situation or in repeated confrontations with that situation. Coherence stability can be studied with a design including measurements at different moments in time (Design XV). To estimate coherence stability use can be made of:

$$\rho^2_{(PSR)T} = \frac{\sigma^2_P + \sigma^2_{PS} + \sigma^2_{PR} + \sigma^2_{PSR}}{\sigma^2_P + \sigma^2_{PS} + \sigma^2_{PR} + \sigma^2_{PSR} + 1/n_T(\sigma^2_{PT} + \sigma^2_{PST} + \sigma^2_{PRT} + \sigma^2_{PSRT;\ error})} \qquad 14$$

The study of coherence is important not only to warrant the adequacy of assessment tools, but also to provide evidence concerning the assumptions of the model. Ozer (1986, p. 59) has advocated the study of coherence in the context of theory-based constructs: 'Coherence... may provide a basis for the explanation of behavioral variability which focuses on the adequacy of underlying theory...' Unlike the true score model we do not assume all three types of coherence to be equally important at the different levels of personality.

At the cognitive–symbolic level, individual strategies are postulated as the major structures governing behavior. Based on social learning, individuals are assumed to develop coherent ways to exploit or transform situations to their benefit. Strategies reflect individual ways to deal with situations, so that in a comprehensive study $P \times S \times R$ will be the major component reflecting coherence.

According to the product assumptions of the open-systems adaptation model, individual experience with specific situations and situation domains will affect the elements of the cognitive structure governing behavior. Assumption 3.1 states that new information will be collected by the personality to yield further differentiation of the situation concepts used. Different situations will be treated differently so that generalization across subsituations will diminish as a function of experience.

Assumption 3.2 points out an increasing integration of responses as a function of experience. Response patterns will become well organized and retain mainly actions that have proven effective in establishing the transformations wanted. As a consequence, generalization of $P \times S \times R$ across subresponses will gradually increase. Thus, at the cognitive–symbolic level internal coherence is the major type of coherence to be expected. In addition, data obtained at the cognitive symbolic level may be expected to exhibit coherence stability.

At the control level of personality functioning the tactical system contains several ST-mechanisms to maintain and restore equilibrium. On biological grounds a definite preference for specific tactical mechanisms is assumed to exist in any individual, yielding $P \times R$ as a coherent component at this level. According to assumption 3.3 tactical mechanisms will be coupled with situations on the basis of conditioning. So $P \times S \times R$ will exhibit stable individual connections and become a coherent component as well.

Assumption 3.4 states that tactical mechanisms will be connected with situations similar to the original situations, so that, eventually, a certain amount of generalization across situations will be established. Therefore, at the control level we expect transsituational coherence to be the dominant type. Also at this level coherence stability will be accomplished.

At the sensorimotor–operational level behavior is assumed to be a function of strategic as well as tactical regulation. Within a specific situation the effects of both subsystems will become apparent so that neither internal coherence nor transsituational coherence may be expected in the study of overt behavior. This prediction is in line with earlier findings concerning T-data (Block, 1977) and observations of overt behavior (Hettema, 1981). According to the model, coherence will become manifest only in the form of stability within situations and in repeated confrontations with the same situation.

To summarize then, consistency in the context of the open-systems adaptation model is conceived as coherence with $P \times S \times R$ as the object of measurement. At the three levels of the personality system coherence takes a different shape. The cognitive–symbolic level emphasizes internal coherence, the control level stresses transsituational coherence. At all three levels of the system a certain amount of coherence stability is postulated[1]. The model does not claim consistency of individual behavior apart from the situation in which behavior is studied. Neither does the model postulate consistency as a function of the situation apart from the individual operating. Coherence is clearly related to the situation specific goals of the individual as well as to reactions to disturbances occurring in the individual while attempting to attain his goals.

SUMMARY STATEMENT

In this chapter I have designed a number of methodological tools for personality assessment in the context of the open-systems adaptation model. The principles of assessment differ according to the levels of personality distinguished in the model.

At the cognitive–symbolic level, measurement occurs with the aid of self-reports, using the verbal medium to present situations and the verbal mode to indicate behaviors preferred in those situations. Predictions at the cognitive–symbolic level are specific for persons as well as for situations. They refer to classes of behavior with the capacity to transform situations in a direction specified by the person. At this level, behavior is expected to be

---

[1] It should be noted, that coherence across different data domains (Block, 1977) or modes (Fiske, 1971, 1978) is not among the claims of the present model. On the contrary, by connecting modes with different levels of personality functioning, we have granted a different status to different modes, theoretically as well as empirically.

internally coherent as well as stable. Using PSR as the object of measurement, generalization can be studied across different responses and across time.

At the control level, measurement is concentrated on physiological reactions occurring in subjects confronted with situations represented with films. At this level predictions are specific for persons and for situations as well as at the cognitive symbolic level. They refer to behaviors with the capacity to maintain or restore the equilibrium between the person and the situation. At the control level generalization is expected reflecting transsituational coherence and stability of control reactions.

At the sensorimotor–operational level, measurement consists of observations of overt behavior occurring in natural settings. At the sensorimotor–operational level, behavior is assumed to be governed by the cognitive–symbolic as well as the control level of personality, viz. to contain elements aimed at transformation as well as equilibrium. Thus, at that level, behavior is assumed to exhibit neither internal coherence, nor transsituational coherence. The only type of consistency to be expected at this level is coherence stability.

Part II

Assessment at the cognitive–symbolic level

3

Self-report: from traits to strategies

JOOP HETTEMA

The validity of trait scores obtained with self-reports is very modest at best. Mischel (1968) claims convergent validity of trait scales hardly ever to exceed 0.30. Wiggins (1980) has qualified the validities of 20 PRF-scales with a median of 0.29 as 'quite respectable in comparison with those typically reported for personality inventories' (p. 415). Why are validity coefficients that low and why have we not made substantial progress regarding validity of trait scales during decades of increased methodological sophistication?

History provides at least the beginning of an answer. Self-report techniques were used originally to replace the psychiatric interview (cf. Wiggins, 1980). The assumptions on which this approach was based were, however, questioned and the criteria for scale construction were changed radically. Rather than being selected to reflect some true state of affairs, items were chosen to represent internal traits. The basis for item selection were statistical properties, the most important of which was internal consistency of trait scales. Thus, it became common practice to narrow down an initial pool of presumably trait-relevant items on the basis of item analysis. Only those items were retained that exhibited high item-total correlations. High internal consistency, however, does not guarantee high validity of the trait scale. It may even be questioned whether boosting consistency is the best way to enhance validity. As long ago as 1946 Meehl and Hathaway raised the point that enhanced consistency may lead to increased measurement of intraverbal sets and habits rather than the internal state under consideration.

A better approach may be to increase *representativity* of the test items rather than their consistency. This approach, advocated by the present author (Hettema, 1967) would serve to delineate more precisely the boundaries of the

Personality and Environment: Assessment of Human Adaptation
Edited by P. J. Hettema. ©1989 John Wiley and Sons Ltd

domains in which the behavior of interest is supposed to be relevant. Self-report measures should ideally be designed as multifaceted instruments in which both situations and actions are representative of domains specified in advance. An argument for this approach may be based on the effects of situations and response modes upon self-reported trait scores. With respect to the effect of situations, Endler, Hunt and Rosenstein (1962) used an S-R inventory of anxiousness to show the impact of that facet. Alston (1975) has emphasized the effect of response modes stating that a particular trait may be expressed via different behaviors and among those behaviors correlations are not necessarily high.

Reviewing the development thus far, one conclusion seems unavoidable: internal consistency will eventually be abandoned as the main criterion for the construction of trait scales. A serious candidate to replace the criterion of internal consistency is *prototypicallity*. Buss and Craik (1980, 1981) the main advocates of the prototypicallity approach, define a trait (or disposition as they call it) as the emission of a large number of appropriate responses given a representative set of situations. The acts subsumed under a particular disposition may be topographically dissimilar but are nonetheless considered to be manifestations of that disposition. Rather than to constitute equivalent representations of the same disposition, the acts will thus show 'family resemblance' (Wittgenstein, 1968) and are subsumed under the same linguistic label. In Buss and Craik's view, dispositions have the status of summary labels, rather than causes of behavior. Thus they agree with Mischel (1973) who has stated: '... Thus while the traditional personality paradigm views traits as the intrapsychic causes of behavioral consistency, the present position sees them as the summary terms (labels, codes, organizing constructs) applied to observed behavior' (p. 264).

This leaves us with the question how self-reports can provide information concerning factors intrinsically involved in the individual's behavior. To find the answer to this question we may turn to recent work in the area of causal attribution of behavior. According to Jones and Nisbett (1972, p. 91), a crucial difference exists between the attributions made by actors as compared with observers of their actions: 'When the actor steps back to view himself, he is probably inclined to emphasize not the superficial topography of behavior but the underlying purposes mediated by the behavior. The actor is consequently more likely to conceive of his personality as a configuration of values and strategies than as a collection of response dispositions'.

Transposed to the area of personality assessment this statement would imply that traits are to a high degree mode-specific, i.e. specific to the mode of ratings rather than self-ratings. To test this proposition the present author (Hettema, 1981) has analyzed data obtained in the construction of rating scales and self-rating scales in The Netherlands during the period 1970–1977. A total of 30 different rating scales and 51 self-rating scales were involved in this study.

The main criterion for the trait character of the scales was internal consistency. The data showed that internal consistency was significantly higher ($p < 0.01$) for rating scales than for self-rating scales (median coefficients were 0.85 and 0.72 respectively).

A remarkable additional finding was obtained while comparing the process of item selection for rating and self-rating scales. For each of the selections involved the number of items eliminated to improve internal consistency was established. For rating scales a median of 17% of the items was eliminated from the original pool, whereas for self-rating scales the median was 35%! The results of this study thus supported the hypothesis that traits are mode-specific and that rating scales constitute the appropriate way to measure them rather than self-rating scales.

The latter mode is particularly suited to reflect the intentional aspect of individual behavior, including the goals of behavior as well as the means to obtain those goals. In the context of the open-systems adaptation model of personality these aspects have been brought together under the heading of strategy.

A strategy is conceived as a structure at the cognitive-symbolic level with the function to direct and guide behavior in concrete situations. It contains a collection of broad behavioral opportunities as well as behavioral preferences existing before the actual execution of behavior is started (cf. Hettema, 1979, pp. 72–74). The strategy is concerned with the question in which direction an individual intends to move if confronted with a particular situation and what means will be utilized to accomplish that intention. The strategy has been more formally elaborated (in: Hettema, 1979) and has obtained the form of a so-called SRS-matrix, a structure composed of representational (S_y) and transformational (R_y) elements. These elements are defined in general (intersubjective) terms, but the connections between them are assumed to be brought about on an individual basis.

Strategic information with respect to a particular individual may be obtained from self-reports, collected with the aid of multi-faceted instruments in which situation concepts and transformation rules are the facets. The elements of those facets will be systematically crossed to yield the necessary information.

A strategic questionnaire will usually be designed to cover a specific domain of situations as well as actions pertinent to these situations. To be able to design questionnaires for different domains, we need elaborate taxonomies of situations as well as of actions. The development of both types of taxonomies will be described in detail in the next chapters.

4

Situation concepts: definitions and classification

GUUS L. VAN HECK

'Every concrete activity is the solution of a situation' (Thomas and Znaniecki 1927, p. 68).

All human action is situated. Therefore, behavior cannot be understood apart from the situation in which it occurs and to which it is a potential adjustment. Antecedent to operative interventions, people have to establish their conception of the situation. The open-systems adaptation model perspective on personality (Hettema, 1979) provides a bridge between a way of conceptualizing people's understanding of the environment and a way of conceptualizing directed behavior. This control-theoretical model gives a framework from which to view the cognitive–symbolic level of the personality system, in particular the interpretation and transformation of the behavioral context via individual strategies. I begin this chapter with a brief sketch of the theoretical orientation toward the analysis of situations and then turn to a description of a comprehensive study aimed at the development of a general taxonomy of situations (see also, Van Heck, 1984).

SITUATIONS CANNOT BE TAKEN FOR GRANTED

In everyday life, no one doubts that situational conditions contribute to the conduct of individuals. Nevertheless, in the scientific study of personality only a small deal of effort has gone into systematic situational analyses.

Of course, the obvious fact that the immediate situation is influential in

Personality and Environment: Assessment of Human Adaptation
Edited by P. J. Hettema. ©1989 John Wiley and Sons Ltd

determining an individual's behavior has been considered in various theoretical models of personality. For instance, situationists (e.g., Dollard and Miller, 1950; Farber, 1964) have stressed that stimuli almost exclusively determine behavior. However, in empirical research, most of the time these situational factors have been held constant but for one manipulated factor (cf. Magnusson and Ekehammar, 1978). Also, within the personologist tradition the role of situations has been given some weight. According to Allport (1961), pressures from the surrounding environment, viz. the companions a person is with, may delay, augment, distort, or inhibit the conduct that normally can be expected to issue from a person's stable characteristics. However, situation perception and doing what the situation 'demands' depend on the individual's system of characteristics. For, differing situations elicit differing tendencies from the repertoire (Allport, 1966).

Cattell (e.g., 1965), although in a limited way (cf. Magnusson and Ekehammar, 1978), takes the psychological situation requirements into account via so-called 'behavioral situational indices' representing the relative contributions of all traits to the performance in a given situation. For the greater part, however, traitists have paid attention almost exclusively to the categorization of response–response connections and the assignment of meaning to these associations (cf. Endler and Magnusson, 1976a), paying only lip service to Lewin's (1935) equation B = f(P, E), which states that behavior (B) is a function (f) of facts within the person (P) and the environment (E).

Other theorists, such as Murray, Angyal, and Lewin, who can be located midway between situationists and personologists, must be mentioned within this context. However, Murray's (1938) need-press units, Angyal's (1941) biospheric terms, and Lewin's (1935) 'life space' have attracted more the attention of psychologists writing historical reviews of personality than of the majority of today's researchers.

An ever-increasing number of publications has shown the existence of behavioral inconsistency across situations, the disappointing predictive power of traditional trait scores and, more generally speaking, the incompleteness and insufficiency of B = f(P) models of personality (for detailed reviews see, e.g., Mischel, 1968; Van Heck, 1981).

Currently, the interest in interactionist approaches to personality (see, for instance, Endler, 1982; Magnusson and Endler, 1977) and environmental psychology (e.g., Stokols, 1978; Wicker, 1979), however, seems to introduce a promising change into this state of affairs.

The interactionist position contrasts sharply with the views held by those who follow classical personological approaches. Interactionism can be regarded as the synthesis of personologism and situationism. According to Kenrick and Dantchik (1983), the interactionist position is that the individual selects environments to play out his or her personal characteristics; that the characteristics of the individual can reciprocally alter the environment he or she encounters; that neither personality factors alone, nor situational factors alone, are sufficient in predicting behavior; and that the patterns of individuals' responses to situations in a particular domain is idiosyncratic.

Also, ecological and environmental psychology emphasize man–environment relations, focusing attention to environmental assessment, environmental perceptions, cognitive representation of large-scale environments, the analysis of behavior settings (Barker, 1968) and personality–environment interactions (cf. Craik, 1973). These emerging fields are mainly responsible for the current interest in the study of the S part of Lewin's (1935) formula. More and more the belief is shared, that in order to understand behavior an understanding of the context of that behavior is sorely needed. According to Frederiksen (1972), a systematic way of conceptualizing the domain of situations and situation variables is needed before rapid progress can be made in studying the role of situations in determining behavior. Dynamic multidirectional process conceptualizations of interaction require the study of environments analyzed in smaller units on the basis of a taxonomy of situations (Hettema, 1979; Secord, 1977).

REQUIREMENTS FOR A TAXONOMY OF SITUATIONS

The problem of definition, measurement, and classification of situations can be 'solved' in quite a number of ways (e.g., Ekehammar, 1974; Magnusson, 1981; Pervin, 1978; Van Heck and Welvaart, 1984). Within limited domains or across domains, at different levels of abstraction, situations can be studied in terms of actual situational properties or person-bound qualities, emphasizing structural or content characteristics (cf. Magnusson, 1981). Moreover, situational analyses can be aimed at high or low consensus among subjects.

Various authors have stated that many different classifications of situations are possible. Therefore, some authors believe that to seek any single basic taxonomy of situations may be futile (e.g., Hoefert, 1982; Mischel, 1977a). It must be added, however, that not all of the possible classifications will be equally useful. For instance, it is impossible to answer questions about the effects of specific situations if one cannot systematically assess or arrange these situations. How to decide whether the situation presented through verbal descriptions, film or video-tape truly reflects negotiation, competition, or accusation? Which ingredients must be represented in scripts for role-playing sessions in order to be certain that it will be situation X or situation Y? How to identify situations in observational studies in real-life conditions? Knowing that a particular situation is rated as 'exciting' and 'interesting', or 'monotonous', 'inactive', and 'peaceful' does not provide the answers to such questions (cf. Argyle, 1976, 1980). Instead, systematic descriptions and classifications in terms of key elements are needed.

THE 'SITUATION CATEGORIES OF THE MIND'

What are the salient components of situations? A distinction is often made between the situation as it actually is, defined by its objective physical-geographical and social characteristics, independent of any observer, and the situation as it is perceived (Magnusson, 1978). This distinction suggests a choice between an analysis of situations in objective terms and an analysis in person terms, viz. individual perceptions, idiosyncratic needs and motives, or very personal ways of responding. Such a partitioning of the field suggests erroneously that the actual versus perceived qualification parallels a shared versus individual distinction. In doing so, one of the most promising approaches to situational analysis is obscured. I refer to the shared psychological meaning of situations based on consensus among observers.

Within this context a very insightful distinction has been made by Block and Block (1981). They distinguish the *canonical situation* (cf. the alpha press of Murray, 1938) and the *functional situation* (cf. Murray's beta press).

> 'Canonical situations are consensually defined, consensually constructed, or consensually accepted situations. It is the psychological demand-quality or structure of the situation as specified by widely established categories of objects, concepts and relations, rules, standards, and normatively provided expectations... To the extent that developing views of the world attain consensuality, they may be said to have canonical form and the canonical form can be identified' (Block and Block, 1981, p. 87).

The functional situation represents the stimulus context as it is effectively understood by any individual. The latter 'situation', however, can only be known afterward from the individual's response. Thus, we understand the situation from the behavior and the behavior from the situation! (Block and Block, 1981). Psychologists who conceptualize situations in person terms run the risk of creating tautological circles from which there is no escape (cf. Barker, 1968; see also Postman and Tolman, 1959). Therefore, several authors have stressed that a clear distinction between the concepts person, situation, and behavior is a preprequisite for making the interactional approach to personality a fruitful one (e.g., Block and Block, 1981; Hettema, 1982a).

Hettema (1979, 1982a) has emphasized the intersubjective and normative character of situation descriptions. He recommends that situations be treated as elements of a public domain and to take as the point of departure the many subtle discriminations that people belonging to a particular group or culture make with respect to the continuous flow of events.

People, in structuring their world, striving for behavioral control, rely heavily on learned verbal responses of labeling. These labels, acquired through cultural teaching, reflect the discriminations and equivalences that have been found useful by generations of trial and error (Dollard and Miller, 1950; Miller, 1948).

Psychological adaptation is not always an easy task, however, because every situation is more or less new. The individual does not find passively ready situations exactly similar to past situations. Instead, he or she must define every situation on the ground of some analogy with known situations 'as an old problem viewed from a new standpoint' (cf. Thomas and Znaniecki, 1927).

The effort to interpret the new in terms of the old is one of the cornerstones in Hettema's (1979) view on the adaptive strivings of human beings. According to that position, people try to reduce environmental uncertainty by categorizing an infinite number of environments via a limited number of situation concepts. In doing so, individuals make use of cultural information, viz. definitions of situations which have been arrived at through the consensus of adults over a period of time (cf. Hettema, 1979; Kluckhohn and Kelly, 1945; Thomas, cited in Volkart, 1951). Systematic confrontation with the accumulated knowledge available in a particular culture will lead to consensually constructed situations. Through language people have at their disposal an intersubjective classification system with far-reaching consequences for behavior (e.g., Berlyne, 1965; Dollard and Miller, 1950; Miller and McNeill, 1969; Pavlov, 1951).

The major aims of the present chapter are to characterize the content of this classification system, and to detect the degree of orderliness in the layperson's everyday 'natural' categorical knowledge about situations. Concepts are situation concepts if they relate to the environment (in its broadest sense) and if their properties or semantic markers (cf. Katz, 1972) may be referred to intersubjectively (Hettema, 1979).

Our approach is very akin to a categorical-prototype analysis (e.g., Cantor, Mischel, and Schwartz, 1982a, 1982b; Eckes and Six, 1984). This latter research strategy is an adaptation of the prototype model (Rosch, 1978) to the domain of naive situation knowledge structures. This model emphasizes the tendency to group elements of the world, viz. objects, people, or psychological episodes, into categories so that non-identical information can be treated as if it was equivalent (Rosch, Mervis, Gray, Johnson, and Boyes-Braem, 1976). According to this position, 'knowledge about any given category is structured around, and represented in, long-term memory as a prototype that captures the meaning of the category' (Cantor, Mischel and Schwartz, 1982b, p. 35). Thus, the ideal member of a category is represented by a set of features commonly associated with members of a category, with each feature assigned a weight according to the degree of association with the category. Prototypes function as standards around which bodies of input are compared. Consequently, these pre-existing situation images have a unifying effect with respect to the complex flood of environmental information. Although idiosyncratic prototypes are conceivable (see Eckes and Six, 1984), until now attention has been devoted mainly to the study of consensual prototypes. These consensual beliefs are conceived of as normative conceptual schemes for organizing situational input, analogous to Hettema's (1979) 'situation concepts' (S_y), a major element of individual behavior strategies.

THE DOMAIN OF SITUATIONS

In developing a taxonomy of situations several other important decisions have to be made. First, a choice must be made regarding the domain of situations. What must be included? The existing classifications of situations are almost without exception based on a limited number of situations unsystematically sampled within one, rather loosely defined, domain, e.g., stressful events, risky tasks, test conditions, school situations, work environments, etc. 'Typically, situations were sampled at the convenience of the investigator or theorist' (Price, 1981, p. 104).

With respect to choice of domains, there seems to exist a great diversity of insight. Some investigators prefer sampling limited to specific domains (e.g., Magnusson, 1971), while others suggest that it will be best to sample over large domains (e.g., Pervin, 1978). In my opinion it is important to take as point of departure a broad sampling of situations. As long as '... the whole matter of the definition of elements of situations is shrouded in clouds and smoke' (Sarason, 1977, p. 267), restriction to a particular type of situations, e.g., work settings or leisure activities, can lead to biased conclusions with insufficient possibilities of generalization. Pervin (1978) advises to avoid getting prematurely locked into a particular classification scheme. In the present study this advice was taken seriously. An attempt was made to investigate the taxonomic structure of the total 'sphere' of situations to which people seem to be responsive.

THE LEVEL OF ANALYSIS

Another issue that required a decision refers to the problem of determining the level of analysis. Environments can be conceptualized along a micro-macro dimension (Bronfenbrenner, 1977; Magnusson, 1978, 1981; Pervin, 1978). Recently, Cantor (1981) has reported some research on perceiver's categorical knowledge about everyday situations. She employed various units of analysis. Categories of situations were studied on three levels of abstraction: superordinate, most inclusive categories like 'ideological situations', middle level categories like 'being at a demonstration for a cause', and even more concrete categories like 'being at a save-the-whales sit-in'. At each level of abstraction subjects were asked to give 'prototype' descriptions in terms of the features characteristic of situations that belong to these categories. Cantor found that middle-level situation categories provided the optimal balance between richness of information (number of features) and degree of redundancy in the information contained in the description for neighboring situations. Cantor's middle-level situations resemble closely the 'situation types' as described by Magnusson (1981). A situation type can be conceived of as '... the general class of a particular kind of actual and/or perceived situations, without specification of time and place, in contrast to momentary situations' (Magnusson, 1981, p. 15). For example, the situation type corresponding to the momentary situation 'having words with a colleague at Monday morning in your office' would be 'a quarrel'. In the present study situation concepts were investigated at a level midway between most concrete and most abstract.

THE CONSTRUCTION OF A GENERAL TAXONOMY OF SITUATIONS

The collection of situation concepts

Via dictionary searches[1] it was tried to obtain a more or less exhaustive set of the everyday terms people use to describe their ecology. Only nouns that refer to situations that can be objectively (that is, with high consensus) perceived were chosen. Selected were those nouns that could be placed meaningfully into sentence frames of the following form: 'a... situation' or 'being confronted with a... situation'. Additional criteria were formulated in order to be able to decide whether or not a particular noun must be included in our collection of situation concepts. Not selected were nouns that refer to very molecular events, inner processes, emotional and motivational states, personality traits, evaluations of acts or events, historical processes, periods, biological processes and bodily states, sociological and economic positions, enduring stable relations between persons or between persons and institutions, roles, specific locations, animals, plants, and objects. Also proper names and geographical names were eliminated. Finally, nouns such as beginning, that are relatively meaningless without knowing the answer of questions like: 'The beginning of what?', or 'With respect to what?', were excluded. Using these guidelines nouns such as accusation, punishment, interruption, conversation, dinner,

[1] Use was made of (a) Weijnen, A. (1975). *Nederlands woordenboek*. Spectrum, Utrecht, and (b) Reinsma, R. (1975). *Signalement van nieuwe woorden, W. P.-woordenboek van 2000 neologismen*. Elsevier, Amsterdam. Moreover, as a check, parts of Van Dale's (1976) *Groot woordenboek der Nederlandse taal, Vol I & II*. Nijhoff, 's-Gravenhage: 1976 were analyzed.

examination, etc. were selected, while sadness, attention, sweetness, marriage, director, meadow, spiny lobster, woodruff, jigsaw puzzle, Helen, Paris, finish, etc. were left out.

Dictionaries were analyzed independently by two judges. Approximately 750 nouns fulfilled all requirements. This initial pool contained many synonyms and also various archaic terms. After elimination of these superfluous words there remained an item pool of 263 situation concepts.

The collection of cues

Our next step was aimed at definition of these concepts in terms of objective situational characteristics or attributes. To compose a pool of situational attributes a sample of 160 subjects were interviewed. The sample was completely balanced with respect to the rural versus urban population, male–female, age (over and under 38 years), and socio-economic class (education level and occupational position).

The total item pool was divided in 10 sets of situation concepts. Each subject was interviewed with respect to one set of 26 (or 27) situation concepts. So, each subgroup of 10 subjects was presented with the total item pool. It follows that each situation concept was presented 16 times.

The procedure employed was derived from Flanagan's (1949) well-known 'Critical incidents approach'. Subjects were asked to bring to mind concrete situations that were, in their opinion, typical examples of the situation concepts offered. In free descriptions subjects generated the essential characteristics (cues) of the situations. Note that subjects did not enumerate attributes. Instead, they told us their vivid stories characterized by rich variety. All the concrete descriptions were recorded on audio-tape.

In the next phase, which can be called 'the inventory of cues', these tapes with a total duration of more than 200 hours, were analyzed according to a coding scheme containing eight content categories. Pervin (1977) describes a situation as a Gestalt containing four major components: place, people, action, and time. In line with this definition, the following content categories were distinguished in the analyses of the tapes:

1. *Context.* The broader context in which situations occur is an often neglected aspect in situational analyses (cf. Price, 1981). Situations are contained within other temporally more extensive situations. According to Shotter (1980), human actions and their settings are necessarily nested. Cues belonging to this Context category refer to the institutional and historical context of the situation. For instance, bombardments occur only under wartime conditions. Moreover, it was found necessary in a small

number of cases to include cues that referred to the immediate cause of a particular situation.

2. *Location/physical environment.* These cues refer to the geographical and topographical aspects of the situation.

3. *Objectively discernible characteristics of the physical environment.* Only those cues were selected that could be expected to show high intersubjectivity among observers. This category contained mostly physical and biological properties of the environment.

4. *Persons.* This category contains the types of people lay psychologists expect to be found in certain kinds of situations (cf. Cantor, 1981). There is no question of a burglary in the absence of a burglar; of medical operations without a surgeon, patients, and nurses; or a wedding without a bride.

5. *Objectively discernible characteristics of the persons concerned.* Only highly observable properties, that is factual conditions and features of the persons involved that can be detected independent of interpretations by single observers, were selected. For instance, drunk, pregnant, naked, dressed in black, wearing a uniform, etc., but not dependent, alienated, pretty, etc.

6. *Actions and activities that are characteristic for the particular situation.* This category comes close to one of Argyle's (1977) basic components of situations, viz. 'special moves'. According to Argyle, 'each situation defines certain moves as relevant and important: e.g., making love—various types of bodily contact; tutorial—read part of essay; dinner party—pass food, pour wine; shopping—try on trousers; interview—ask personal questions' (Argyle, 1977, p. 364).

7. *Objects/equipment.* In any particular situation a number of different objects may be present that are necessary for the activities that 'belong' to the situation.

8. *Temporal aspects.* Sometimes a situation can be characterized by the period when it is occurring. Furthermore, situations do have beginnings and ends—they do have duration.

Data resulting from the content analyses were processed as follows. From each situation concept and each category of cues all the cues mentioned by our subjects were brought together. With respect to virtually all the situation concepts rich sets of cues were obtained. As a next step, a team of six judges was intensively trained in rewriting the overwhelming amount of concrete situation ingredients. Using extensive directives this group of judges worked on all the unassorted lists of cues. In order to reduce the large number of discrete feature units to a manageable number of cues, they collapsed certain variations in phrasing into one category that was identified with the morpheme, called a 'keyword', common to each member of the category (cf. Rosenberg and Jones,

1972; Gara and Rosenberg, 1981). So, synonyms were left out and the various concrete instances of a more general class were relabeled at a more abstract level. For instance, gun, rifle, shotgun, automatic pistol, stiletto, bayonet were relabeled as weapon.

For each situation concept a matrix of cues × subjects was obtained. Inspection of these matrices revealed that in a limited number of cases subjects generated disjunctive sets of cues with respect to a particular situation concept. As a consequence, the initial item pool of situation concepts was slightly adapted. Furthermore, it appeared that some situation terms were poorly understood by our subjects. Therefore, some concepts, for instance, pogrom, were removed.

The final result of this phase of the study was a list of 248 situation concepts and a list of 659 separate cues. Of these cues, 34% were actions. The percentages for the other content categories were: 5% (context), 13% (locations), 8% (characteristics of the physical environment), 11% (persons), 9% (person characteristics), 14% (objects/equipment), and 6% (temporal aspects). These 659 cues formed the total set found in the more than 4000 situation descriptions we collected. The list of situation concepts is presented in Appendix A of this book.

The classification of situations

In a next stage of the present study the situation concepts were presented to a new group of subjects ($N = 744$). They were asked to describe situations in terms of the complete set of cues. The task was to indicate on seven-point Likert-type scales how essential and characteristic each of these cues were for the situation in question. Each situation was described by four subjects, viz. a male below the age of 30, a male above the age of 30, a female younger than 30, and a female older than 30.

The immediate result of this phase was a 248×659 matrix with cells containing average scores reflecting the degree that a particular cue was judged to be a characteristic of a particular situation

This matrix was analyzed for each cue category with Johnson's (1967) hierarchical clustering procedure (maximum method)[2] in order to group the 659 separate cues into clusters of cues. This analysis resulted in 254 clusters of cues. Appendix B presents these clusters of situation cues.

New scores were calculated in order to be able to define situations in terms

---

[2] The following coefficient of convergence was used:

$$CC_{jk} = 1.00 - \left[\frac{1}{n} \sum_{i=1}^{n} \left(\frac{X_{ij} + X_{ik}}{X_{ij} + X_{ik}} \right)^2 \right]^{1/2}$$

This coefficient is related to Clark's (1952) distance measure given in Sokal and Sneath's (1963) *Principles of numerical taxonomy*.

of these cue clusters. In this manner a 248 (situation concepts) × 254 (cue clusters) matrix was developed. Subsequently, the 248 × 254 matrix was analyzed aimed at the discovery of clusters of situations based upon (dis)similarities of these new cue profiles. Again, a hierarchical cluster analysis (Johnson, 1967; maximum method) was carried out. The number of situation clusters retained was set equal to 100. So, the final result of this clustering technique was a matrix (with new scores) of 100 (clusters of situation concepts) × 254 (cue clusters).

The last phase of data analysis involved the calculation of Pearson correlation between clusters of situations. Factor analysis of the 100 × 100 correlation matrix produced our general taxonomy of situations. Ten factors meeting an eigenvalue criterion of 2.0 were extracted and Varimax rotated. The outcomes of the principal factor analysis are given in Appendix C, presenting only loadings in excess of 0.30.

Factor 1

The situations defining this first, large factor reflect fighting and *interpersonal conflict*. Thus, this factor was labeled accordingly.

Factor 2

The second factor is defined by clusters of situations reflecting *joint working*, and the *exchange of thoughts, ideals, and knowledge.*

Factor 3

Situation clusters with high loadings on this factor mainly reflect male–female sexual activity, *intimacy, and interpersonal relations.*

Factor 4

The fourth factor is defined by situations such as reception, dancing-party, inauguration, dinner, birthday party, concert, show, etc. The factor emphasizes festivities, either with an official character, or informal and without ceremony. Common aspects of all the situations loading high on Factor 4 are amusement, entertainment, or diversion. Therefore, a suitable label seems to be *recreation*.

Factor 5

This factor contains eight clusters of situations involving travel, transport, and being on the way. Furthermore, this factor is defined by situations reflecting all sorts of disasters that can happen when people are en route. The factor is labeled *traveling*.

Factor 6

Four clusters of situations are included in this factor, representing two somewhat related events. On the one hand, situations reflecting religion and religious ceremonies, and on the other hand, situations in which a deceased person plays a central role, viz. funeral, cremation, or autopsy. An adequate label is difficult to formulate. Because funerals and cremations have much in common with divine services, perhaps religious and other *rituals* is the most adequate label.

Factor 7

This factor reflects situations involving sport activities, competition, and physical exercise, and is labeled *sport*.

Factor 8

This factor contains the situations fornication, obscenity, orgy, drinking-bout, turning night into day, night-duty, hypnosis, and gambling. A tentative label for this factor is *excesses*.

Factor 9

This rather small factor reflects *serving*.

Factor 10

This factor contains situations in which the act or process of buying and selling is the central aspect. Therefore, the factor is labeled *trading*.

TAXONOMIES AND DIFFERENT TYPES OF CUES

To gain more insight into the taxonomic structure obtained, some additional analyses were carried out. The major purpose of these analyses was to reveal the relative impact of the various cue categories. What will happen when place features are left out? Do time features have their own specific contribution to the ultimate categorization? Are locations, persons, and actions relatively independent, each producing distinct groupings when considered in isolation? Is a taxonomic structure based on locations alone, or persons alone, much more global compared with the fine-grained nuances obtained by way of the analyses of action patterns? Or, alternatively, are the different types of cues interdependent, so that they produce highly similar taxonomies?

In order to be able to answer these questions, a set of 25 situation concepts was selected from the original item pool. The choice was guided by two principles: taxonomic representativeness and ecological representativeness.

First, it was tried to represent the whole gamut of situations. Therefore, three situation concepts were chosen from each of the first five factors of the taxonomy of Appendix C, and two situation concepts from each of the remaining, smaller factors. In addition to taxonomic representativeness, our second selection criterion was the ecological validity of the situations. In consequence, it was tried to sample those situations that were as nearly representative of the daily livings of our subjects as possible (cf. Brunswik, 1956; Pervin, 1977). The set of 25 situations is given in Table 1. Using the data of our group of 744 subjects, six matrices were formed:

1. 25 situation concepts × 24 cue clusters reflecting context and time features (see Appendix B).
2. 25 situation concepts × 49 clusters of location cues and location characteristics.
3. 25 situation concepts × 57 cue clusters containing persons and their physical features.
4. 25 situation concepts × 80 clusters of action cues.
5. 25 situation concepts x 44 clusters of cues indicating objects and equipment.

Table 1 List of 25 situation concepts used in the comparisons of classifications based on different types of cues

Number	Situation concepts	Number	Situation concepts
1	Farewell (5)	14	Feast (4)
2	Meeting/encounter (3)	15	Cremation (6)
3	Sale (10)	16	Queue (5)
4	Quarrel (1)	17	Housekeeping (9)
5	Dinner (4)	18	Rapprochement/advances (3)
6	Examination (2)	19	Divorce (3)
7	Job application (2)	20	Orgy (8)
8	Discussion (2)	21	Address/speech (4)
9	Religious ceremony (6)	22	Contest (7)
10	Obscenity (8)	23	Criticism (1)
11	Drill (5)	24	Market (10)
12	Nursing (9)	25	Holiday (5)
13	Accusation (1)		

Note. Numbers in parentheses refer to the factors of Appendix C.

Table 2 Degrees of correspondence (Pearson *r*) between correlational structures derived via different sets of cue clusters

	C + T	A	P + CP	L + CL	Ob	200
Context + temporal features (C + T)	—	50	42	41	42	64
Actions (A)		—	61	53	71	88
Persons + person characteristics (P + PC)			—	41	51	71
Locations and location characteristics (L + CL)				—	50	50
Objects (Ob)					—	75
200 Cue clusters (200)						—

Note. Decimal points omitted.

6. 25 situation concepts x 200 randomly selected[3] cue clusters spread over all the eight cue categories.

For each matrix, a correlation matrix was computed across cue clusters. The degree of relatedness between these six matrices of correlations was determined by product–moment correlations. These Pearson *r*s are presented in Table 2. Of course, these correlations between correlation matrices cannot be interpreted in terms of amount of variance explained or significance level, because they are based on non-independent observations (cf. Block, Weiss, and Thorne, 1979). Nevertheless, these intermatrix correlations positively have a descriptive value, yielding interpretable figures, which indicate how well one can predict from one set of measurements to other sets (cf. Shweder and D'Andrade, 1979).

The inspection of Table 2 reveals a number of interesting things. Firstly, the patterns of interrelations for judgements in terms of only one type of cues were strongly related to the pattern of interrelations obtained via an analysis incorporating all types of cues. It must be admitted that it is not so remarkable that the pattern of intercorrelations for, e.g., actions was like the pattern of a larger set of features, actions included. For, 32% of the 200 selected cue clusters were clusters of action cues. Much more remarkable is the fact that also a substantial correspondence was found between the pattern derived via 'context and time'-features (8.5% of the 200 cue clusters) and the overall pattern. Secondly, substantial degrees of correspondence were found between correlational structures based on separate cue categories, viz. actions, persons and their physical characteristics, etc. I think that these results make clear that the various kinds of cues are interdependent. Actions are closely linked with types of persons, and to a lesser extent, with all sorts of places. It seems that

[3] This selection was necessary because of limitations of the computer program we used.

only certain combinations of places, persons, equipment, and actions, etc. are possible. The present results underline Argyle's (1980) view that the features of situations form a system.

In addition to the computation of the intermatrix correlations, Johnson's (1967) hierarchical clustering procedure (maximum method) was used to obtain situation clusters and dendrograms. As index of relatedness between each pair of situations product-moment correlations were used. The three most important tree structures are shown in the Appendices D-1 (actions), D-2 (persons and person characteristics), and D-3 (locations and location characteristics).

From the graphs, it is clear that these three hierarchical clustering configurations are closely related to each other. For instance, the following 10 cluster solution was obtained for *actions*:

1. Farewell, religious ceremony, cremation.
2. Quarrel, accusation, criticism, discussion.
3. Address.
4. Drill, contest.
5. Encounter, rapprochement/advances, dinner, feast.
6. Obscenity, orgy, divorce.
7. Sale, market.
8. Queue, holiday.
9. Examination, job application.
10. Nursing, housekeeping.

The 10-cluster groupings for *place and person* features are:

1. Farewell, Rapprochement/advances, encounter.
2. Dinner, feast, housekeeping.
3. Obscenity, orgy.
4. Religious ceremony, nursing, cremation.
5. Divorce.
6. Sale, holiday, queue, market.
7. Quarrel, accusation, criticism.
8. Drill, contest.
9. Examination, job application.
10. Discussion, address.

For locations and characteristics they were:

1. Farewell, drill, criticism.
2. Queue.
3. Quarrel, discussion.
4. Obscenity, contest.
5. Sale, examination, job application, market.

6. Nursing, accusation.
7. Housekeeping, divorce.
8. Encounter, feast, rapprochement/advances.
9. Dinner, orgy, holiday.
10. Religious ceremony, address, cremation.

It can be seen in Appendices D-1, D-2, and D-3 that the 10-cluster solutions are obtained when rather lenient cut-off points are used: 0.04, 0.10, and 0.10, respectively, for action-, person-, and location cues. When a less tolerant cut-off point is selected, for instance, 0.30, then there are 15, 16, and 17 clusters of situations, respectively for action-, person- and location cues.

So it appears that compared with dimensional or perceptual approaches (e.g., Forgas, 1978, Magnusson and Ekehammar, 1975) a componential approach as used in the present study reveals that situations do not fall readily into equivalence classes.

CONCLUDING REMARKS

Summarizing, it can be said that the interpretation of the obtained factors provided no insurmountable difficulties. The obtained taxonomic structure is a very clear one. Though our road to the grouping of situations was a rocky one, it turned out that it was not impassable.

It is rather remarkable that these empirical results fit fairly well in an *a priori* classification suggested by Krause (1970). Krause offers a set of classes of social situations, such as joint working, trading, fighting, sponsored teaching, serving, self-disclosure and playing. Furthermore, the obtained empirically derived classification shows some relation with ideas put forward by Argyle (1977). Argyle has stated that goals are probably the best starting point for situational analyses. Based primarily upon Krause's (1970) article and the work of Harré and Secord (1972), he has proposed the following list of goals that could serve as a basis for a classification of situations: Primarily social/cooperative, including most family life, play, eating together; male–female sexual activity; competitive games; aggressive conflict; negotiation, buying and selling; joint work, with cooperation and supervision; joint discussion, problem solving, decision taking; teaching, therapy; lectures and other public performances; interview, interrogation; religious and other rituals.

I am not implying that our taxonomy is mainly a classification in terms of goals. Rather, I try to underline the soundness of the empirically derived structure by pointing to some striking similarities with classes of situations distinguished within the context of theoretical analyses of situational conditions.

Most remarkable, however, is the finding that situations can be grouped in meaningful classes based on analyses in terms of objectively defined characteristics of situations. This finding is even more surprising because of the fact that all these cues were weighted equally. Persons involved, physical properties of places, the occurrence of behavioral activities, but also at first sight rather trivial aspects like ash-trays, spoons, cups of coffee, a table, or the presence of a microphone, received equal weight in characterizing situations.

According to Magnusson (1981), there are several reasons for making situations a subject of analysis: Firstly, physical, biological, social and cultural aspects of the environment are of decisive importance for the development of more permanent ways of conceptualizing and dealing with the actual world. Secondly, behavior cannot be understood in isolation of effective situational variables. Thirdly, systematic knowledge about situations is needed, so that situational conditions can be considered in a known, predictable, and controlled way. Finally, knowledge about situations can contribute to effective applications of psychology. The results of the present study can be used with respect to all these issues.

Only when presentation of stimulus conditions is based on systematic conceptualizations of situations, is it possible to test differentiated hypotheses about the interactions between persons and specific environments. The present taxonomy provides a general background for the definition of situations that can be used in various media of stimulus presentation, for instance, questionnaires, films, simulations, and observation systems.

Some years ago, Mischel (1977, p. 250) stated that it will be important '...to avoid emerging simply with a trait psychology of situations, in which events and settings, rather than people, are merely given different labels'. He rightly pointed out that the task of naming situations cannot substitute for the job of analyzing how situations interact with the people in them. I believe that the present study avoided most of the pitfalls of classical trait psychology. Consequently, the constructed situation taxonomy will prove to be a useful element in process oriented studies of situated actions.

5
Transformation rules: towards a taxonomy of everyday behavior

JOOP HETTEMA

ADAPTATION AND BEHAVIOR

In the context of adaptation, behavior has specific effect with respect to human ecology. Earlier (Hettema, 1979) I have conceptualized human ecology by making a distinction into three different areas. Those areas were represented as three concentric circles of which the central area is the domain where biological functioning is guaranteed directly. Around that area a second domain was postulated where transformation to the first area is possible through evolutionary determined behavior. Together the two inner areas of human ecology constitute the environment of evolutionary adaptedness (Bowlby, 1969). Behavior in areas I and II was deemed to be the province of ethology, the biology of behavior. Area III was defined as the special domain of psychology. It contains a collection of relatively new and unknown environments that can be adequately controlled only if a new dimension is added to the behavioral equipment: psychological adaptation. The vital function of adaptative behavior is to enlarge the range of environments in which the human species can survive, to extend the ecological niche defined by species-specific behavior.

Psychological adaptation is acquired and extended gradually during the ontogenetic development of individuals. The information assumption (2.2.) states: 'The individual collects information either from personal experience or social learning to help him control the environment'. While elaborating this assumption, I have pointed out that language plays an essential role in

Personality and Environment: Assessment of Human Adaptation
Edited by P. J. Hettema. ©1989 John Wiley and Sons Ltd

encoding and transmitting the information relevant for psychological adapt-ation. Two main elements have been distinguished to conceptualize the contribution of learning to adaptation: situation concepts (S_y) and transform-ation rules (R_y). With respect to the former elements a comprehensive study has been reported in the previous chapter to specify situation concepts.

Here our task will be to develop a taxonomy of behaviors that are presumably fit to exploit situations as well as to transform situations into new situations with more advantage for the individual. Clearly, to accomplish this task we cannot resort to the typical mainstay of ethology, i.e. species-specific behavior governed by survival value. Instead, we will have to define behaviors in terms to make them effective to transform ill-defined and uncertain environments.

The basis to accomplish a taxonomy of the type mentioned are situations and their basic features as defined earlier. Earlier I have defined the situation as 'a culturally specified cue structure of a spatio-temporal nature, that has been provided with a particular meaning' (Hettema, 1979, p. 86). Obviously, to transform situations answering to this description always means to trans-form their spatio-temporal elements or cues. Transformation rules have to be defined in a way allowing them to be tied on to the structural elements of the situation.

Furthermore, transformations should be *directed* transformations to be psychologically adaptive. The transformation assumption (2.3) states that 'Directed activities can modify the environment, and produce feedback to the personality system'. This means that transformation rules must be defined in a way to make them fit to bring about specific modifications or a particular new situation. As has been pointed out before (Hettema, 1979, pp. 90–92), to perform their directional function, transformations have to satisfy criteria of legitimacy. This implies that a particular situation imposes restrictions upon the kinds of behavior that may be effectively executed in that situation. And, on the other hand, each behavior imposes a particular direction upon the situation. The direction imposed may or may not coincide with the direction already present in the initial situation. Both aspects of restrictivity and directionality should be explicitly included in a taxonomy of transformational behavior, in order to act as a key element in the context of psychological adaptation.

To summarize this section a taxonomy of transformational behaviors will henceforth be developed based on linguistic concepts referring to transform-ational activities. For obvious reasons the taxonomy should be as comprehen-sive as possible within the linguistic context chosen. Two more specific requirements have emerged from the discussion. First, with respect to each behavior we will have to be able to indicate whether it can transform (particular aspects of) the situation in which it occurs. And, secondly, the direction of the transformations presumably occurring will have to be indicated. Only if these conditions are satisfied, will we be able to ascertain whether the behavior is effective either in transforming the situation into a new one, or in exploiting it while leaving the initial situation essentially unaffected.

THE ANALYSIS OF VERBS

Transformation rules may be referred to intersubjectively while being represented in language. They can be defined with the aid of semantic markers that will by nature demonstrate a different emphasis as compared with the markers used to define situation concepts. To define transformation rules the linguistic elements coming to mind first are verbs. However, an important question to be asked is, whether verbs always refer to actions. An elaborate analysis by Schank (1973) has shown that verbs are not necessarily representative of particular underlying actions. In fact, most of the time, an English verb is a description of a resulting state of some unknown action or a relation of many unknown actions rather than the action itself (Schank, 1973, p. 209). What we really need is a system of actions rather than verbs to represent transformation rules. On the basis of conceptual dependencies existing in natural languages, Schank (1973) has managed to reduce the information encompassed by language utterances into complexes involving just a few basic elements. According to Schank, his conceptual dependency theory is able to adequately represent all the information underlying English verbs with the aid of a limited number of so-called primitive actions plus a number of states (Schank, 1973, p. 228). *Primitive actions* are meant to account for the concepts underlying an action that people talk about, and they serve to organize the inferences that can be made about the results of an action (Schank and Abelson, 1977, p. 86). Clearly, to represent transformation rules, primitive actions offer an important aspect that should be taken into account.

Schank and Abelson have distinguished between 11 different primitive actions and provided them with a code:

ATRANS = the transfer of an abstract relationship, e.g. possession.
PTRANS = the transfer of the location of an object or of oneself.
PROPEL = the application of a physical force.
  MOVE = the movement of body parts.
 GRASP = the grasping of an object by an actor.
 INGEST = the taking in of an object to the inside.
  EXPEL = the expulsion of an object from the body into the physical world.
MTRANS = the transfer of mental information between or within indivi-
             duals.
MBUILD = the construction of new information from old information.
  SPEAK = the actions of producing sounds.
ATTEND = the actions of attending or focusing a sense organ towards a
          stimulus.

According to Schank (1973), the primitive actions can conveniently be classified into physical actions (PTRANS, PROPEL, GRASP, INGEST, EXPEL and MOVE), mental actions (MTRANS, MBUILD and ATTEND) and instrumental actions. Each of the primitive actions ties on to a specific aspect of the situation to which they are applied. Thus, for instance, in PTRANS the location of an object or subject may be the starting point, whereas in PROPEL one or more objects and in MTRANS one or more subjects are involved. Each primitive action assumes a particular state of affairs to exist in the initial situation. Furthermore, primitive actions appear useful to indicate all kinds of activities an individual may carry out to transform specific elements of the situation. Thus, if an individual intends to transform the location of an object or of himself, he may use PTRANS; if he intends to transform the actions prevailing in the situation, he can use PROPEL, MOVE, GRASP or other actions, but he can also use MTRANS to have other persons act in a particular way.

In each of the examples given a proviso is made concerning the intentions of the subject. Primitive actions as such do not specify the goal aspects of the actions involved, the intended state. As stated before, verbs generally do provide information on the state of situational aspects intended to be acquired by means of primitive actions. In Schank and Abelson's (1977) view 'often a verb is represented as a particular combination of primitive actions and states none of which are unique to that verb, but whose combination is entirely unique' (p. 12). Thus, verbs may be conceptualized to involve goal aspects as well as primitive action aspects so that they can be used to communicate complete actions. With respect to the relationship between the two aspects, Schank and Abelson have pointed out that primitive actions can be taken to be arranged according to plan boxes, each of which is subsumed under one or more goals. Thus, if goals are conceived as intended transformations of situational aspects, primitive actions may be conceived as the appropriate means to bring about the desired transformations. What we obviously need is a second system to classify the relevant goal aspects of verbs. Only then will it be possible to satisfy our second requirement, the directional aspect of transformational behavior.

The goal aspects to be chosen here cannot be derived from general theories of motivation or biological needs. Instead, within the present context, we must rely on the major process assumption of the open-system theory, the control assumption (2.1). This assumption states that 'Internal and external activities of the individual are governed by the leading principle to acquire and maintain control over the environment'. Its implication is, that the goal aspects of behavior should be conceptualized in terms of an individual's intentions to gain, maintain or increase control over specific aspects of the situation.

Once again, Schank and Abelson (1977) have provided us with a useful system based on the analysis of natural language. We are referring to the so-called *delta goals* or d-goals, conceived by those authors to organize information on the intended change of state of an object (p. 86).

These d-goals reflect intentions to increase knowledge, power, proximity, generally to gain control over specific aspects of the situation. The following d-goals have been distinguished:

D-SOCCONT = the intention to gain power or authority.

D-CONT = the intention to gain control over physical objects.

D-PROX = the intention to move to a new location or to another person.

D-KNOW = the intention to increase knowledge.

D-AGENCY = the intention to get someone else to pursue a goal on one's own behalf.

In addition to the five d-goals outlined, Schank and Abelson have defined I-PREP, to classify all activities with a preparatory character regarding specific d-goals.

The d-goal system is not meant to imply that in a particular situation actions are restricted to the attainment of just one of the goals. Several d-goals may be strung together to form elaborate plans, organizing a number of subsequent transformations intended to be brought about. Thus, d-goals provide us with a language that is appropriate to indicate detailed transactions between an individual and a situation to gain control. Together with primitive actions they may be used to define types of transformational behavior to be applied in different situations and aiming at different transformations to occur. Clearly, the directional aspect of behavior is accounted for by the d-goal system.

A TAXONOMY OF TRANSFORMATIONAL BEHAVIOR

Having defined the two main aspects of actions in the context of psychological adaptation, we will henceforth turn to the development of a taxonomy of transformational behavior. This will be done by classifying verbs according to primitive actions and d-goals.

A major problem to be solved to establish that classification is the problem of ambiguity. This problem is especially to be expected in the classification of the d-goal aspect. For instance, a verb like 'to ask' can be classified to represent D-KNOW, but also to represent D-CONT or D-AGENCY. As D-KNOW to ask means to ask for information, as D-CONT it means to ask for an object, and as D-AGENCY it means to ask somebody to do something. What we obviously need in a case like this is a further specification of the verb to be able to unambiguously classify it in any of the three ways. Suffixes like 'for' or 'about' might shed some light here, although 'ask for' as in D-CONT may as well be elaborated to 'ask for help' as in D-AGENCY.

In the Dutch language prefixes would be more appropriate to discriminate between several d-goal aspects of the same verb. For instance, the verb 'vragen' (to ask) may be accompanied by prefixes like 'onder-' 'over-' 'na-' 'uit-' 'door-' 'aan-' 'af-' or 'op-' to indicate subtle specifications of its d-goal aspect. Obviously, verbs differ largely in the amount of generality-specificity with respect to the goal-aspect indicated. Thus, if a taxonomy of transform-ational behavior is to be defined in terms of verbs, it should preferably be restricted to verbs containing specific goal references. If, on the other hand, more general and ambiguous verbs are included, they should be accompanied by specific goal indications to serve their purpose.

Before turning to the establishment of the taxonomy a preliminary study was done in our laboratory by Wings (1979) to test whether the Schank−Abel-son categories could be meaningfully applied to classify specific behaviors in concrete situations. Wings took 10 situations from Van Heck's situation taxonomy and asked his Ss how they would act when confronted with those situations. The Ss were 55 undergraduate students majoring in psychology. The situations were selected primarily to be familiar for a student sample. They included: a concert, a meeting, an exchange of thoughts, an inquiry, a visit to a bar, a teasing situation, a visit, a car ride and a party. All situations were briefly described in terms of the main cues derived from the situation taxonomy. The method used was an open interview to allow for additional questions to be asked in case of ambiguous answers. Specifically, if a subject would give an answer that was inconclusive with respect to the d-goal aspect of the behavior indicated, Wings would ask 'Why would you do that?'. Using this procedure he managed to classify 86% of the actions reported ($N = 746$) unambiguously with respect to the primitive action aspect as well as to the d-goal aspect. The remaining 14% concerned actions that, even after repeated questioning, could not be classified in any of the d-goal categories. In those cases, the Ss would give comments like 'I do that just because everybody does that' or 'One ought to behave that way in a situation like that'. Obviously, although not surprisingly, a number of actions appear to be carried out, not to transform situations or to exploit them, but simply to preserve their original form. An action frequently mentioned in this context was 'await', indicating a passive and open attitude of the S waiting for the situation to take its own course. Since this type of 'activity' could not be subsumed under one of the Schank− Abelson primitive action categories, Wings recommended to add a new category to the system, i.e. AWAIT.

A few general conclusions may be drawn from this study. First, the Schank−Abelson classification of primitive actions does not cause serious problems when applied to verbs used in free descriptions of behavior in concrete situations. Secondly, the application of d-goals requires a distinction into general (ambiguous) verbs on the one hand and more specific verbs on the other: only the latter can be meaningfully classified in terms of d-goal categories. And, finally, besides behavior intended to exploit or transform the situation, a third category is needed to encompass behavior meant to preserve the situation in its original form.

With respect to the behavior taxonomy to be developed both the primitive action and the d-goal classification systems were slightly adjusted. In the primitive action system the category EXPEL was replaced by the category AWAIT. In the d-goal system a category was added to include the general verbs. With these principles in mind the construction of the taxonomy was started. The classification matrix contained 77 different categories, resulting from the systematic combination of 11 primitive action categories and seven d-goal categories. All the verbs ($N = 225$) emerging from the situation taxonomy (cf. Van Heck, Chapter 4) were taken and it was attempted to classify them all. For each verb on rational grounds the proper categories were ascertained with respect to primitive actions as well as d-goals, to determine the cell where it belonged. It turned out that very few verbs could not be classified (examples are 'to die' and 'to give birth'). After the verbs had been classified, only 37 of the 77 cells had actually been used (it should be pointed out here that this classification refers to Dutch verbs and is restricted to the verbs appearing as cues in the situation taxonomy). A tentative conclusion may be that not all actions are fit to bring about all changes intended. The only row filled up completely is MTRANS and the only column filled up completely is the general column. Rather than making any statements on the completeness of this classification, we decided to take it as a first approximation to the behavior taxonomy wanted.

The final step in the construction of the taxonomy was the selection of verbs that could be considered to be more or less pure representations of behavior for each of the 37 cells. Apart from being impractical for the purpose of measurement the distribution obtained showed some ambiguities, so we attempted to retain only those verbs that fitted quite well into the definition obtained by combining a particular d-goal with a particular primitive action. For each cell a maximum of four verbs was taken into account. At the end of a second careful rational analysis of all verbs a final set of 104 verbs was retained. They were distributed over the 37 cells according to Appendix E.

THE PROTOTYPICAL PACKAGE

Having defined transformation rules in terms of primitive action aspects and d-goal aspects, I will henceforth turn to the question whether or not a particular transformation rule will be effective in actually transforming a particular situation.

Earlier I have distinguished between three different types of transformation rules on the basis of their effectivity to maintain or transform a specific situation. Some rules will be effective in *preserving* the original situation, others will *transform* the situation into a new one, whereas still others do *not affect* the situation at all. Earlier (Hettema, 1979) I have located the first category of transformation rules on the main diagonal of a matrix representing the exploitative system. The second category was located in the off-diagonal cells of the same matrix. The third category was not represented in the matrix because it is not effective at all.

In the present section the discussion will focus on prototypical behavior, i.e. behavior that can be expected to preserve the original situation. In each situation a set of behaviors can be defined answering to the restrictions imposed by that situation, but not transforming the situation into a new direction. This set of behaviors, designated here as the *prototypical behavioral package* of that situation, can be taken to be effective in preserving the situation, eventually to bring the situation to a natural end, but not to transform it into any new direction. To identify this set of behaviours for each situation the data gathered in the context of the situation taxonomy provide a solid basis. What obviously needs to be done, is to take all the verbs that are characteristic of a situation and to categorize them according to the viewpoints developed in the context of the behavior taxonomy.

Since those verbs are very characteristic of that situation, they may be taken to represent its restrictional aspects as well as its directional aspects. An analysis of the pertinent verbs according to the aspects mentioned will give us the prototypical package of the situation, specified according to restrictional and directional aspects. To provide an example of the procedure outlined, a sample of situations was taken from Van Heck's taxonomy and analyzed accordingly. The sample ($N = 33$ situations; for an overview see Appendix F) was meant to represent different factors as well as different clusters within factors. Care was taken to represent each cluster by more than one situation.

The analysis aiming at the definition of prototypical behavior packages for each of the situations, was started by isolating the 104 verbs used to define the behavior taxonomy. The scores of each situation for each of the verbs were arranged according to the 37 categories of the behavior taxonomy, and mean scores for the categories were determined. Thus, each situation could be characterized in terms of the behavior taxonomy categories.

The next step of the analysis was meant to obtain a hierarchy of primitive actions for each situation. Since in the matrix representing the behavior taxonomy a number of cells were blank, a special analysis was needed to establish that hierarchy. First, paired comparisons were made between the scores for different primitive action categories within d-goal categories. From the matrix (cf. Appendix E) it follows that a total of 113 paired comparisons could be made. The results of these comparisons were brought together in an 11×11 dominance matrix of primitive actions. Each cell of that matrix contained from one to five comparisons. The results per cell were all reduced to a single dominance score on the basis of a simple comparison of the number of plus and minus signs per cell. (If the number of pluses exceeded the number of minuses, the cell was scored plus and vice versa. If they were in balance the result was scored as zero.)

Finally, these dominance matrices were subjected to a method developed by Coombs (1964) for the reduction of a single set of pair comparisons. Using weak stochastic transitivity as a criterion, the elements of the matrices were rearranged according to the number of times each element was considered to be more characteristic. The results of this analysis were taken to represent the hierarchies of primitive actions wanted for each of the situations. They are brought together in Appendix F-a.

A closer look at this Appendix reveals an interesting feature of the primitive action hierarchy. As has been stated before, primitive actions are the basis used to classify actions according to the restrictions imposed by the situation. This would imply that they will to a large extent be domain specific. That this is actually the case, can readily be seen if the 33 situations are arranged according to the factors found in the situation taxonomy study. After the three primitive actions with highest ranks for each situation are categorized according to physical, mental and instrumental acts, the following picture (Table 1) is obtained. We see then, that factor I is dominated by physical acts and factor II by mental acts. Factor III seems to combine both physical and mental acts, whereas factor IV shows a tendency to be dominated by instrumental and mental acts.

The final step of the analysis concerned the d-goal hierarchy for each situation. The procedure used was much the same as the previous one. Thus, paired comparisons were made once more but now for any pair of d-goals within primitive action categories. A total of 31 comparisons were possible on the basis of the behavior taxonomy. The results were brought together in a 6×6 dominance matrix of d-goals (the general category was left out of consideration). The cells of this matrix contained from one to five comparisons. Per cell the results were reduced to single dominance scores according to the same procedure as used in the analysis of primitive action

Table 1 Distribution of prototypical physical, mental and instrumental acts over situation factors

| | | Acts | |
	Physical	Mental	Instrumental
Factor I	12	3	9
Factor II	6	41	13
Factor III	3	6	0
Factor IV	0	3	3
Total	21	53	25

hierarchies. Subsequently the items were rearranged to produce d-goal hierarchies for each of the situations. The results of this analysis are collected in Appendix F-b.

Having obtained hierarchies of primitive action categories as well as of d-goal categories, we could henceforth set out to determine the prototypical behavior package for each of the 33 situations. It was argued that, in order to qualify as part of the prototypical package a transformation rule should be applicable to, as well as codirectional with the situation. This means that only those transformation rules are to be taken into consideration that combine primitive actions and d-goals both occupying a high position in their respective hierarchies. Arbitrary criteria were set to include the three highest ranking primitive action categories as well as the two highest ranking d-goal categories. In addition to the latter, the general category was always included in the prototypical package. By combining the categories mentioned for each situation a set of transformation rules is defined, that together constitute the prototypical package.

PRINCIPLES OF SITUATION TRANSFORMATION

This final section deals with the problem of situational transformation by means of behavior. After distinguishing between different transformation rules we have managed to define situations using a limited amount of transformation rules together determining the prototypical behavior package for each situation. In this context the obvious way to approach situation transformations is to point out changes occurring in the prototypical package to produce a prototypical package representing a new situation. Thus, the introduction of transformation rules *not* included in the prototypical package will tend to transform the situation. As has been pointed out before, however, to be effective the primitive action aspect of those rules should form part of the primitive actions included in the prototypical package. This leads to an important conclusion: situational transformation can be brought about only by changing its directional aspect. Or, in other words, *transforming a situation by means of behavior means changing one or more d-goals of its prototypical package.*

In different areas of scientific investigations it is customary to represent directional aspects with the aid of vectors. Assuming d-goals to represent more or less independent directions a six-dimensional space would be adequate to represent all directions included in the prototypical packages of the situations in the taxonomy. Since we need only two d-goals to describe the directional aspect of any particular situation, a two-dimensional subspace would suffice to define a situation. Within that subspace a specific direction is established by combining the vectors representing both relevant d-goals, taking their relative magnitudes into account. This representation of the directional aspect of situations provides a basis to define situational transformation. It can be represented either as a change of direction within the two-dimensional subspace, or as a change of the dimensions involved. Depending upon the kind of change, two different types of situation transformation can be defined:

1. *Moderate transformation*, involving change in the hierarchy of d-goals defining the initial situation.
2. *Radical transformation*, in which a new directional dimension is introduced by replacing one of the d-goals of the initial situation by a new d-goal.

Both types will be elaborated here, since they are both considered legitimate situational transformations in the context of psychological adaptation.

In moderate transformation the hierarchy of d-goals can be changed on the basis of behavior *emphasizing the subordinate d-goal* of the prototypical package. For instance, a situation originally defined as a talk situation may be moderately transformed by one of the actors who starts cracking jokes. In doing so the subordinate d-goal of the talk situation, D-PROX, is emphasized. It can eventually become dominant to redefine the situation as rapprochement. In terms of d-goals the initial hierarchy showed I-PREP dominating D-PROX, while in the final situation the order was reversed in that D-PROX dominated I-PREP. The order of events outlined may as well be reversed. This will occur, for instance, if an individual attempts to persuade somebody else to have a date together, and finally ends up discussing merits of several restaurants to be considered as the place to visit. The initial situation of this example can be labeled rapprochement in which D-PROX dominates I-PREP. In the final situation I-PREP dominates D-PROX to constitute a talk situation. On the basis of the principle of reversal, moderate transformations may be expected to occur between different pairs of situations taken from the set of 33 situations discussed in the previous section. Obviously, the transformation rule to be used to accomplish moderate transformations differs according to the pertinent situations. A few examples are given in Figure 1.

It is obvious that moderate transformations can only be accomplished between any two situations sharing the same d-goals albeit in a different order. Those situations may be expected to be close to each other in terms of the situation taxonomy. The latter is not true for the second type of situational change: radical transformation. As a matter of fact, a situation may be transformed into a situation that is quite different from the initial one, if new dimensions or d-goals are introduced.

For example, a lecture can turn into a quarrel if the lecturer is systematically criticized by his audience. The initial situation, directionally defined as [D-KNOW, D-CONT] is then transformed into [D-SOCCONT, D-CONT] by the introduction of D-SOCCONT. On the other hand, it is conceivable to transform a quarrel into a lecture by asking the other party to explain his point of view. In that case [D-SOCCONT, D-CONT] is transformed into [D-KNOW, D-CONT] by introducing D-KNOW behavior. As another example, a situation of misunderstanding can be changed into cooperation on the basis of reconciliation behavior. In that case [D-SOCCONT, I-PREP] is transformed into [I-PREP, D-PROX] on the basis of D-PROX behavior. And, once again, the reverse can be accomplished as well, if cooperation is disturbed by continuous remarks. In that case [I-PREP, D-PROX] turns into [D-SOCCONT, I-PREP] by the introduction of D-SOCCONT as the new d-goal. On the principles outlined here, radical transformations may be expected to occur as shown in Figure 2. Thus far, moderate as well as radical transformations have been pointed out within pairs of situations. What happens if the principles derived are applied to a larger sequence of activities may be illustrated with the following example.

Suppose the manager of a large organization summons his executive staff for a gathering. As everybody is present, he calls attention to a specific problem of management, i.e. an increasing failure to delegate particular activities to subordinates in the organization. In a plea for improvement he urges his staff to take measures with respect to the issue.

Situation	Transformation	Situation
Manipulation	D-SOCC	Accusation / Interference
Intrigue	D-CONT	Quarrel / Conflict
(D-CONT, D-SOCC)		(D-SOCC, D-CONT)
Plea	I-PREP	Discussion / Deliberation
Address	D-CONT	Assembly
(D-CONT, I-PREP)		(I-PREP, D-CONT)

Figure 1　Examples of moderate transformation of situations

Situation	Transformation	Situation
Examination / Report / Interview	D-SOCC / I-PREP	Judgement / Criticism / Failure
(D-KNOW, I-PREP)		(D-SOCC, D-KNOW)
Meeting	D-AGENCY	
Rendezvous	D-PROX	Appointment
(D-PROX, I-PREP)		(D-AGENCY, I-PREP)

Figure 2　Examples of radical transformation of situations

His argument is, however, not received by his audience as benevolently as he would like. One of the executives in particular takes offence and starts criticizing the manager, stating that he is obviously not aware of what is really going on at the lower levels of the organization. The atmosphere becomes chilly and a quarrel seems unavoidable. At that moment, one of the other executives asks whether the others have the same experience with respect to the delegation issue. They all give their opinions and exchange views on the subject. Another executive summarizes what has been said thus far and he tries to reconcile the different points of view. Finally, they deliberate the issue at length and deal with the question of what can be done about it.

Surveying this sequence of events, it can be stated that a number of transformations have occurred here, although most situational aspects (e.g. the setting, the location, actors, attributes, and the like) have remained essentially the same. However, especially the actions, and presumably the state, of the actors show major changes. Those changes are considered here to be sufficiently radical to constitute a number of different situations emanating from each other. Thus, what started as a neutral gathering of company executives successively evolves into a discussion, a plea, a misunderstanding, a judgment situation, an exchange of thoughts, a rapprochement, and, finally, a cooperation. Each new situation is introduced by a change of d-goals brought about by one of the participants. As a consequence, the directional aspect is changed almost continuously. Table 2 gives an overview of the transformations occurring and shows each new d-goal emanating indicated by a circle. A closer examination reveals that two transformations ($2 \rightarrow 3$ and $7 \rightarrow 8$) are of the moderate type, whereas the other are radical transformations.

One may wonder whether we really need eight different situation concepts to describe what is going on in this example. After all, one might as well have designated the whole sequence as just one single situation. In doing so, one would however have failed to appreciate all the more subtle transactions occurring between individuals and environment. Another question to be asked here is, whether the cues and features actually changing over time are essential or merely adventitious in defining each of the situations. For instance one could ask whether a real plea can take place in a company's meeting room at 3.00 p.m. The answers to these questions should obviously be derived from the situation taxonomy. A crucial part is played by the level of abstraction chosen to define situations. The abstraction issue has been dealt with in some detail earlier and it has been decided to define situations at an intermediate level of abstraction. The situation taxonomy constructed on that basis indicates that it is quite possible for the different situations mentioned to occur within the same location. The major aspect differentiating between those situations are actions, and, within that category, the goal aspects of actions. This does not imply, however, that all situation transformations are restricted to mere actions. Many transformations will involve a change of location, of actors, of

Table 2 Situation transformations occurring as a consequence of behavioral goals

D-Goals	1 Gathering	2 Discussion	3 Plea	4 Misunderstanding	5 Judgment	6 Exchange of thoughts	7 Rapprochement	8 Cooperation
D-SOCCONT								
D-CONT	×	×	⊗	⊗	×			
D-PROX							⊗	×
D-KNOW	×				⊗	×		
D-AGENCY								
I-PREP		⊗	×	×		⊗	×	⊗

attributes and the like. But even in those transformations a decisive part is played by actions and their goal aspects, causing other changes to occur in non-action aspects of the situation.

The principles concerning situation transformation outlined here have not been fully elaborated as yet. In their present form they are considered to constitute a first step into the direction of a full-fledged 'situational algebra' defining elements and transformations in more detail. With respect to the transformations suffice it to restate the rules derived from the previous analysis.

1. To transform situations through behavior d-goals is the decisive factor.
2. D-goals that coincide with the first d-goal of the prototypical hierarchy will leave the situation unchanged.
3. D-goals coinciding with the second d-goal of the hierarchy will cause moderate transformations to occur. As a consequence a new situation is brought about of which the d-goals have changed positions compared with the initial situation.
4. D-goals that differ from both prototypical d-goals cause radical transformations to take place. The d-goal hierarchy of the new situation emanating as a consequence, contains the new d-goal as well as one of the d-goals of the initial situation.

6
The assessment of behavioral strategies

JOOP HETTEMA

and

DORIEN P. HOL

INTRODUCTION

Strategies are cognitive structures governing behavior so as to attain individual goals. From a macro-perspective individual goals can be conceived as elements of life tasks (Cantor and Kihlstrom, 1987) or personal projects (Little, 1983). They involve long-term sequences or chains of actions to accomplish a career, a marriage or a public image. However, for assessment purposes these global descriptions do not offer a solid basis. To solve this problem, in the open-systems adaptation model strategies are conceived as sequences of situation transformations, ultimately directed at the attainment of some long-term personal goal(s). Information on those sequences may be obtained by dividing them into their elements—discrete situations—and studying behavior in each situation separately. While systematically confronting a subject with different types of situations emerging in a sequence, a complete picture may be obtained concerning the sequence as a whole. Thus, in the context of the present model, strategic assessment comes down to confronting subjects with situations of different types and establishing the choices they make with respect to behaviors, maintaining, modifying or transforming the situations offered.

Personality and Environment: Assessment of Human Adaptation
Edited by P. J. Hettema. ©1989 John Wiley and Sons Ltd

ELEMENTS AND PRESENTATION

To establish his strategy, the subject has to be confronted with specific situations. With respect to those situations he has to indicate which behaviors he would preferably show if he would be in a situation of the given type. Furthermore, he would have to indicate which final situation he would intend to bring about by means of that behavior.

Regarding the medium and the mode to be utilized it has been pointed out before that both should be of a verbal nature. The verbal medium allows situations to be presented in a clear way. It is important to mention a number of concrete situational elements to avoid ambiguities as are present in, for instance, situation labels. The situation taxonomy provides the opportunity to do this. Based on the cue packages collected by Van Heck a vivid image can be portrayed of each of the situations in terms of locations, actors, actions and other situational cues.

The behaviors that the subject demonstrates in a particular situation can be collected in either of two ways: the free response format or the precoded response format. An advantage of the first approach is that the subject is enabled to consider freely his most preferent behavior as well as the intended products of his behavior. A disadvantage is that an elaborate instruction would be necessary to explain to the subject what the strategic behavior aspect is all about, before he can deliver his preferences. Another disadvantage is that many subjects will give an incomplete picture of their actual preferences because they are not able to imagine all the possibilities at that particular moment.

By offering a number of precoded alternatives the decision process will be relatively simple. A disadvantage of this method is that the response options offered may have a steering effect regarding the subject's behavior. To combine the advantages of both approaches the following procedure was designed. First, the subject is asked to consider the situation and give his response preferences by means of free responses. Subsequently, the subject obtains a number of response alternatives and is asked to indicate which of those alternatives he would consider to demonstrate when actually confronted with the situation. Further studies will have to decide whether this procedure offers real advantages over the mere precoded response approach.

As well as situation descriptions the response alternatives given have to be stated in concrete terms. The formulations should preferably be borrowed from daily usage to minimize ambiguity. From the definition of a strategy it follows that in general different behavioral options are to be solicited rather than one single behavior. Essentially each individual is considered to have more strings to his bow regarding the goal aspect (the preferred final situation) as well as regarding the means aspect (the preferred action) of behavior. To do justice to this principle in the questionnaire, the subject is asked to indicate all alternatives he would consider in the pertinent situation and furthermore to accomplish a preference order among the alternatives chosen. Order may be obtained with the aid of either rating or ranking procedures.

THE SELECTION OF SITUATIONS AND RESPONSE ALTERNATIVES

Strategies are specific to domains, i.e. is is not possible to extrapolate to an individual's strategy in domain B on the basis of information concerning his strategy in domain A. Thus, the study of the strategic aspect of behavior will have to occur within the boundaries of a well-specified domain of situations. One could, for instance, study strategies in school situations, in industrial situations or in interpersonal situations. In a particular study it is therefore important first to delineate the domain of interest with the aid of an ecological analysis (cf. Brunswik, 1943). The frequency of occurrence of each situation within the domain can be established using the situations derived from the situation taxonomy as elements. On the basis of this analysis a sample of situations can be defined that is representative of the domain studied. Within that domain the sample does not have to be homogeneous in any respect: representativity is the main criterion of interest (cf. Hettema, 1979).

Regarding the response alternatives to be offered it is important to represent all possible alternatives: completeness is the main criterion here. This requirement implies that with respect to each situation a systematic exploration of the responses possible in that situation has to be carried out. The taxonomy of behavior provides an indispensable expedient here. By systematically scanning all cells of the taxonomy one can make sure that no important alternatives are overlooked. In view of the relatively abstract character of the behavior taxonomy it is advisable to use a second procedure next to the one mentioned: free generation of responses, preferably by experts in the pertinent domain.

FORMULATION OF THE ITEMS

The description of situations for the questionnaire is based on the cue packages established in the context of the situation taxonomy study. For each of the situation concepts identified the scores of the different cue-clusters are known. Per situation concept the most characteristic, i.e. highest scoring cue clusters are selected among the 254 clusters used.

The following rules are taken into account in the selection process:

1. Find the 15 cue-clusters with the highest score (group I).
2. Find the 15 cue-clusters with the next highest scores (group II).

The 30 cue-clusters obtained provide the ingredients for the description of the situation. All clusters included in group I should be represented by one or more cues. Group II provides optional clusters that may or may not be used to complete the group I cues. The other cues, not occurring in either the group I or group II clusters, are considered to be not characteristic for the situation. Consequently they are not allowed to be taken up in the description of the situation. Thus, situations are always described in terms of the cues minimally necessary to characterize them. This procedure, that we have indicated as the *method of minimal cues*, will return later in the context of the representation of situations via the film medium. Based on the package of cues so defined the situation description should be as concrete as possible. It should be closely connected with the circumstances in which the subjects live their lives, and, in addition, it should have a somewhat problematic character.

Against the background of those situation descriptions response alternatives are formulated. As has been pointed out before, a particular situation imposes restrictions regarding the type of behavior that can be effectively carried out. The crucial aspect in this regard are the primitive actions (PA). Thus, only those primitive actions are represented that are effective in the pertinent situation (prototypical primitive actions). In the formulation of the response alternatives the specific d-goal (dG) aspect is emphasized as well. This can be done with the aid of the specific verb used or by stressing the intended state of affairs by mentioning the goal of the action. All potential alternatives are scrutinized with respect to clarity and unequivocallity of the formulation used. Thus, for each situation a list of maximally 3 (PA) $\times$ 7(dG) = 21 response alternatives is compiled. This list may occasionally be extended with responses that contain a non-prototypical primitive action. The list of alternatives consists of responses preserving the original situation (the prototypical package) as well as responses transforming the original situation (the transformational package). To complete the process of item construction the order of the response alternatives is randomized and subsequently put in a fixed order. The different situations are presented in a fixed order as well.

The instruction

The questionnaire is presented with an instruction stating that its goal is to obtain insight in the behavior of people in slightly problematic situations, occurring regularly in daily life. It is pointed out that in that kind of situations several actions are usually possible and that the test is meant to collect information on the subject's individual way of behaving. The subject is confronted with a short situation description and a number of response alternatives. He is asked to study the situation description and to imagine what he would do in that situation and with what purpose. Subsequently he may check whether his preferred action is present among the alternatives offered. In case no alternative corresponds very well with his own solution, the subject is asked to write the latter down on a separate card.

After the first option is established he is asked to think if alternative behavioral options would be considered in this situation. If so this is indicated on the answer sheet. Usually the subject will indicate some other actions and he is asked to rank order them, or, in the case of ratings, to point out the degree of preference for each action on a five-point Likert scale. It is always possible for the subject to create new alternatives and order or rate them among the others. In case new alternatives are added to the ones present, the investigator will categorize them afterwards in terms of the response taxonomy.

THE SRS-FORMAT AND THE COHERENCE OF STRATEGIES

The preferences indicated by the subject are the basis to determine his strategy. To do this use is made of the behavior taxonomy's property that each behavior alternative can be categorized with respect to its primitive action as well as its d-goal aspect. Based on that property of the behavior taxonomy it is possible to indicate for each behavior alternative chosen which final situation is intended, and which activity is used to attain that goal.

The questionnaire method developed here differs from existing techniques. The classical personality questionnaire does not usually specify the initial situation, whereas all responses are referring to the same trait and can be viewed as more or less precise replications of each other (cf. Hettema, 1967). A more advanced type of questionnaire, the SR-questionnaire (cf. Endler, Hunt and Rosenstein, 1962; Van Heck, 1981) does give a specification of the initial situation, but again the responses all refer to the same trait (e.g. anxiousness, hostility). The present technique specifies the initial situation but it also conceives of the response alternatives as reflections of behavioral options with a different strategic meaning. That meaning is exacerbated in the final situations intended to be brought about by means of the actions. Thus, it appears justified to refer to this procedure as a new technique. We have called it the SRS-questionnaire, stressing the final situation as well as the initial situation, and distinguishing it from the SR-questionnaire.

Special requirements are to be taken into account with respect to the reliability of SRS-questionnaires. Those requirements may be specified starting from the reliability of classical personality questionnaires. Classical personality questionnaires require the items to be consistent, i.e. that they all refer to the same trait or personality disposition. For the investigator this comes down to the claim that individual differences are replicable over items, e.g. with the aid of Kuder–Richardson formulae. The SRS-questionnaire is not primarily directed at homogeneity but at coherence (cf. Magnusson and Endler, 1977). Coherence implies that individuals may be characterized on the basis of stable individual response patterns as a function of the same or different situations.

Obviously, in the context of our interactional approach, there is no need for a particular strategic preference in a particular situation, to generalize to other situations (transsituational consistency). However, behavior of the same type should be preferred as well (internal coherence), whereas in the same situations the behavior preferred originally should be preferred again (coherence stability). In addition, it would be nice if we could generalize to somewhat broader classes of situations in order to increase the range of convenience of the SRS-questionnaire (transsituational coherence).

To test the generality of our assessment technique several studies were done with SRS-questionnaires in which the effect of variation of responses and of situations were explored. The first investigation was directed at the effect of different operationalizations of transformation rules as distinguished in the behavior taxonomy. This study, reported by Begeer (1984) was restricted to d-goals as response types. Begeer developed an SRS-questionnaire taking into account the guidelines given here for the development as well as the reliability study of SRS-questionnaires. His study was directed at leader strategies in specific problem situations occurring in a particular company. Subjects were 42 executives working in that company.

First Begeer did an ecological analysis to identify the problem situations and on that basis he developed a 15-items SRS-questionnaire. For each of the 15 situations Begeer used six response types corresponding to six different d-goals. For each response type he formulated three different items that he considered to be parallel items, each reflecting the same d-goal and the same primitive action. Preference scores for each response alternative were obtained with ratings using five-point Likert scales.

The data of Begeer's study were analyzed according to a three-facet ANOVA design, with situations, response types and responses nested within response types as facets (design XI^b, cf. Chapter 2). The coefficient of generalizability was computed using the following (Equation 13, Chapter 2):

$$\rho^2_{(PSR)r\,:\,R} = \frac{\sigma^2_P + \sigma^2_{PS} + \sigma^2_{PR} + \sigma^2_{PSR}}{\sigma^2_P + \sigma^2_{PS} + \sigma^2_{PR} + \sigma^2_{PSR} + 1/n_r(\sigma^2_{Pr\,:\,R} + \sigma^2_{PSr\,:\,R;\ error})} \qquad 1$$

The result was 0.70, indicating a fair amount of internal coherence of the SRS-questionnaire. Begeer concluded that we can safely put together the scores derived from different behaviors referring to the same delta goal, thus warranting the internal coherence of the SRS-questionnaire.

More recently, one of us (Hol, 1990) studied the internal coherence of strategies, using two 15-item SRS-questionnaires. Fifteen social situations were carefully selected from the situation taxonomy to represent all combinations of two d-goals in their prototypical packages. Each situation had 21 response alternatives, seven d-goals with three different responses each. All responses in this questionnaire were of the MTRANS type.

Two versions of the SRS-questionnaire were developed, one with male social counterparts, one with female counterparts in the situations. The first version was administered to 73 subjects (39 females and 34 males), the second version to 74 subjects (40 females, 34 males). All subjects were students of higher professional education. Data were analyzed with a three-facet ANOVA design, using situations, response types and responses nested within types as facets (design XI^b). Coefficients of internal coherence were computed according to equation 1 (Equation 13, Chapter 2), yielding the same value of 0.69 for both versions. These results, corroborating the Begeer study, provide a solid basis for the internal coherence of the SRS-questionnaire.

The next reliability study had a different aim. Its purpose was to investigate if strategic response preferences can be generalized beyond single situations to broader equivalence classes of situations. Those classes were defined on the basis of the prototypical packages of situations. We argued that, if two situations can be characterized with the same primitive actions and d-goals, they can be taken to be functionally equivalent, at least insofar as behavior is concerned. Consequently, we expected some generalization to be possible over situations of the same prototype. Since the study directed at this issue has not been reported elsewhere, we will present it in more detail.

A STUDY OF INTERPERSONAL STRATEGIES WITH THE SRS-QUESTIONNAIRE

The selection of situations

In order to obtain insight in the assessment of strategies with SRS-questionnaires, a study was done in the area of interpersonal behavior. This is a very broad domain, so that a formal ecological analysis can hardly be carried out. Instead, a number of interpersonal situations were selected on the basis of a systematic inspection of the situation taxonomy. Representativity with respect to the major interpersonal factors of the taxonomy was the main criterion for selection. The choice of situations was codetermined by the intention to represent situations occurring frequently in daily life. Furthermore the consideration to eventually represent the situations in films as well as in simulations of natural settings was taken into account. Finally, 17 situations were selected from factors I, II, III and IV of the situation taxonomy to be included in the SRS-questionnaire of interpersonal behavior (see Table 1). For each situation a description was made according to the directives given before,

Table 1 Selected situations with prototypical packages

	Primitive actions	Delta goals
Assembly	MBUILD–AWAIT–MTRANS	I-PREP–D-CONT
Deliberation	MTRANS–MBUILD–AWAIT	I-PREP–D-CONT
Discussion	MTRANS–MBUILD–SPEAK	I-PREP–D-CONT
Examination	MBUILD–MTRANS–ATTEND	D-KNOW–D-CONT
Gathering	MTRANS–AWAIT–MBUILD	I-PREP–D-CONT
Interview	MBUILD–AWAIT–MTRANS	I-PREP–D-KNOW
Job application	MBUILD–MTRANS–ATTEND	I-PREP–D-KNOW
Lecture	MBUILD–SPEAK–MTRANS	D-KNOW–D-CONT
Manipulation	MTRANS–AWAIT–PROPEL	D-CONT–D-SOCCONT
Meeting	MTRANS–ATTEND–MBUILD	I-PREP–D-PROX
Negotiation	MTRANS–MBUILD–AWAIT	I-PREP–D-CONT
Officialdom	MBUILD–ATTEND–PTRANS	I-PREP–D-CONT
Rapprochement	MBUILD–MTRANS–GRASP	I-PREP–D-PROX
Rendez-vous	PTRANS–MTRANS–MBUILD	I-PREP–D-PROX
Report	MBUILD–MTRANS–ATTEND	D-KNOW–I-PREP
Talk	MTRANS–MBUILD–SPEAK	I-PREP–D-PROX
Thought exchange	MTRANS–MBUILD–ATTEND	I-PREP–D-KNOW

and, in addition, for each situation a number of appropriate response alternatives were formulated. An example is given in Table 2.

Subjects

The 17 items of the SRS-questionnaire were presented to 118 students of different schools for higher professional education in Tilburg. Those schools included academies for teaching, engineering, sports, arts, traffic and libraries. The student group was composed of female ($N = 55$) as well as male students ($N = 63$). Ages ranged from 17 to 27 years.

It was assumed that all members of this group had either personal experience or at least sufficient knowledge of the situations presented. A pilot study directed at the issue of familiarity of the situations confirmed that assumption.

Procedure

The questionnaire was administered in small groups containing from 10 to 15 persons at a time. After a brief general introduction of the study as a whole, the subjects were asked to quietly and attentively read the written instruction of the test. In this study the task of the subjects was to rank order the preferred response alternatives rather than to rate them. Use was made of a card form of the questionnaire in which each response alternative was written on a separate

Table 2 Example of an SRS-item: the situation 'assembly'. An assembly is held by the district council on the housing policy of the municipal authorities. The municipality has issued an announcement that some new companies will be established in the district in order to enhance employment. House building will consequently be stopped. An official has explained those intentions to be assembly. A teacher of the district's elementary school takes down what is said. Several participants ask questions and the discussions are fierce. At a certain moment you have made an important observation but it goes by unnoticed and it is not entered on the minutes. What would you do?

	PA	d-goal
1. Ask somebody to repeat your observation	MTRANS	D-AGENCY
2. Start a quarrel in the assembly	MTRANS	D-SOCCONT
3. Quit talking and do not participate in the deliberations any longer	AWAIT	D-SOCCONT
4. Discuss the course of the assembly with acquaintances	MTRANS	I-PREP
5. Start making remarks at every occasion	MTRANS	D-SOCCONT
6. Resign as an active member of the council	MTRANS	D-SOCCONT
7. Wait for an opportunity to repeat your observation	AWAIT	GENERAL
8. Ask the teacher to take down your remark	MTRANS	D-AGENCY
9. State your remark to the people sitting next to you	MTRANS	I-PREP
10. Address the chairman until he gives you the opportunity to make your observation	MTRANS	D-CONT
11. Repeat your remark at the top of your voice	MTRANS	D-CONT
12. Quit talking and leave it at that	AWAIT	GENERAL
13. Start discussing other matters with the people next to you	MTRANS	D-PROX
14. Start yelling until you attract attention	SPEAK	GENERAL
15. Rise to attract attention and repeat your observation	MTRANS	D-CONT
16. Put down your observation in district's newspaper	MBUILD	GENERAL
17. Leave and do not participate any longer	PTRANS	D-SOCCONT
18. Make noise to attract attention and repeat your remark	MTRANS	D-SOCCONT
19. Start talking with the official to see what he thinks of your observation	MTRANS	D-KNOW
20. Present your remark to the secretary in writing and have it entered on the minutes	MBUILD	I-PREP
21. React later at another point to be able to repeat your observation	MTRANS	GENERAL
22. Start asking questions at every occasion for the rest of the assembly	MTRANS	D-SOCCONT
23. Start counteracting the assembly	MTRANS	D-SOCCONT
24. Bring in a motion of order to the chairman and have him make your observation still	MTRANS	D-CONT

card. In case of ambiguities, an additional explanation was given, preferable using the same terms as the instruction. To illustrate the procedure, an example was treated with the whole group. The importance of making one's own individual choices was emphasized and the subjects were encouraged to rank order the cards at their own personal pace.

Results

To allow for a detailed analysis of the results of the SRS-questionnaire, scores were obtained per subject per situation for the primitive action aspect as well as for the delta goal aspect. This was done by determining the percentage of items endorsed for each aspect separately. If, for instance, a situation had six items referring to PTRANS and a subject endorsed two of those items, his score would be 0.33.

To answer the main question of this study—the effect of the junction of situations into prototypes—we proceeded as follows. First we selected clusters of situations on the basis of shared prototypical packages. The clustering was done for primitive actions and for d-goals separately, so that two different sets of clusters emerged. For primitive actions the problem was, that the vast majority of the situations shared MTRANS and MBUILD in their proto-typical package. So we had to rely on the third primitive action to make clusters. We decided on one cluster sharing AWAIT as the third primitive action, containing the situations assembly, deliberation and negotiation. The second cluster was based on SPEAK as the third primitive action and contained discussion, lecture and talk as situations. And the third cluster was based on ATTEND as the third primitive action and was composed of examination, job application and thought exchange.

With respect to d-goals almost all situations had I-PREP in their proto-typical package, so that the other d-goal was taken as the basis to form clusters. The first cluster contained D-CONT and consisted of assembly, deliberation, discussion and negotiation. The second cluster was based on D-KNOW and contained interview, job application, report and thought exchange. The third cluster shared D-PROX and contained meeting, rappro-chement, rendez-vous and talk as situations.

The obvious analysis of primitive actions as well as d-goals is gen-eralizability analysis with persons × situation types × reactions as the object of measurement. The data were analyzed according to the P × (s : S) × R partially nested ANOVA design. In this study the factor R (primitive actions or d-goals) was conceived as a fixed factor and the factor P as random, whereas the other factors were conceived as samples from finite universes (cf. Brennan, 1978). As the numbers of situations and situation types are quite large in the universe, there seemed to be no point in conceiving the corresponding factors as random. Thus it was decided to analyze the data according to a mixed model with the factor responses fixed and the other factors random. Eleven components of variance were obtained following design XIa and used to determine the coefficient of generalizability according to equation 2 (equation 12 Chapter 2).

$$\rho^2_{(PSR)s\,:\,S} = \frac{\sigma^2_P + \sigma^2_{PS} + \sigma^2_{PR} + \sigma^2_{PSR}}{\sigma^2_P + \sigma^2_{PS} + \sigma^2_{PR} + \sigma^2_{PR} + 1/n_s(\sigma^2_{Ps\,:\,S} + \sigma^2_{Ps\,:\,SR;\;error})}$$

For primitive actions the coefficient of generalizability was 0.263 and for d-goals we obtained 0.495. The conclusion from these results must be that it is not easy to generalize to situation prototypes on the basis of information obtained with single situations, neither on the base of primitive actions nor on the base of d-goals. This conclusion implies that a radical simplification of the situation taxonomy on the basis of prototypical packages would probably deprive us from valuable strategic information, compared with the taxonomy in its present form. Thus, we will henceforth have to restrict conclusions on strategic preferences to the single initial situations eliciting those preferences. This conclusion does not, however, pertain to the final situations, intended to be brought about by the behavior preferred. In the next section attention will be drawn to that issue.

COMPETENCE AND INTENTIONALITY AS FACETS OF A STRATEGY

The predictive validity of strategies has been investigated by Hettema (1984) in a preliminary study.

The results of that study showed that predictions of overt behavior based on strategic information are reasonably accurate. A closer inspection of the data revealed however, that the positive findings could to a considerable extent be attributed to general, super-individual factors rather than to individual strategies *per se*. As an explanation Hettema (1984) formulated the hypothesis that shared competence had played a decisive part in determining the results. In addition to competence the intentionality of individuals was suggested to be tapped by the SRS-questionnaire, This latter factor was assumed to add an individual component next to the more general competence aspects.

Hettema (1984) suggested trying to separate these aspects in the measurement of strategies, because

'the aspects of intentionality and competence are inseparably tied together in self-report measures, but both of them seem important in the prediction of individual behavior. To untie those aspects seems to be an important task for investigators working with self-report measures in the context of interactional personality psychology' (p. 176).

To bring about the distinction between competence and intentionality empirically as well as theoretically the behavior taxonomy was extended to include d-goals as well as primitive actions. As was pointed out in the previous chapter, a particular situation imposes restrictions upon the kinds of behavior (primitive actions) that may be effectively executed in that situation. Alternatively, each behavior imposes a particular direction upon the situation on the basis of its d-goal aspect. Knowledge of situational restrictions may be taken to be an important aspect of competence, whereas the direction into which a situation is transformed is obviously related to the intentionality of the behaving individual. Thus, the aspects of primitive actions and d-goals were included especially to reflect competence and intentionality separately.

Empirical discrimination between competence and intentionality might be achieved if different laws would govern primitive actions and d-goals. Up to this moment, however, we have not been able to demonstrate such differences between the two aspects. Both have become manifest as $P \times S \times R$ interactions and for neither of the two it appeared to be possible to establish them at a more abstract level of analysis. We have searched for the solution of this problem by a more thorough examination of intentionality as a major aspect of strategies. We have stated that d-goals are related to intentionality. However, it is not the d-goal as such, but rather the product of the d-goal, the final situation, that represents intentionality. Therefore, instead of assuming a particular individual to have a preference for a particular d-goal, we should assume a particular individual to have the intention to attain a particular situation with the aid of d-goals. Which d-goal is to be preferred is also a function of the situation in which the behaving individual finds himself. Thus, we should focus upon transformation products rather than transformations to analyze intentionality.

The behavior taxonomy provides a basis to study transformation products. The prototypical package of the initial situation together with the transformation rule produce a final situation that can be defined unequivocally with respect to its prototypical package (cf. Chapter 5). To study intentionality we have used the same data as we did before to study d-goals. But rather than arranging the data according to d-goals we arranged them according to the final situations to be obtained. This was done by applying the principles of situation transformation developed earlier. Those rules imply that the initial situation is retained as long as either general actions are shown or actions, the d-goal of which is the first in the prototypical package of the initial situation. In all other cases a transformation will be accomplished into a direction specified by the new d-goal (cf. Table 3). The situations for this analysis were selected from the clusters used to study delta goals. The first cluster consisted of the situations assembly, deliberation and negotiation with D-CONT as the second d-goal. A second cluster contained interview, job application and thought exchange with D-KNOW, and the third cluster contained meeting,

Table 3 Transition matrix with d-goals preserving or transforming three types of initial situations

		Final situation type			
	IS	IC	IP	IK	IA
Initial situation type					
IC	S	GEN/I	P	K	A
IP	S	C	GEN/I	K	A
IK	S	C	P	GEN/I	A

rendez-vous and talk with D-PROX as the second d-goal of the prototypical package. Table 3 indicates that only radical transformations were taken into account in this analysis, so that the same five situation types (IS, IC, IP, IK and IA) could be obtained starting from each of the initial situations.

For each subject ($N = 118$) the preference for final situations was expressed as the percentage endorsement of items the delta goal aspect of which led to any of the five final situations. The scores were subjected to ANOVA, with persons, initial situation types and final situation types as factors. Final situation types were treated as a fixed factor, persons and initial situation types were random factors. Variance components were obtained to estimate the generalizability of the preference for final over initial situation types, according to:

$$\rho_{PS_2}^2 = \frac{\sigma_P^2 + \sigma_{PS_2}^2}{\sigma_P^2 + \sigma_{PS_2}^2 + \dfrac{1}{n}(\sigma_{PS_1}^2 + \sigma_{PS_1S_2}^2)} \qquad 3$$

This generalizability coefficient was 0.977 indicating a high degree of generalization of final situations over initial situations. This unusually high coefficient clearly called for a replication. With this aim in mind, the data of the study mentioned earlier by Hol (1990) were partly reanalyzed. Two sets of data were isolated within each of the two versions of the SRS-questionnaire. One set contained five situations with I-PREP in their prototypical packages, i.e. cooperation, game, job application, negotiation, and visit. The other set consisted of four situations sharing D-SOCCONT, i.e. judgment, physical violence, quarrel, and thrashing. The scores were subjected to ANOVA, with persons, initial situations and final situations as factors. In this study, persons were treated as a random factor, whereas situations were fixed. Using formulas to determine generalizability of the preference for final over initial situations, Hol obtained coefficients of 0.67 and 0.70 for the I-PREP cluster, and 0.73 and 0.65 for the D-SOCCONT cluster. Although substantially lower, these results do confirm our conclusion, that the preference for d-goals in

SRS-questionnaires is determined by final situation types to be obtained, rather than by the type of initial situations offered. This finding provides a solid basis to further conceptualize strategies assessed with the aid of SRS-questionnaires.

DISCUSSION: THE STRUCTURE OF BEHAVIORAL STRATEGIES

Strategies have been loosely defined by Hettema (1979) as: 'broad behavioral opportunities as well as...behavioral preferences existing before the actual execution of behavior is started...' (p. 174). The findings with the SRS-questionnaire reported here, allow us to be more specific with respect to strategies. Within strategies an important distinction can be made between a competence aspect and an intentional aspect. Our data suggest that these aspects function according to different principles so we assume that different structures are involved as well.

The *competence structure* refers to the effectivity of particular kinds of actions in particular situations, without specifying the goals to be obtained. Thus it connects actions with initial situations. For instance, in a class situation talking or thinking may be considered generally effective but not walking or yelling. But in football matches the latter activities may be more effective. Learning processes, social or individual, may provide the basis for the conception of general effectiveness of particular primitive actions in specific situations. Taken together, those conceptions of effectivity constitute the competence structure of an individual.

The *intentional structure* on the other hand is concerned with the preference for particular situations to be attained rather than others. Its function is to connect behavior with final situations by means of d-goals. Learning experiences will be important here as well, but in addition characteristics of temperament, e.g. introversion or sensation seeking may be relevant to determine situational preference. Our data have indicated that the intentional structure is simpler than the competence structure, since it provides a categorical preference for some kinds of situations, relatively irrespective of the situation actually prevailing.

Both the competence structure and the intentional structure may be assumed to be involved in the process of directed thinking. That process has been conceptualized by Hettema (1979) as a process in which situation concepts (S_y) and transformation rules (R_y) are the core elements. By alternating S_y and R_y elements chains may be built on the symbolic level, finally leading to a situation that is particularly preferred by the individual. The direction of this type of thinking has been conceived as founded on two considerations: the

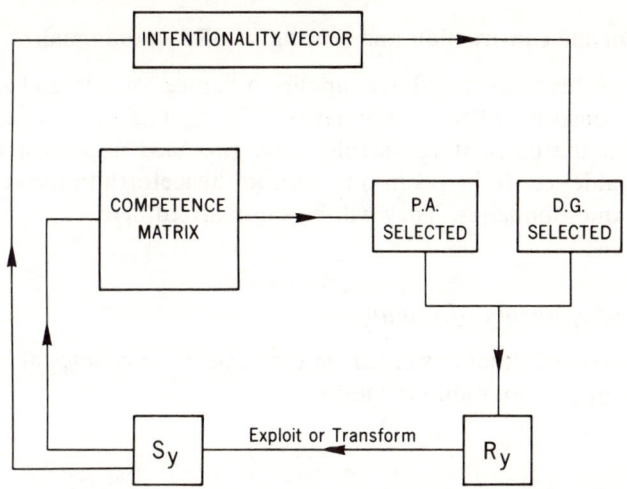

Figure 1 Hypothetical strategic decision structure

probability of obtaining the situation wanted and the utility of that situation for the individual (cf. Hettema, 1979).

The first aspect, *probability*, can now be elaborated and attributed to the competence structure. It rests on the question which primitive action will be most effective under the circumstances prevailing. *Utility* on the other hand, can be defined as the hierarchical position of the situation to be obtained in the intentional structure of the individual. Together, the competence structure and the intentional structure will at any moment determine the transformation rule actually chosen to be applied in a particular situation. The decisions made to select the R_y have been summarized hypothetically in Figure 1. In this figure competence is represented as a matrix indicating the degree of effectivity of several primitive actions in different situations. Intentionality is conceived as a vector of situation concepts arranged according to their preference values. The aspects of primitive actions and d-goals merge to form transformation rules (R_y) to either exploit or transform the original situation (S_y). Repetition of transformational activities may have the effect of gradually ascending in the intentional structure and finally reach an optimal situation. The intentional structure provides the opportunity to reach an optimal state, relatively independent of the initial state. Thus, by separating intentionality from competence, we have provided a basis for *equifinality*, one of the major characteristics of open systems (cf. Rapoport, 1972). The second major characteristic of open systems, dynamic equilibrium between the system and its environment, is conceived at the control level of the system and will be treated in part three of this book.

Directives for the construction and scoring of SRS-questionnaires

At the start of this chapter we have supplied a number of rules to be taken into account to construct SRS-questionnaires. The findings with questionnaires composed on the basis of those rules have provided us with a number of additional guidelines to be taken into account henceforth in the construction of strategic questionnaires. They will be summarized here.

The choice of a domain of situations

Define a domain of situations either on the basis of an ecological analysis, or on the basis of the situation taxonomy.

The choice of situations

Compose a set of situations belonging to the domain chosen and make sure that the situations are balanced with respect to d-goals in the prototypical package. Since there are six different d-goals two of which are represented in the prototypical package, 30 situations are necessary to cover all prototypes (taking into account the order of prototypical d-goals). So a standard SRS-questionnaire will contain 30 items.

The formulation of response alternatives

Response alternatives should be formulated to cover at least the prototypical primitive actions of the situation as well as all d-goals. Both aspects should be completely counterbalanced.

The response scale

Each response alternative should be provided with a Likert-type scale representing the probability that one would show the particular behavior in that situation.

Scoring: The preference for primitive actions

The preference for primitive actions is determined per situation by obtaining the score per primitive action averaged over d-goals. So the standard SRS-questionnaire would contain $30 \times 3 = 90$ preference values for primitive actions.

Scoring: the preference for situations

First, per situation the preference for d-goals is obtained by averaging over primitive actions. Then per situation the preference for final situations is determined on the basis of the rules specified in the previous chapter. These rules imply that in each situation the preference values for six final situations are obtained. Each final situation type will recur six times over the whole questionnaire so that preference values may be obtained by averaging over the six values obtained. Thus, a standard SRS-questionnaire produces 30 preference scores for situations.

The representation of strategies

An individual's strategy for the domain studied is represented in the form of two different tables:

1. *The competence matrix*, containing preference values for primitive actions in 30 different situations, and
2. *The intentionality vector*, containing preference values for 30 situation types.

SUMMARY STATEMENT

For the study of behavior strategies we have developed a new type of questionnaire. The SRS-format provides separate representations of the stimulus situation, the actions considered in that situation, as well as the situations emerging as a result of those actions. Individual preferences regarding means and goals in a balanced set of situations are the basis to design a person's strategy within a particular domain of situations.

Our first analyses with this new type of questionnaire have shown that strategies are internally coherent, but that they do not exhibit transsituational coherence. Further analysis has shown that the behavioral means preferred are situation specific as well as person specific. The behavioral goals preferred show convergence, i.e. the same goal situations are preferred, relatively independent of the stimulus situations offered. The latter result is interpreted as equifinality, a major aspect of open systems.

Part III

Assessment at the control level

7
Psychophysiology: from temperament to tactics

JOOP HETTEMA

The biological aspects of personality have traditionally been studied in the context of temperament. One of the leading experts in this area, Strelau (1984), conceives of temperament as the result of biological evolution, available in man as well as in animals from the very moment of birth. Unlike content, temperament is concerned with formal dimensions of behavior including aspects like intensity, behavioral dynamics and sensation seeking. Modern theories of temperament have been largely inspired by Pavlov's conceptions on the functioning of the nervous system. For instance, Eysenck (1967, 1970) who started with the assumption that people differ on a hereditary basis in the reactivity of their autonomous nervous system, adopted Pavlov's notion of excitatory and inhibitory processes occurring at the level of individual nerve cells. Eysenck assumed those processes to have some sort of mass effect on the entire nervous system and to be important for the explanation of individual differences in behavior. Processes of excitation and inhibition could be of different strength or potency in different individuals and this difference would account for the amount of introversion versus extraversion characterizing individual behavior.

Strelau (1984) has made a distinction between activity and reactivity as basic features of temperament. Activity determines the amount and range of actions undertaken by the individual, and reactivity determines the amount of stimulation necessary for the individual to initiate action. The aspect of reactivity is assumed to be related to the concept of strength of the nervous system (Pavlov, 1950; Teplov, 1964; Nebylitsyn, 1972) low reactivity referring

Personality and Environment: Assessment of Human Adaptation
Edited by P. J. Hettema. ©1989 John Wiley and Sons Ltd

to a strong nervous system and high reactivity referring to a weak nervous system. Zuckerman (1979, 1980) has developed the conception of sensation seeking and assumed it to be related with strength of the nervous system as well. Individuals high on sensation seeking would have a strong nervous system and those low on sensation seeking would possess a weak nervous system (cf. Feij, 1984).

Traditionally, temperament has been studied with the aid of self-report questionnaires. In the factor analytic tradition temperament scales have been developed by Guilford and Zimmerman (1956), Cattell (1966) and Eysenck (1970). Those scales encompass broadly defined categories of formal aspects of everyday behavior, presumably relevant for the domain of temperament. Recent developments in the construction of temperament scales tend to be directed at more specific issues specified in advance on the basis of theoretical considerations. Examples are Strelau (1972) and Zuckerman (1979).

As temperament scales are based on biological aspects of personality, the obvious way to validate them consists of demonstrating correlation with physiological measures. But with respect to this issue the results have not been very encouraging. For instance, Terry (1953) used a variety of physiological measures like skin conductance, blood pressure and heart rate to validate Guilford and Zimmerman's temperament scale. He had to conclude that 'there are no clearly demonstrable relationships between measures of temperament and sets of scores in autonomic reactivity'. A recent review by Strelau (1988) has corroborated this statement. Averill and Opton (1968) concluded a review of correlational studies connecting temperament questionnaires with measures of autonomic reactivity stating that:

1. Most correlations between psychophysiological reactions and personality measures are low.
2. There is little overlap among the studies carried out.

In trying to explain the negative results in this field those authors have called attention to three major factors: the dispositions studied are defined too broadly; psychophysiological reactions show a considerable amount of autonomous response specificity; and investigations have not paid enough attention to confounding variables. With respect to the first issue it may be noted that more recent conceptualizations of temperament like e.g. Zuckerman's sensation seeking have been defined more narrowly than the classical dimensional scales. Recent work with the sensation seeking scale has produced some promising results (cf. Fey, 1984; Kulcsár, Kutor and Arató, 1984).

A major problem, however, pointed out earlier by Eysenck (1970) has as yet not adequately been solved: the problem of *autonomous response specificity*. Investigators are confronted with this problem at the very moment they start selecting the physiological variables for the purpose of validation. To obtain meaningful correlations the variables chosen should unequivocally reflect processes like activation. In older research this did not seem to raise a special problem since many variables were assumed to represent this concept. It was assumed that in order to emit any form of overt behavior, the organism has to mobilize energy in the anticipation as well as in the execution of behavior (cf. Duffy, 1972). Gradually it became clear, however, that a unidimensional conception of activation is too simple (cf. Lacey, 1959). Different variables all meant to reflect activation showed very low correlations. Different subjects exhibited highly idiosyncratic reaction patterns when confronted with the same arousing stimuli. And, in addition, as a result of specific stimulus conditions, physiological response systems showed 'dissociation', i.e. variables hitherto assumed to reflect the same process reacted in different directions (cf. Lacey, 1959, 1967).

According to Averill and Opton (1968) autonomous response specificity can be subdivided in different components:

1. *Individual response specificity*, i.e. the tendency of individuals to react with specific physiological responses rather than other responses.
2. *Stimulus–response specificity*, i.e. the capacity of specific stimuli to elicit specific physiological responses.
3. *Motivational response specificity*, i.e. the tendency of a physiological response pattern to be specific to the subjective appraisal of the stimulus.

To explain the consequences of autonomous response specificity for personality assessment, Averill and Opton (1968) have used the framework of analysis of variance. If in a repeated measures design the subjects are confronted with situations in which several physiological reactions are recorded, response specificities become manifest as *interactions of response modes* with either persons, situations or both persons and situations. The first variance component represents individual response specificity, the second component reflects stimulus response specificity and the third component refers to motivational response specificity. In correlational analysis all components contribute to the error term thus reducing the correlation with any external variable. This analysis shows that it is hard to string different physiological variables together under the heading of activation. Instead, several authors have suggested to conceive of physiological reactions as multidimensional patterns rather than single dimensions.

If stable patterns of autonomic reactivity can be demonstrated the problem of response specificity becomes easier to handle. Individual response specificity might then refer to a categorical preference for particular patterns with the exclusion of others for each individual. Stimulus response specificity could imply that specific situations have the capacity to elicit specific patterns. And, finally, motivational response specificity might indicate that the mobilization of a particular pattern in a situation is a function of subjective appraisal of that situation.

There are theoretical as well as empirical arguments to support this conception. Especially Lacey (1967) has provided neurophysiological and psychophysiological evidence to support this way of thinking. He proposed the conception:

> 'that activation or arousal processes are not unidimensional but multidimensional and that the activation processes do not reflect just the intensive dimension of behavior but also the intended aim or goal of the behavior, or, as I phrased it in an earlier paper, the nature of the transaction between the organism and its environment...The emphasis on multidimensionality of, and the non-energizing aspects of, the arousal process is tantamount to saying that different somatic processes have different roles to play in the execution of different kinds of behavior and different interactions with other concurrent responses, and hence appear in different amounts and temporal evolution, depending on the requirements of the intended interaction between the organism and its environment' (Lacey, 1967, p. 25).

The interaction between the organism and the environment can take many different forms. Earlier Lacey (1959) had already distinguished between patterns of *environmental intake* versus patterns of *symbolic manipulation* aimed at problem solving. Generalizing this line of reasoning Lacey (1967) distinguished between autonomic, electroencephalographic and motor responses that are presumably mediated by different types of dissociation.

The physiological specificity of passive intake–oriented processes and active performance–oriented processes has been stressed by Pribram (1971) as well. This author refers to them as *arousal* versus *activation*. In Pribram's view arousal processes are concerned with the regulation of input, with preparation, anticipation and feedback. Activation processes on the other hand are concerned with the execution of plans, with output regulation and forward feed. More recently, in the context of the control of attention, Pribram and McGuiness (1975) have defined another process, called *effort*. This process in which both stimulus and response oriented processes are involved, has the function to bring about a change of actions originally intended.

A major difference between the approaches outlined by Lacey and Pribram concerns the principle on which the processes are assumed to operate. Lacey (1959) has used terms like *facilitation* versus *hindering* the dealings ('transactions') of the organism and the environment. The image coming up here is that of a valve that can be opened up or closed depending upon the response pattern available. Pribram (1971) on the other hand conceives of the processes as bringing about change in the configuration present before the process started. The principle of *configurational change* enables the organism to adjust the course and the direction of his behavior anywhere from the incoming stimulus to the response emitted. Apart from this basic aspect the views of Lacey and Pribram are to a high degree compatible. Both authors have stressed that autonomous responses can only be interpreted as parts of the total behavior of the organism. In Lacey's transactional conception the relation between organism and environment is much to the fore, whereas Pribram's approach focuses primarily on cognitive transformations and internal regulatory processes.

While conceptualizing psychological adaptation I have designed a control structure based on the principles outlined by Lacey, Pribram and others (cf. Hettema, 1979, p. 105 *et seq.*). The main purpose was to provide a physiological basis for several state-transition mechanisms defined to maintain or restore control over the environment (cf. Figure 1).

The structure represented in Figure 1 has two dimensions. The horizontal dimension represents intake versus manipulation (Lacey) or arousal, effort and activation (Pribram *et al.*). The system includes three different phases: the first phase is concerned with the initial situation (S_1), the second phase is concerned with the transformation (R), and the third phase concerns the final situation (S_2) established as the effect of R acting upon S_1. The vertical dimension is particularly concerned with the relation between the organism and the environment. The system comprises three levels: the top level contains representational elements of a cognitive symbolic nature (indicated with subscripts y), the bottom level contains actual environmental elements (indicated with subscripts x), and the middle level contains elements of control.

The environmental elements (x) may or may not be congruent with the representational elements (y). If so, the system is said to be in a state of control. If not, ST-mechanisms at the control level will become active to

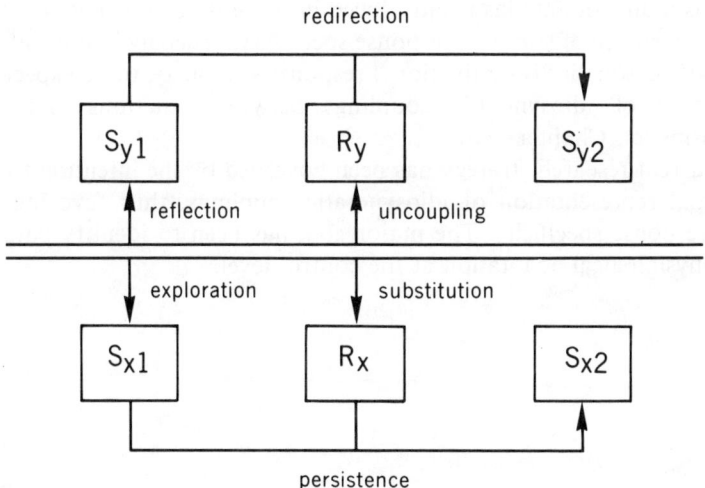

Figure 1 State transition mechanisms affecting different system elements

change the configuration in one or more of the system elements. Configurational change may occur either at the cognitive–symbolic level or at the sensorimotor–operational level. Six different ST-mechanisms are defined corresponding to the elements of the system: reflection, exploration, uncoupling, substitution, redirection, and persistence.

The system and mechanisms outlined here are meant to provide a control structure for psychological adaptation. Obviously this does not preclude other systems and processes to be available and active as well. In the original presentation of the system some of these have been mentioned (cf. Hettema, 1979). The ST-mechanisms have the function to maintain equilibrium by causing more or less subtle changes to occur in the course of an ongoing stream of behavior. They accomplish formal changes like tuning, switching and intensifying behavior within the context of a comprehensive strategy adopted earlier. The ST-mechanisms represent tactical aspects of behavior with the function to maximize control given the limiting conditions prevailing. Other tactical aspects of behavior include disruption mechanisms activated to minimize loss of control if the ST-mechanisms fail.

The present conception of behavioral tactics has the potential to provide an explanation for the occurrence of autonomous response specificity. State transition mechanisms as well as disruption mechanisms are assumed to have specific patterns of concomitant physiological reactivity. Individual response specificity will become manifest as a consequence of innate 'preferences' to use specific tactical mechanisms rather than others (cf. Chapter one). Stimulus–response specificity might be explained on the basis of conditioning and generalization processes (cf. Assumptions 3.3. and 3.4 of the open-systems adaptation model). As soon as learning processes become institutionalized as in schools a directional bias is introduced in those processes that can account for the occurrence of stimulus-response specificity. Specially important for the domain of personality is motivational response specificity, to be expected as a consequence of idiosyncratic couplings between situations and tactical mechanisms (cf. Chapter two).

Our current research strategy has been governed by the intention to obtain an optimal representation of idiosyncratic couplings, thus favoring motivational response specificity. The major goal has been to identify patterns of psychophysiological adaptation at the control level.

8

The representation of situations through films

JOOP HETTEMA,

GUUS L. VAN HECK,

and

COR BRANDT

INTRODUCTION

The study of tactical mechanisms is complex with respect to stimulus conditions as well as responses. In daily life tactics are assumed to be activated by an apparent discrepancy arising between external stimuli and information present at the cognitive–symbolic level of the system. According to the open-systems adaptation model if an individual is confronted with a specific environment a situation concept will be activated accompanied by a set of expectancies concerning future developments. A discrepancy becomes manifest as soon as expectancies prevailing in the system are invalidated or violated by the actual course of events. Which tactical mechanism is activated as a reaction to the discrepancy is a function of the person as well as the situation. Assumption 3.3. of the open-systems adaptation model states: 'State transition and disruption mechanisms tend to be coupled with the situation concepts with which they initially occurred'. Assumption 3.4. states: 'Via processes of generalization state transition and disruption mechanisms are coupled with elements of the symbolic behavioral structure, which resemble characteristics of the environment, where the disruption initially occurred'. Both assumptions lead to the expectation that tactical mechanisms are coupled with situation

Personality and Environment: Assessment of Human Adaptation
Edited by P. J. Hettema. ©1989 John Wiley and Sons Ltd

concepts. Thus, as a result at the control level, tactics represent stable connections between person and situation. To study those connections persons may be confronted with situations containing unexpected events, that is events that are non-prototypical for that situation.

To elicit tactical responses, we considered creating experimental settings by means of simulation. This approach, however, has some severe drawbacks. Besides being highly impractical, simulation is hard to control experimentally. An individual acting in a simulated situation can transform that situation in any direction so that the original stimulus is redefined. Furthermore, an exact replication of simulated situations is difficult to obtain.

These problems can all be solved by using films instead of simulation. Films can be arranged to represent any situation in the situation taxonomy. They are not influenced by the subject and they can be used repeatedly without any difference occurring between presentations. The use of films will also enable us to carefully study psychophysiological reactions representing tactical responses.

THE SELECTION OF SITUATIONS

The purpose of the production of films in the context of the present program was threefold. First, the films are to be used to *elicit patterns* of psychophysiological reaction that can be meaningfully interpreted as representations of specific ST-mechanisms and disruption mechanisms. Second, the films should be used in the context of *validation* studies. Finally, the films will eventually have to be useful for *assessment* purposes in various applied

Table 1 Situations classified according to domains and positive/negative/stressful character

Domain	Positive/neutral	Negative	Stressful
Clinical	Pregnancy (III)	Accident (I)	Dying-bed (III) Operation (IX)
Interpersonal	Thought exchange (II) Love-making (III) Rapprochement (III)	Quarrel (I) Gossip (III)	Rape (III) Divorce (III)
Educational	Exam (II) Test (II) Lesson (II)		Failure (II)
Organizational	Job application (II) Report (II) Assembly (II) Overwork (II)	Officialdom (II) Intrigue (I) Dispute (I) Interruption (I) Misunderstanding (II)	Discharge (II)

settings. These goals have guided the process of selecting the situations to be filmed.

Using stimulus tapes consisting of dramatic, short segments from already existing commercial movies (see, e.g., Davis, Hull, Young, and Warren, 1987) was considered to be inadequate. For reasons of replicability and representativity, discussed in more detail below, it was felt necessary to produce our own films.

As regards the first purpose—eliciting physiological reactions—divergence of the situations in terms of content was considered an important option. The second purpose—validation—led to the option of selecting situations occurring more or less frequently in the context of daily life. Furthermore, the situations were to be chosen with an eye on replicability in role playing settings that would act as criterion situations. The third purpose—assessment—led to the option for the situations to pertain to domains that can be considered to be relevant for applied psychology.

Summarizing, then, the situations to be selected should be divergent, closely connected with everyday life, replicable in role playing, and psychologically relevant regarding the domains to be covered.

Connection with everyday life as well as replicability led to a choice among the situation factors found in the situation taxonomy (see Van Heck, Chapter 4). The factors 2 and 3 were considered the most appropriate ones in this respect. In addition, some situations were derived from factor 1 and factor 9 to represent the more harsh aspects of life as well. The requirement of divergence was effectuated by selecting from many *situation clusters*. With respect to domains a crude categorization was made into situations that have relevance for clinical, interpersonal, educational or organizational psychology. Within each of the domains mentioned, care was taken to represent *positive* or *neutral* situations and more aversive situations including situations that are usually considered as downright *stressful*. Budget limitations finally imposed a numerical restriction to the production of 25 films. The final set of situations has been brought together in Table 1.

The degree of representativity as well as divergence of the situations selected can be traced looking at their positions in the factor structure presented by Van Heck (Chapter 4). For convenience the factors 2 and 3 have been represented here with the 25 situations located according to their loadings on these factors (Figure 1).

THE FILM SCRIPTS

A primary concern in the production of films has been to represent a number of situations from the taxonomy as adequately as possible. The principle of situational isomorphism, stated in Chapter 2 of this book, holds that situations

116

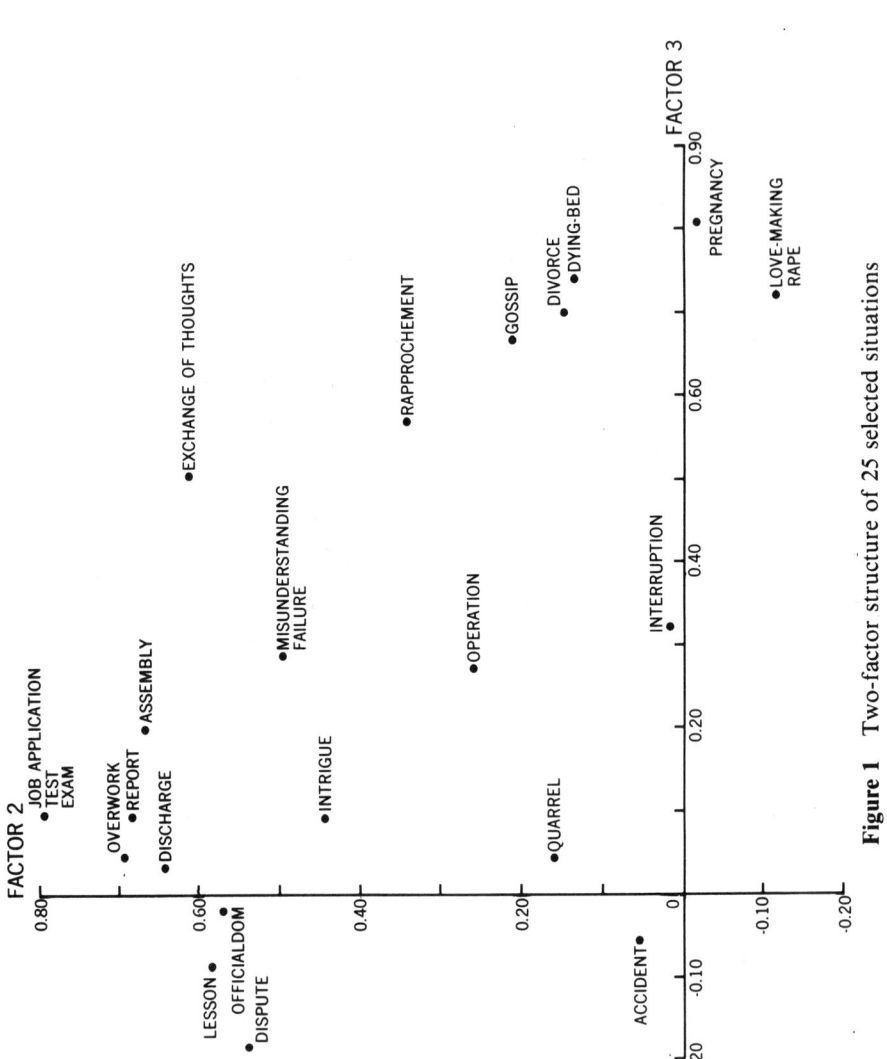

Figure 1 Two-factor structure of 25 selected situations

should be maximally congruent represented at the cognitive–symbolic level and at the sensorimotor–operational level. Thus, the translation procedure from the taxonomy to situation description at both levels was kept constant.

Cues to be represented in the films were selected in much the same way as in the SRS-questionnaire. Thus, the 15 highest ranking cue clusters from each situation were derived from the situation taxonomy and each cluster provided one cue. In addition, the 15 clusters next in line provided cues to be considered as options.

The cue packages thus obtained for each of the situations were handed over to our scriptwriter to write a provisional scenario. He was cautioned to include only the cues mentioned in the scenario, and to leave out all other cues. Thus, the method of minimal cues developed in the context of strategic measurement was applied here as well.

In cases where the scriptwriter could not manage to write an adequate story based on the cues provided, he would come back and ask for alternatives. Those were always provided taking into account the rules for cue selection given earlier. The scriptwriter was free to either visualize the cues or include them in the dialogues. Often the choice among those two alternatives was very simple because the duration of each film was limited and some cues could not be visualized within the limits given. In all cases it appeared possible to write a script that was satisfactory. A problem that could not always be solved was to exclude the cues not wanted. Therefore, a final check on the adequacy of situational representation appeared necessary. We will come back to this issue later in this chapter.

The provisional scenarios were carefully scrutinized by the project team with respect to all cues included as well as all cues not included. Once approved the scenarios were translated into story-boards in which the films were represented as strips. For an example the reader is referred to Figure 2. The story-boards were scrutinized again to check whether any inequity had slipped in during the translation process. After final approval the production of the films could be started. The scripts of each of the films produced will be briefly described hereafter.

Pregnancy

Mrs M is pregnant. She is very happy to tell her husband this good news. Together with him she plans, buys and prepares all the necessary things they need for the baby.

Accident

A housewife preparing dinner wants to use her mixer. But it does not work. She tries unsuccessfully to mend it. When she takes the vegetables out of the

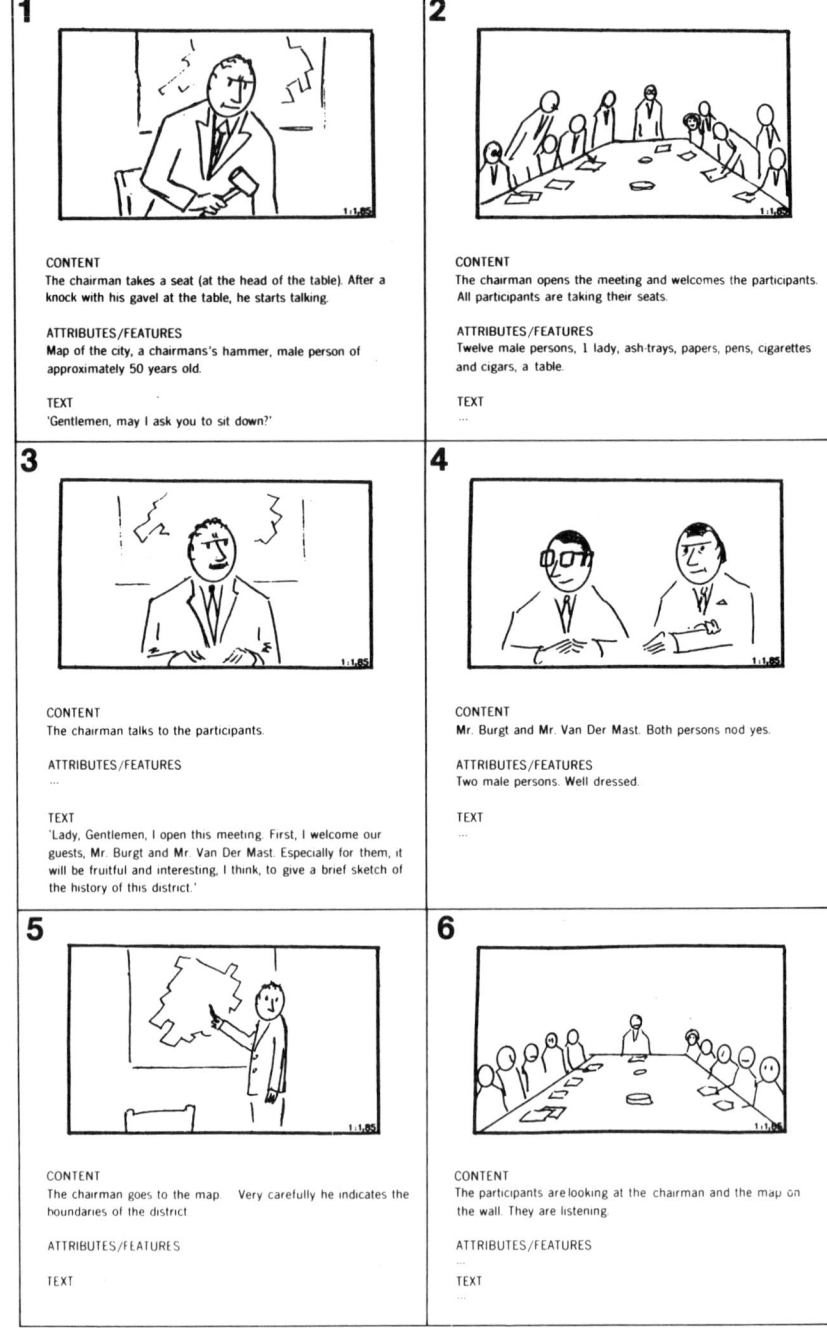

Figure 2   Fragment of the story-board of the assembly film

mixer the apparatus suddenly starts off and the sharp knives cut her fingers. She tries to call her doctor but fails and, on top of that, her neighbour does not seem to be at home either.

Death-bed

A clergyman, family and friends stand around the dying-bed of a rather young woman. In the middle of the night the nurse wakes up the woman's husband and her daughter. Then she calls for a doctor. All the doctor can tell them is that the woman has died.

Operation

A man is run over by a car. From that moment on ambulance drivers, doctors and nurses decide what has to be done with him. Severe internal injuries make an immediate operation necessary. Preparations are made and the operation takes place. Afterwards the man is recovering.

Thought exchange

A publisher of leftish pamphlets meets one of his opponents. They exchange thoughts about how to propagate their different opinions.

Love-making

A young man with a cut-out ad in his hand, in which a tent is offered, rings at a door. He looks very surprised when the door is opened by a girl. She has just moved in and he helps her placing the furniture. Then, they talk about the tent. He needs it for his holidays in Greece. After a while he suggests she should come with him. She is delighted and accepts his offer. He accepts her invitation to stay with her that night.

Rapprochement/advances

Henk Van Der Meulen works in a building opposite the music school. Looking out of the window he falls in love with a 'cello teacher. He approaches her by telling her that he wants to go on with his 'cello lessons. He borrows an instrument from a friend and tries to draw some acceptable sounds out of it, which is very annoying for his neighbours. When he shows up at her place he has to make two confessions: first, that he never played a 'cello before, and second, that he fell in love with her.

Quarrel

When Mr and Mrs F have returned from an office-party she is very angry because her husband spent too much time entertaining his secretary. On top of that she is furious about his boss's bold behavior and she blames her husband for a spoiled evening. He blames her for being narrow-minded.

Gossip

At about four o'clock Mr K, a high school teacher, walks to his car. There he is welcomed by an attractive young girl who kisses him. Two of his colleagues watch this scene. That day Mr K and the girl are seen in several public places. The next morning Mr K is told that the headmaster wants to see him right away because an intimate relation between teacher and pupil is still taboo.

Rape

Marianne has done some overtime and it is already dark when she leaves the chemist's shop. In spite of warnings she takes her bike and goes home. In front of her apartment she is rudely taken into the bushes and violated.

Divorce

After the quarrel of the night before Mr A tells his wife that he is going to see a lawyer. He wants a divorce. Her bitter reply is that she will do the same. They both tell their story to their lawyers. At the end Mr A picks up his belongings, kisses the children and drives away.

Exam

After a last driving lesson the instructor assures Mrs S that she will pass the driving test as long as she stays calm. When she returns after the the test she is glad to tell her instructor he was right.

Test

Harry applies for a job in a museum. He thinks he is the right man for it, although he has no diploma. The museum wants him but demands a diploma and Harry starts a swot. At the exam he has to hurry to finish his paper, but he succeeds. After the exam he returns to the museum where he is welcomed by the staff.

Lesson

Mr van Tilburg is a physics teacher. The lesson he gives is often disturbed by latecomers and inattentive pupils. Nevertheless, he manages to explain a difficult topic.

Officialdom

Mr T wants to send a package to England. The package contains a bathroom tile. At the post office he is told that he has to go to the customs for special export forms. At the custom-house he is sent from office to office. The very last counter clerk tells him that he does not need any form at all and tears the already collected forms to pieces. Back at the post office his package is still not accepted. Mr T gets very angry and leaves.

Failure

Marian has to do an oral examination, but on almost every question she fails to give the correct answer. Above that the examiner's conduct makes her very nervous. After a while she is sent away.

Job application

Mr S. calls his daughter Esther. In the morning paper he reads an advertisement in which a job is offered for which he thinks his daughter is the right applicant. A few days after the interview she receives a letter and she is very glad to tell her father the good news.

Report

Mr N a very self-confident man, faces a large number of people when he gives a lecture on automation. After the report he will answer some questions from the audience. But some questions are hard to answer. Then a minor accident makes him a laughing-stock.

Assembly

There have been many meetings about the future of an old quarter of Maasburg. Some useful ideas from previous meetings of the assembly are suddenly forgotten. A solution for the problems of the old quarter seems far away.

Overwork

A big hydraulic press is out of order and the plant manager needs two volunteers to repair the machine overnight. Very tired, but happy now the press works again, the two workers leave the factory at dawn.

Intrigue

One evening Mr S is told that the manager of his department will be promoted, so there will be a vacancy to fill. His wife suggests that Mr S should take some actions against his competitors.

Dispute

The board of a football club meets after the A-team becomes champion of the league. It is not a happy meeting because many players, egged on by drunken supporters, misbehaved. One of the board members blames the chairman for it because he, a brewer, provided the beer. The chairman leaves the board.

Interruption

Garage owner Robben wants his mechanic to mend Mr W's car first of all. He himself has an appointment and cannot help. The mechanic starts working on the car but he is very often interrupted by customers, telephone calls, tools that do not fit and so on and so forth. When after hours his boss returns and is told that Mr W does not need his car anymore, he nearly explodes.

Misunderstanding

Unsuspectingly, Mr N leaves his house in the morning. When he wants to get in his car he is rudely arrested. At the police station they look very glad. At last they've caught this very much wanted man. However, Mr N does not understand what he is accused of. At last he is allowed to make one 'phone call. In this call he asks his wife to come over with his passport.

Discharge

At the factory, where Mr Sanders works, some sections will be closed down. So his redundancy is not unexpected. Nevertheless it is a hard fact for him to take. Back home, he tells his wife this bad news. She begins to cry.

THE PRODUCTION OF FILMS

A major concern of this study was to confront our subjects with a selection of situations taken from the taxonomy and to make sure that those situations and nothing else would act as stimuli. To acquire this aim a number of special precautions were taken with regard to casting and locations, as well as to the composition of the films and the way of presentation.

The cast of the films was extensive. A total number of 335 persons acted in front of the camera at any time during the project, 38 of them played a leading part. This group was expected to be familiar with stage directives and to be able to learn long dialogues by heart. They were recruited from amateur theatrical companies and selected initially by the directors of those companies. The final selection was done by our own director, who also chose actors for the 80 additional parts. The latter did not require much acting experience. The other 217 persons were extras recruited mainly by means of advertisements. The large number of persons involved was the consequence of the requirement that none of them could play in more than one film. Violation of this rule would have caused recognitions to occur and have lowered the credibility of the films.

The films were shot on a number of different locations in different parts of the country specially selected to represent the environmental cues of the situations as truthfully as possible. Recording the pictures was influenced by the need to put the film spectator in the centre of the action. The desired position of the spectator can best be described as that of a 'tacit participant'. Thus, the camera was always located in a position where a spectator would go if he had been present at the event. A major consequence of this option was that the camera replaced the spectator and did not have any narrative or interpretative function.

In 90% of the recordings a standard recording lens (focal distance equals the diagonal of the film image) was used because that lens registers perspective in much the same way as the human eye. Some of the film shots, referring to scenes where the location was considered relatively unimportant compared with the action going on, were registered sharply with the lens completely opened up. The depth edge then amounts to only a few centimeters. This recording technique known as 'Rembrandt-lighting' requires a long period of illumination but it avoids uncredible double shadows and strongly reduced pupils to occur. Another advantage of this technique is that the presence of the camera, usually threatening to actors, is less pronounced and the atmosphere is more like the one meant in the situation to be filmed.

All films were provided with stereophonic sound. To accomplish this we first had to solve the problem that while registering sound stereophonically on location every change of position of the microphones causes the background noise to change as well. This has some nasty effects on the presentation. For instance, cars seem to be passing the spectator sometimes in front of him, sometimes beside him. In dialogues involving two persons who are located at both sides of the screen the sound alternates continuously between the left and right channel. This is highly unrealistic and causes much confusion to occur in the spectator. To avoid this problem the microphones were kept rather closely together during recording. In each new camera position a new position of the microphones was found as well.

The situations filmed were usually not restricted to just one location or one time unit. Therefore, mounting had to be applied to string different scenes together. This technique, in film circles considered to be an art form by itself, can cause a world of difference to occur regarding the final product. This is especially important with respect to the films produced here, in which situations had to be represented as adequately as possible. Each intervention can give rise to new cues not at all included in the original cue package. Thus the mounting editor had to be very careful to avoid additional cues to slip in. To determine the optimal order of events the editor as a rule asked himself this question: 'What would I look for and at what moment in time would I go and see this or that?'.

Because the human eye cannot make 'freezing frames' and is unable to establish overflows, the application of these opticals has been avoided with one or two exceptions. Those had become necessary because budgetary restrictions did not allow for additional shots of a particular scene to be made.

FIDELITY OF THE FILMS

The development of the films described thus far has removed us step by step from their origin, the situation taxonomy. First, situations have been translated into lists of cues and those lists have been restricted to only a few very typical cues. Subsequently, the cues have been included in scripts. And, finally, the scripts have been transformed into films. The question can be rightfully asked whether the films still represent the situations that were intended to be represented.

Some evidence concerning this question can be obtained by comparing the structure based on relations between films with the structure represented in Figure 1 that was based on relations between situation concepts. To find the film structure we proceeded as follows. First, all films were watched by three expert observers, who had studied the list of cues thoroughly. For each film they made an independent rating on each cue, answering the question whether the cue was present or absent. Then, the results of the raters were compared. In case of discrepancies the raters discussed whether or not the cues were actually present. Discussion was continued until a complete agreement was obtained. At that moment the films were defined as cue vectors. On the basis of

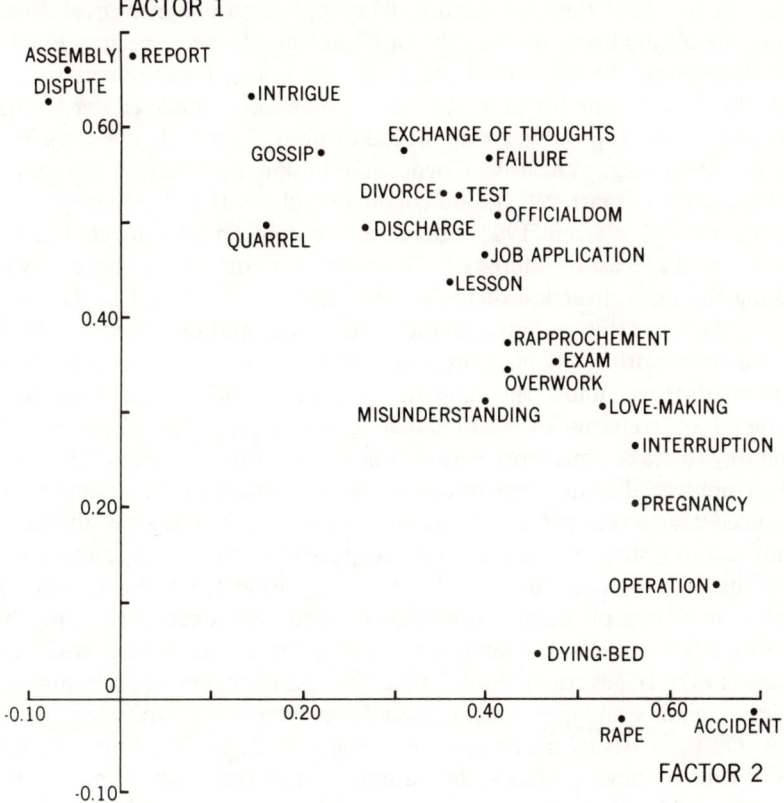

Figure 3 Two-factor structure of the 25 filmed situations

those vectors it was possible to compute the relationship between any pair of films. As a measure we used the phi-coefficient for dichotomized data. The phi-coefficients were brought together in a correlation matrix and this matrix was factor analyzed by principle components with the option to produce two factors. The results of this analysis are shown in Figure 3. A comparison of Figures 1–3 reveals a close correspondence between the factor structure obtained in the taxonomic study of Chapter 4 (Figure 1) and the structure obtained via the ratings of the films. Thus, the present outcome substantiated the isomorphism requirement mentioned earlier.

THE PRESENTATION OF THE FILMS

In the present project, several circumstances have been an impediment with respect to the impact of the films. As mentioned in the previous section a number of so-called opticals could not be applied to enhance involvement, because the original definition of the situations had to be respected. Furthermore, in general, the content of the situations selected was not very sensational, thus contrasting the present study with attempts made earlier to study psychophysiological processes with the aid of films. Especially the work in the areas of stress (e.g., Lazarus, Coyne and Folkman, 1962), violence (e.g. Carruthers and Taggart, 1973), and cognitive and emotional empathy (Davis, Hull, Young and Warren, 1987) offered a fair chance that subjects watching the film would at least be interested. This issue is important here because while watching the films diversion of the subjects had to be avoided at the risk of exposing them to other stimuli than the situations meant. Our primary concern with the presentation of the films has been to maximize the impact of the situations portrayed and at the same time to minimize the effect of background features of an irrelevant or even disturbing character.

One way to make films more penetrating is to enlarge the screen. During the 1950s, commercial filmmakers doubled the optic angle of their cameras and introduced wide screen projection systems to enhance the impact of their films. In wide screen systems the display angle surpasses the human optic angle to the extent that for a spectator it is hard to withdraw from the picture. An explanation of this phenomenon may be derived from experimental psychology. The effects of display angle upon performance have been studied by Sanders (1963). In general he found a decay of performance in discrimination, reaction, vigilance and memory tasks as a function of the magnitude of display angles. On the basis of his results Sanders has made a distinction into three types of functional visual fields: the stationary field, requiring no movement at all; the eyefield, requiring just eye movements; and the headfield, requiring head movements as well. The three fields corresponded roughly with display angles of $0° - 25°$, $25° - 85°$, and $85°$ and beyond. If subjects change from one field to another (i.e., from the stationary up to the headfield) a decay in performance occurs as a rule. Sanders (1963) attributed those performance drops to a change of the selective strategies used in each type of field.

In the context of studies of perceptual style, one of the present authors (Hettema, 1966, 1968) has hypothesized two different processes to occur in dealing with focal stimuli compared with contextual stimuli. Focal stimuli elicit processes of information transmission but contextual stimuli tend to be equivocated and become active as anchor stimuli. The latter stimuli exert a considerable effect as a background against which the focal stimuli are evaluated. This principle might provide an explanation of the impact of motion pictures presented with the aid of wide screen techniques. Stimuli shown near the periphery of the screen would tacitly influence the perception of the main focal events in the picture.

In the context of the present study the authors have considered working with a headfield in the sense of Sanders. This would, however, cause gross head

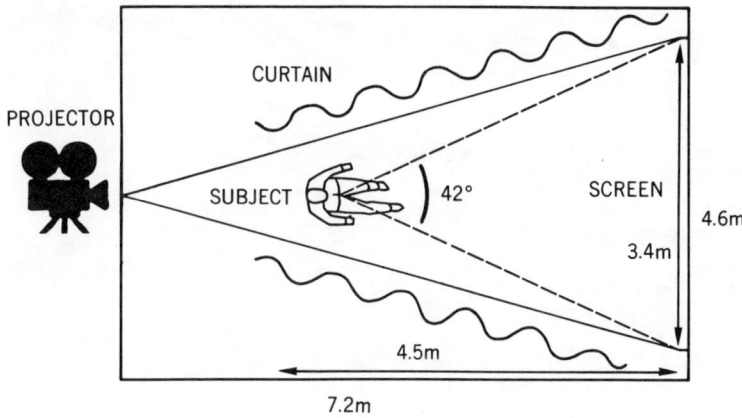

Figure 4   Plan of the experimental room

movements to occur in our subjects and possibly influence the physiological measures taken simultaneously. Thus, it was decided to merely use the eyefield. The size of the screen used in all experiments with films was 3.4 × 1.8 m, and the subject was seated in front of the screen at a distance (between his head and the screen) of 4.5 m (cf. Figure 4). In this arrangement the display angle was 42° which is well beyond the boundaries of the stationary field. The same contextual effect as in the visual domain was intended in the auditory domain by the use of earphones. The reproduction of stereophonic sound by earphones offers a completely separate perception through the left and right channels. The contrast between the two channels creates an impression of being in the centre of action and adds to the liveliness of the presentation.

Besides actively manipulating contexts on the basis of situational cues all other context influences should be eliminated. To achieve this, care was taken to get rid of all other visual as well as auditory stimuli. The film room was completely dark during the presentation. The walls as well as the floor and the ceiling were painted black and in addition a large curtain of black velvet enclosed the space between the subject and the screen. The use of earphones was an efficacious measure to avoid any disturbing sound to slip in. Thus, external visual as well as auditory stimulation appears to be controlled to a high degree.

9

Patterns of physiological and biochemical reaction during films

JOOP HETTEMA,

AD J. VINGERHOETS,

and

GUUS L. VAN HECK

INTRODUCTION

In the present study, subjects were confronted with films and simultaneously monitored with respect to a number of selected physiological and biochemical variables.

Obviously, films have been used before to elicit physiological reactions. After the pioneering efforts of Lazarus, Speisman, Mordkoff and Davison (1962) films have been used by Levi (1972) to study reactions as a function of film content. Using films containing humour, horror or natural scenery Levi could demonstrate how the level of urinary catecholamines is influenced by their content. Carruthers and Taggart (1973) used violent film and TV programs and found that in spite of increased catecholamine secretion slowing of the heart occurred, indicating increased vagal tone. Interesting as the results mentioned may be in and of themselves, they do not permit us to draw conclusions beyond massive effects over subjects of films of a highly dramatic character. The studies mentioned are primarily concerned with stimulus–response specificity and leave open questions with respect to personality and individual reactions. To be of value for the study of personality it appears necessary to use films of a less 'heavy' character and, most important, to work

Personality and Environment: Assessment of Human Adaptation
Edited by P. J. Hettema. ©1989 John Wiley and Sons Ltd

Table 1 Hypothetical state transition mechanisms for short-term adaptation (after Hettema, 1979)

	Arousal	Effort	Activation
Cognitive–symbolic	Reflection	Uncoupling	Redirection
Sensorimotor–operational	Exploration	Substitution	Persistence

in the context of a theoretical framework, conceptualizing physiological reactions as reflections of specific person × situation interactions.

The use of physiological measures in the context of personality assessment has been advocated by e.g. Averill and Opton (1968) and Fiske (1971). Spectacular findings have, however, been scarce in this area. More finesse has been introduced at the theoretical as well as the empirical level by the work of Lacey (1967) and Pribram (1973). The conception of control developed in the context of the open-systems adaptation model builds on the results of the authors mentioned and will hopefully offer a perspective for obtaining better results in the area of psychophysiological assessment of personality.

The link between personality on the one hand and psychophysiological variables on the other is based on our conception of psychological adaptation in which a number of basic connections between person and situation are postulated. Those connections, designated as state transition (ST)- and disruption-mechanisms, are conceived as means to achieve and maintain stable person–situation relationships. Links between persons and specific situations are assumed to be established on an idiosyncratic basis as a consequence of the individual learning history. On theoretical grounds six ST-mechanisms were postulated and each of those mechanisms is assumed to be represented in terms of a specific pattern of physiological reaction. The mechanisms are summarized in Table 1.

DESIGN OF THE STUDY

To identify patterns of physiological reaction representing ST-mechanisms, an experiment was designed using films as eliciting variables. The analysis of the data obtained in the present study has been focused on motivational response specificity. First, with respect to each of the variables studied the question was raised whether it would qualify as an element of patterns to be identified. Single variables were analyzed to obtain person × film interactions rather than individual differences or effects of films *per se*. The reactions obtained were conceived as a joint function of persons as well as films. Thus, a physiological variable was required to show substantial and stable person × film interaction effects. To qualify as an element of the patterns P × F interactions should generalize over different moments in the same film, thus exhibiting coherence stability.

A second analysis was directed at the issue of aggregation of the variables retained into patterns. The physiological patterns looked for are conceived as state patterns, to be compared with other patterns of the same individual, rather than with patterns shown by other individuals. Thus, in the analysis of the data an ipsative approach has been used instead of a normative approach. Finally, on the basis of the content of the patterns as well as their biochemical correlates an attempt was made to interpret the patterns in terms of the theory.

METHOD

Subjects

Since blood samples had to be collected for the biochemical analyses, a major criterion for the recruitment of subjects has been familiarity with blood donation for medical purposes. It was decided to select the subjects from among student nurses who may be assumed not to become frightened at the sight of an injection needle.

Thirty eight students agreed to act as subjects after being told what the experiment was about. The group consisted of 27 males and 11 females. During the experiment for 14 subjects it appeared impossible to collect blood samples due to problems with the canula. Their results have been discarded for the main analyses so the sample consisted of 24 subjects, 23 males and one female. All subjects were volunteers and they received dfl. 25 as a reward.

Films

The films were selected to be of interest for subjects of this age and background. Divergence with respect to content was considered important to elicit different states. Thus from each of the four domains distinguished in Chapter 8 one film was chosen. The situations represented by those films—quarrel, interruption, failure and accident—are all more or less aversive. Two films representing more agreeable situations, i.e. wedding party and endurance test, were added to complete a set of six experimental films. A seventh film acted as a buffer film for the subjects to get used to the procedure. The buffer film showed a number of shots of a party, in which people were having a good time, dancing, drinking and talking with each other. The six experimental films are described in order of presentation:

1. *Endurance test.* A young man is pushing himself up on parallel bars as often as he can manage. He gets visibly tired and the last push-ups cost him

a lot of effort. A coach is standing by his side and encourages him to go on. Finally he gives up, completely exhausted.

2. *Quarrel.* A young married couple come home at night after a party. They start an argument on their behavior at the party, accusing each other of paying too much attention to other people—especially of the opposite sex—and of neglecting each other. Finally, the man takes off and slams the door behind him.

3. *Interruption.* A garage owner gets a telephone call and has to leave immediately. He asks his young assistant to repair a particular car and urges him to finish the job within two hours. The assistant starts working but is very soon interrupted by a customer who needs fuel. From that moment on, about every five minutes a new disturbance takes place in the form of new customers with all kinds of requests as well as several telephone calls. But the mechanic nevertheless manages to get his work done. Finally, the boss returns and tells him that there was no particular hurry with the car after all.

4. *Wedding party.* A newly married couple accompanied by a number of formally dressed guests, arrives at an expensive looking restaurant to have their wedding dinner. The dinner is led by an MC, directing the speeches and toasts. Suddenly, the proper course of affairs is disturbed by a penetrating smell of dog's dirt. The guests start accusing each other of having caused the smell, and start inspecting their shoes. The end is a complete chaos.

5. *Failure.* A female student takes an oral exam and is questioned by a professor. She has obviously not prepared the exam very well and starts to guess hesitantly, while watching the professor's face. She does not manage to pull through, however, and gets the message that she failed, accompanied by some unpleasant remarks from the professor.

6. *Accident.* While preparing dinner in the kitchen, a woman uses a device to grind vegetables. As the apparatus refuses to function, she puts her hand in it to rearrange the vegetables. Suddenly the motor starts, injuring her hand quite seriously. She panics, starts running around crying and finally flees to her neighbor to ask for help.

Physiological variables

The physiological measures used in this study were chosen on the basis of sensitivity for environmental stimuli as demonstrated in studies on stress, emotional behavior, cognitive tasks and films. Heart rate was an obvious choice in this context. Besides being one of the most prominent psychophysiological variables (cf. Gunn, Wolf, Block and Person, 1972) this measure has played an important part in the work of Lacey (1959) on intake versus rejection. As a score we have used mean interbeat intervals, that is the mean time elapsing between two heart beats over a period of time. The standard deviation of interbeat intervals was used as a measure of heart beat regularity. A third measure in this group was the mean amplitide of T-waves from the electrocardiogram. This measure was chosen because recent research has shown it to be a relatively pure index of sympathetic arousal during stress (cf. Heslegrave and Furedy, 1979).

The measure probably used most frequently in psychophysiology is galvanic skin conductance. Next to heart rate it appeared to be important in Lacey's work. In our study skin conductance reactivity as well as skin conductance level was used (cf. Edelberg, 1972).

A well-known variable reacting to environmental change is peripheral vasoconstriction. Direct measurement of this variable is complicated. However, it appears to covary with finger temperature (cf. Duffy, 1972) so the latter measure was included.

Finally the subjects' respiration was registered as a variable reflecting emotionality (cf. Grossman, 1983). Three different measures of respiration were derived, i.e. respiration frequency, mean inhalation time and mean expiration time.

Summarizing, then, nine different psychophysiological measures were studied:

1. Heart beat
   (a) Mean interbeat intervals.
   (b) Standard deviation.
   (c) T-wave amplitude.
2. Respiration
   (a) Frequency.
   (b) Mean inhalation time.
   (c) Mean expiration time.
3. Skin conductance
   (a) Response.
   (b) Level.
4. Temperature
   (a) Finger temperature.

Biochemical variables

Several endocrine products are known to vary as a function of external as well as internal stimulation. Among them, different hormones have been used to study specific film effects. They have been included in the present study to provide additional information on the physiological patterns. The most prominent hormones studied are undoubtedly the products of the adrenals. The catecholamines, epinephrine and norepinephrine are sensitive to stress and have been connected with emotions such as fear and anger (cf. Lang, Rice and Sternbach, 1972). They have also been successfully studied to investigate the effect of films. The corticosteroids have been investigated in the context of stress for a long time already. They have been studied in films by Levi (1972). We decided to include epinephrine and norepinephrine as well as cortisol as dependent variables. Other hormones listed by Mason (1972) to be sensitive to stressful events are growth hormone and testosterone. In addition, triglyceride, glucose and cholesterol were included because their levels are known to vary as a function of the hormones mentioned (cf. Mason, 1972; Guyton, 1976) and effects of films have been demonstrated by Carruthers and Taggart (1973).

Summarizing, then, the effects of films upon the levels of epinephrine, norepinephrine, cortisol, growth hormone, testosterone, triglyceride, glucose and cholesterol have been investigated in this study.

Procedure

All subjects were informed that the experiment was meant to study bodily reactions to films. They were asked to abstain from alcoholic beverages, coffee and smoking during the morning before the experiment started. All sessions started at 9.00 a.m. Upon arrival, the subjects were seated in an easy chair in the film space described earlier (cf. Chapter 8) and the catheter for taking blood samples was inserted in the left arm and secured with tape. Subsequently, the electrodes and thermistors for the registration of heart beat, skin conductance, respiration and temperature were attached. The experiment was started with the films shown in the order indicated, starting with the buffer film. At the end of each film a blood sample was obtained with the aid of a Venoject vacuum collecting tube. Between any two films a pause was given during which soft music was played in the earphones. The duration of the pauses was different: duration was determined to keep the periods elapsing between two adjacent collections of blood constant at 15 minutes.

Registration and analyses

Physiological registration occurred continuously during all films. Heart beat was registered with the aid of surface electrodes: one right of the sternum, one at the lower false ribs and the earth applied to the left wrist. Galvanic skin conductance was registered with electrodes attached to the middle and fore finger of the left hand. The thermistor for registration of temperature was applied to the left thumb. Respiration speed was registered with the aid of a thermistor attached to the nostril. All signals were recorded on an eight-channel Beckman polygraph. They were analyzed for two separate minutes per film. The first minute was started one minute after the film onset. The second minute was located near the end at a salient moment of the film specified in advance.

The blood samples for the analysis of biochemical reactions were placed in a centrifuge for 5 min (3000 rpm). After that the plasma was stored at $-70°C$ until analysis. Plasma catecholamines were analyzed according to the radioenzymatic method reported by Endert (1979). Testosterone was determined by the method of Pratt, Wiegman and Lappöhna (1975). Growth hormone was analyzed by a radioimmunoassay kit, on the principle of competitive protein binding. Cortisol was measured by radioimmunoassay as well. The Technicon SMAC-system was employed to determine glucose, triglyceride and cholesterol.

RESULTS

Selection of physiological variables

To be included in state patterns physiological variables should exhibit stable person × film effects (coherence stability).

In order to investigate which of the physiological measures chosen are adequate to be included in the patterns, the question was raised to which universe each of the measures generalizes. There are several possibilities here, the most interesting are the universe of persons (μ_P), the universe of films (μ_F) and the combination of persons and films ($\mu_{P \times F}$). To obtain an answer to this question an analysis of variance was done with films (F) and replications (R) as facets, according to a 24 (persons) × 6 (films) × 2 (replications) factorial design. Variance components were estimated according to Cronbach, Gleser, Nanda and Rajaratnam, (1972) for P, F, R as well as the interaction terms P × F, P × R, F × R and the remainder P × R × F; error. Generalization to μ_P was estimated on the basis of

$$\rho_P^2 = \frac{\sigma_P^2}{\sigma_P^2 + \dfrac{1}{n_F}\sigma_{PF}^2 + \dfrac{1}{n_R}\sigma_{PR}^2 + \dfrac{1}{n_F n_R}\sigma_{PFR,\ \text{error}}^2} \qquad 1$$

The size of this coefficient indicates to what extent individual scores can be generalized over films and replications. Generalization to μ_F was estimated with the aid of:

$$\rho_F^2 = \frac{\sigma_F^2}{\sigma_F^2 + \dfrac{1}{n_P}\sigma_{PF}^2 + \dfrac{1}{n_R}\sigma_{FR}^2 + \dfrac{1}{n_P n_R}\sigma_{PFR_1,\ \text{error}}^2} \qquad 2$$

This coefficient indicates the amount of generalizability of film scores across persons and replications. Generalizability to μ_{PF} was obtained with

$$\rho^2_{PF} = \frac{\sigma^2_P + \sigma^2_{PF}}{\sigma^2_P + \sigma^2_{PF} + \dfrac{1}{n_R}\sigma^2_{PR} + \dfrac{1}{n_R}\sigma^2_{PFR,\,error}}$$

3

This coefficient gives the amount of generalizability of a person's score over replications within a particular film.

The results of the computations mentioned are represented in Table 2. From this table it can be seen that all measures show a considerable amount of generalization to μ_P. This means that all variables reflect stable individual differences. On the other hand none of the variables exhibits much generalizability to μ_F indicating that the films hardly have effects plain enough to become visible in all subjects at any moment of the film.

Generalization to μ_{PF} is generally high, but there are differences. Four measures (heart beat intervals, T-wave amplitude, galvanic skin conductance level and finger temperature) show extremely high values, whereas coefficients for the other variables are lower. It should be noted that ρ^2_{PF} values have to a considerable degree been determined by σ^2_P that has been included in the numerator as well as the denominator of the formula. This variance component may be assumed to reflect mainly constitutional factors varying between individuals.

Averill and Opton (1968) have advised to discard this component in the context of psychophysiological assessment, preferably by using ipsative instead of normative scores. An estimate of how this intervention would affect generalizability to μ_{PF} can be obtained by removing σ^2_P as well as σ^2_{PR} from the

Table 2 Coefficients of generalizability of physiological reactions to different universes of generalization

		Generalization to:		
	μ_P	μ_F	μ_{PF}	μ'_{PF}
Heart beat				
Interbeat intervals	0.966	0.669	0.970	0.829
Standard deviation	0.860	0.445	0.654	0.000
T-wave amplitude	0.997	0.338	0.998	0.886
Respiration				
Frequency	0.918	0.166	0.793	0.113
Inhalation time	0.765	0.000	0.682	0.371
Expiration time	0.914	0.119	0.824	0.277
Skin conductance				
Response	0.939	0.000	0.720	0.000
Level	0.992	0.187	0.988	0.739
Temperature				
Finger temperature	0.936	0.361	0.972	0.918

formula. The generalizability coefficient thus becomes

$$\rho_{PF'}^2 = \frac{\sigma_{PF}^2}{\sigma_{PF}^2 + \dfrac{1}{n_R}\,\sigma_{PFR,\ error}^2} \qquad\qquad 4$$

The outcomes obtained with this formula are presented in the last column of Table 2. This column shows a clear dichotomy of variables that can be generalized to μ_{PF} and those that cannot be generalized to μ_{PF}. On the basis of this result it was decided to continue the search for patterns with the aid of heart interbeat intervals (IBI), T-wave amplitude (TWA), galvanic skin conductance level (GSL) and finger temperature (TEMP).

Pattern analysis

After selecting the variables the search for patterns was started. First, all scores were ipsatized, i.e. for each variable the 12 scores for each individual were transformed to z-scores with zero means and unit variances. The raw material now consisted of $24 \times 6 \times 2 = 288$ different patterns, each containing four scores. To guide searching it was assumed that the states would manifest themselves as recurrent patterns of physiological variation to form pattern clusters. In addition, we assumed that between the state patterns, transitional forms would become manifest to constitute clusters of state change patterns. The latter would show resemblance with both states between which they vary.

Six states have been assumed to exist, so that 15 change patterns might be expected to become manifest in the data as well. Consequently, the analysis was started with a cluster analysis with the option to produce 21 different clusters. The analysis used was a hierarchical cluster analysis (Ward's method, cf. Clustan, 1978) on the squared euclidean distances between each pair of 288 patterns. The clusters derived from this analysis are represented in Figure 1.

The next step was directed at discrimination between state patterns on the one hand and state change patterns on the other. For that purpose a configurational analysis of all 21 pattern clusters was carried out. The argument for this analysis was that state change patterns are defined as intermediate forms between states. A configurational analysis on the basis of resemblance may be assumed to locate the real state patterns at more extreme positions as compared to the change patterns. Thus, this analysis would simplify the search for state patterns since only the extremely located patterns would qualify. The 21 patterns were subjected to smallest space analysis with the aid of a Minissa program (Minissa, 1977; Lingoes and Roskam, 1973). Three dimensions were necessary to give a fair account of the pattern relations (the obtained stress of 0.068 can be qualified as 'moderate fit'). Given the fact that 21 points have been located in a three-dimensional space, the positions of the clusters may be considered to be metrically determined (cf. Shepard, 1966).

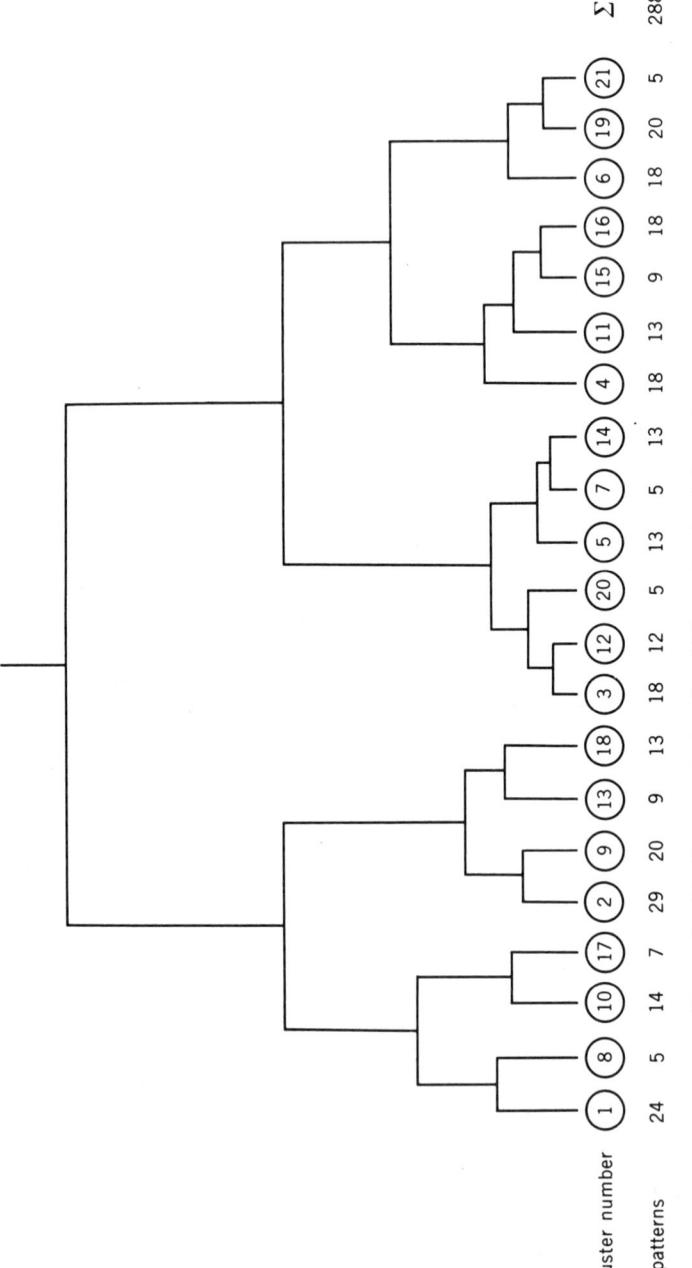

Figure 1 21-Cluster solution for 288 psychophysiological patterns

The real state patterns are most likely to be found in the clusters with high scores on either of the three dimensions. The patterns answering to this criterion are patterns 7, 8, 11, 13, 20 and 21.

Pattern allocation

Thus far we have dealt with state and state change patterns as separate categories, but presumably single patterns belonging to state change clusters are located closer to one or the other state between which they vary. In this section an attempt will be described to reallocate single change patterns to real states if they are close enough. The problem was to develop criteria to determine whether a pattern is close enough to classify it under the heading of a real state. Of course it is possible to determine distances between patterns and clusters. However, with respect to the critical distances to be observed, no satisfactory criteria are available.

In the present study a criterion for allocation was developed empirically, with the aid of rules derived from signal detection theory (see e.g., Gescheider, 1976). First, distances were computed between all state patterns and the means of each of the six real state clusters. Subsequently, the patterns were allocated on the basis of the shortest distances, i.e. the smallest of the six distances constituted the criterion for allocation. The result is a collection of patterns for each real state. This collection can be considered to contain a number of correctly classified patterns as well as a number of so-called false positives, i.e. patterns that do not really belong to the cluster. To determine the best cutting point this distribution was conceived as a 'signal + noise distribution'. In addition a second distribution, containing all other patterns, was conceived as the 'noise distribution'. Obviously both distributions show some overlap (cf. Figure 2). The cutting point was defined as the point where both distributions are equally represented. Thus, the critical distances for each of the real state patterns could be determined. Classification according to these criteria resulted

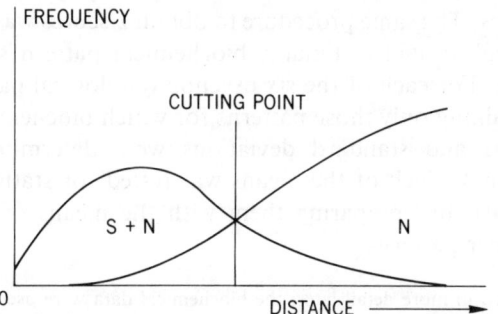

Figure 2   Noise (N) and signal + noise (S + N) distribution (after Gescheider, 1976)

Table 3   Mean patterns for each of the states after allocation of 208 single patterns

State nr	RR-intervals	Psychophysiological variables T-wave amplitude	GSL	Temperature
7	0.17	0.74	− 1.01	− 0.94
8	− 0.85	− 1.22	1.42	0.65
11	0.94	0.54	− 0.06	0.73
13	− 0.85	− 0.99	− 0.71	− 0.74
20	− 0.91	0.65	− 0.47	0.17
21	1.18	− 0.23	− 0.27	− 0.84

in 72% unequivocal classifications; the other 28% were considered to be unclassifiable. Allocation of the classifiable patterns did change the mean values of the four psychophysiological variables in each state pattern. The new values are given in Table 3. These values were currently considered to be the final values defining the six patterns.

Biochemical correlates

Before starting with the main analysis of the biochemical data, each component was subjected to an analysis on the effects of circadian biorhythms. As the administration of the films took more than two hours it was quite possible that this source of variance would have exerted considerable influence on the data. Data were investigated by means of trend analysis for repeated measures (Winer, 1971) on the mean values for every component for each of the subsequent films (for the results see Figure 3). All patterns were tested for linear trends and the test revealed two trends (for cortisol and glucose) to be significant at the 0.01 level. It was decided to eliminate those trends from the data because otherwise they would inconveniently interfere with the results. For each of the two variables least square fits were computed and the raw scores were corrected by diminishing each score with the corresponding value of (b − ax). The corrected scores were subsequently ipsatized by converting them into z-scores. The same procedure to obtain z-scores was followed for the other biochemical variables. Finally, biochemical pattern scores were computed as follows. For each of the six psychophysiological patterns a selection was made, containing only those patterns for which biochemical evidence was available. Means and standard deviations were determined and brought together in Table 4. Each of the means was tested for statistical significance (t-test, one-tailed)[1] by comparing them with the means over the combined values of the other patterns.

[1] As will be explained in more detail later, the biochemical data were used to test a number of directed hypotheses, derived from the interpretation of psychophysiological patterns. Therefore, the application of one-tailed tests seemed appropriate.

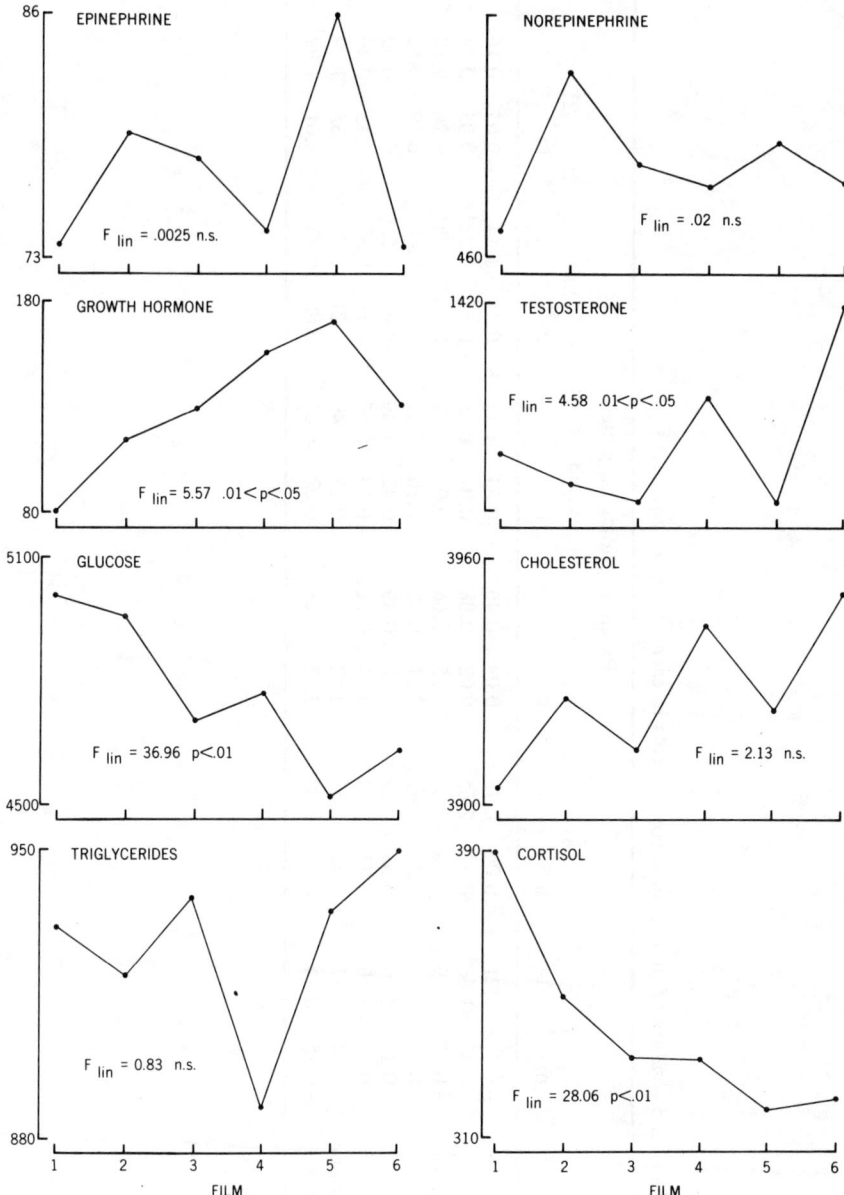

Figure 3 Mean biochemical values for six films

Table 4 Means and t-values of biochemical components in each of six state-patterns

| | Psychophysiological pattern | | | | | | | | | | | | df |
| | 7 | | 8 | | 11 | | 13 | | 20 | | 21 | | |
	m	t	m	t	m	t	m	t	m	t	m	t	
Glucose	-0.33	1.21	0.06	0.18	0.09	0.46	0.33	1.11	0.31	1.14	-0.05	0.16	100
Cortisol	-0.45	1.66[1]	0.82	2.65[2]	0.02	0.08	0.04	0.14	0.51	1.81[1]	0.05	0.14	98
Norepinephrine	-0.05	0.19	-0.16	0.47	-0.55	2.66[2]	-0.09	0.27	0.56	2.08[1]	0.26	0.80	98
Epinephrine	-0.15	0.55	0.21	0.62	-0.21	0.98	-0.10	0.41	0.15	0.60	-0.19	0.58	98
Cholesterol	-0.18	0.70	0.05	0.18	0.13	0.49	0.42	1.49	-0.40	1.56	-0.15	0.49	100
Triglycerides	-0.30	1.10	0.73	2.33[1]	-0.04	0.21	-0.20	0.67	0.16	0.59	-0.15	0.46	100
Growth hormone	-0.24	0.87	-0.46	1.43	0.52	2.54[2]	-0.15	0.49	0.21	0.77	-0.38	1.19	100
Testosterone	-0.15	0.54	0.63	2.00[1]	0.27	1.28	0.02	0.06	0.08	0.27	-0.61	1.92[1]	99

[1] $p < 0.05$ (one-tailed)
[2] $p < 0.01$

Pattern interpretation

The interpretation was primarily based on the psychophysiological data. Biochemical results were used only to confirm or reject the conclusions drawn there. First, within the six patterns a distinction was made into patterns reflecting sympathetic dominance and patterns reflecting vagal dominance. This distinction was based on the cardiac measures, i.e. T-wave amplitude in combination with RR-intervals. In the literature on T-wave amplitude ample evidence is now available to take this variable as a measure of neural sympathetic activity, decreased amplitude referring to increased sympathetic activity (Mitchell and Shapiro, 1954; Simonov, Frolov and Sviridov, 1975; Matyas and King, 1976; Punch, King and Matyas, 1976; Heslegrave and Furedy, 1979). As is evident from Table 3 two of the patterns (8 and 13) clearly demonstrate decreased T-wave amplitude. In addition, those two patterns show considerably decreased RR-intervals, again demonstrating increased sympathetic activity.

The other four patterns are less clear with respect to T-wave; obviously none of them reflects sympathetic dominance. Consequently, they were scrutinized with respect to possible vagal dominance. Usually, RR-intervals are taken to reflect both sympathetic and vagal effects, low heart rate (large RR-intervals) referring to increased vagotonicity. From Table 3 it is evident that patterns 11 and 21 do reflect vagal effects. In addition, for pattern 11 the biochemical data demonstrate vagotonicity as well, including increased plasma growth hormone (cf. Carruthers and Taggart, 1973) and low norepinephrine. Thus, patterns 11 and 21 were interpreted as parasympathetic patterns.

The two remaining patterns showed large T-wave amplitudes, but they also showed intermediate (pattern 7) too small (pattern 20) RR-intervals. If the latter result is attributed mainly to increased humoral sympathetic activity (as shown by the increased norepinephrine level of pattern 20), one is left with the conclusion that in both patterns vagal and sympathetic neural activity are approximately in balance. Summarizing, then, two patterns reflect sympathetic dominance, two other patterns reflect vagal dominance, whereas the two remaining patterns seem to reflect sympathetic-vagal balance.

The next step was to fit these results into the theoretical framework of the present study. On the basis of the descriptions offered by Pribram (1971) it seems obvious to identify vagal overactivity as reflecting passive, emotional 'stop'-mechanisms and sympathetic overactivity as reflecting active, motivational 'go'-mechanisms.

In the two remaining patterns (7 and 20) vagal and sympathetic activities seem to be in balance. Thus, they are interpreted as reflecting states of effort, of which Pribram and McGuiness (1975) have indicated that the stop-mechanisms as well as the go-mechanisms are involved.

Summarizing then, we come to the conclusion that two patterns (11 and 21) are arousal patterns, two patterns (7 and 20) are effort patterns and two other patterns (8 and 13) are patterns of activation.

The final step to be taken in the interpretation of patterns concerns the distinction between cognitive–symbolic versus sensorimotor–operational patterns. To make this distinction, it was argued as follows. In all sensori-motor–operational states (exploration, substitution and persistence) a certain amount of muscular action and increased muscular tonus may be assumed to be involved. Orienting and searching, trial and error behavior and increased vigor (as in persistence) will thus be accompanied by an increase in the mobilization of energy. In effect, skin temperature may be hypothesized to rise and the galvanic skin conductance level will also be elevated. [As a matter of fact and contrary to more sophisticated interpretations, one of the leading workers in this field i.e. Edelberg (1972) considers this to be a major cause of galvanic skin reactivity.]

On the other hand, there seems to be no obvious reason to assume skin temperature and galvanic skin reaction to be elevated in purely cognitive states. Thus, it was decided to view both measures as indices to discriminate between cognitive and operational states. In the biochemical area increased plasma cortisol was considered to be a major index of energy mobilization (cf. Selye, 1976). In addition, increased catecholamines, growth hormone and testosterone as well as glucose and triglycerides were all conceived as indications of energy mobilization (cf. Guyton, 1976). Careful inspection of the six patterns against this background led to the following results. The skin temperature criterion produced a clear dichotomy, classifying the patterns 8, 11 and 20 as sensorimotor–operational states and the patterns 7, 13 and 21 as cognitive–symbolic states. This dichotomy was largely confirmed by the GSL-criterion, where the patterns 8 and 11 obtained the highest scores. The patterns 8 and 20 showed an increase in plasma cortisol, whereas furthermore in pattern 8 triglycerides as well as testosterone were increased. In pattern 11 growth hormone level was elevated and so was norepinephrine in pattern 20. All these results point in the direction of higher energy mobilization in the patterns mentioned. The only exception to this picture was decreased norepinephrine in pattern 11.

In the assumed cognitive state patterns the picture was reversed in that pattern 7 showed decreased plasma cortisol and pattern 21 showed decreased testosterone. These coherent results, together with the conclusions drawn before on arousal, effort and activation states, led us to the final conclusion, that

1. Pattern 7 represents a state of uncoupling.
2. Pattern 8 represents a state of persistence.
3. Pattern 11 represents a state of exploration.
4. Pattern 13 represents a state of redirection.

Table 5 Distribution of identifiable states over films (initial and final recordings)

		Films						
		Endurance test	Quarrel	Interruption	Wedding party	Failure	Accident	Σ
STATES	Reflection	1 0	1 1	2 1	2 2	2 4	5 4	25
	Exploration	4 2	8 5	8 1	11 8	6 8	9 4	74
	Uncoupling	2 0	0 3	2 6	2 7	8 8	6 2	46
	Substitution	3 1	2 5	2 7	5 3	4 3	2 4	41
	Redirection	7 4	4 3	7 9	3 1	3 2	3 0	46
	Persistence	7 12	5 3	3 1	0 0	1 0	0 4	36
	Σ	43	40	49	44	49	43	268
	Unidentified	19	22	13	18	13	19	104
								Σ 372

5. Pattern 20 represents a state of substitution.
6. Pattern 21 represents a state of reflection.

Film effects

Now that the psychophysiological patterns have been classified into six states, it becomes possible to inspect the eliciting effects of different films with respect to the states. In this analysis seven Ss originally removed from the sample, were included because they had complete physiological data. Table 5 gives an overview of film effects in terms of the distribution of state patterns over films. The results are unbiased in the sense that up to this moment film content has neither been used as a basis for pattern analysis nor for pattern interpretation. The results are striking in several respects. First, there is only one state pattern demonstrating an appreciable difference with respect to time of occurrence (early versus late within films). Pattern 11 (exploration) was found more often in the beginning of the films as compared with the end. This result could be expected on the assumption that exploration is more likely to occur in situations of novelty and uncertainty (cf. Berlyne, 1960).

The impact of film content may best be explored on the basis of the final states in each film when the Ss did have a more definite conception of the situation presented. It turns out then, that the distributions of states over films are far from random: different films elicit different states. Furthermore this distribution corresponds to some extent to what one might expect on *a priori* grounds. For instance, the dominant reaction to the film 'endurance test' is a state of persistence. No less than 12 out of 19 identifiable reactions are of this type. The film 'quarrel' elicited more diversity, the dominant reactions being sensorimotor–operational states. Strikingly absent in this film is reflection, a result that might well be typical for this type of situation. The dominant reaction to the film 'interruption' is effort. This result is in good harmony with a situation in which an ongoing job activity is interrupted continuously.

The film 'wedding party' mainly gives rise to states of exploration and uncoupling, the first being a natural reaction to the film's high degree of diversity. The film 'failure' elicits roughly the same states as its predecessor, perhaps to be explained here as a reaction to uncertainty and negative feedback. The film 'accident' finally led to divergent reactions including exploration, reflection and substitution as well as persistence. The first two states are in agreement with the finding of Carruthers and Taggart (1973) that violent situations are frequently followed by states of a predominantly vagal nature.

10

Construct validation of psychophysiological state patterns

Joop Hettema,

Ad J. Vingerhoets,

Margo van der Molen,

and

Fons J. van de Vijver

INTRODUCTION

The patterns identified by Hettema, Vingerhoets and Van Heck (cf. Chapter 9) presumably represent specific processes to acquire or maintain control over the environment. In order to demonstrate that they perform the function attributed to each of them in the context of the open-systems adaptation model, construct validity studies are needed. The design of those studies has to be based on theoretical notions regarding the state transition mechanisms underlying the patterns. State-transition mechanisms then are conceived as intermediate instances that determine behavior in a purely formal way. They accomplish tactical changes in an ongoing stream of behavior. As such they have the status of intervening variables rather than predictors of overt behavior. Thus, validation of the patterns can only be accomplished indirectly.

ST-mechanisms are conceived as mediators between cognitions on the one hand and overt behavior on the other. According to assumption 3.3 of the theory they tend to be coupled with specific situations in an idiosyncratic way. This statement implies that for each individual person a specific situation

Personality and Environment: Assessment of Human Adaptation
Edited by P. J. Hettema. © 1989 John Wiley & Sons Ltd

would be required to elicit any one ST-mechanism in particular. It may be assumed, however, that conditioning processes will have the effect of making the coupling between situations and ST-mechanisms less idiosyncratic, especially in situations that are frequently met and require specific states to deal with. Coming first to mind in this context are cognitive problem situations that can be considered to be unambiguous regarding the processes required to solve them. Thus our primary task is to select specific problem situations answering this general description. Once selected, these situations can be used in construct validation studies in either of two ways.

The first way rests on the view that particular situations will have the capacity to *elicit* particular states. In terms derived from psychophysiology this approach comes down to the principle of stimulus–response specificity of physiological reaction patterns (cf. Averill and Opton, 1968). In a now classical study Lacey (1959) has shown that particular problem situations elicit particular psychophysiological state patterns. Lacey employed 12 different stimulus situations to represent as wide a range of stimulus situations as seemed expedient. The situations ranged from 'visual attention' and 'empathic listening' to 'thinking' and 'withstanding pain'. As psychophysiological measures Lacey, for instance, used heart rate and galvanic skin conductance. In the 'visual attention' and 'empathic listening' tasks the subjects predominantly showed cardiac deceleration, whereas in the 'thinking' and 'withstanding pain' tasks they showed cardiac acceleration. In all tasks galvanic skin conductance was increased. On these results Lacey based his famous dichotomy of tasks for 'environmental intake' versus 'environmental rejection'. The intake–rejection hypothesis has not gone by unchallenged as critical reviews of e.g. Elliott (1972), Hahn (1972) and Kjellberg and Magnusson (1979) demonstrate. The main point here, however, is that Lacey has shown specific cognitive and other tasks to have the capacity to evoke specific patterns of psychophysiological reaction, thus providing a basis for construct validation studies of patterns of the type identified here.

A second approach to the problem of construct validation may be based on the assumption that within a specific problem situation, particular ST-mechanisms are better suited to deal with the problem than others. Thus, for instance, in a searching task exploration will be particularly helpful, whereas in a thinking task reflection will be more beneficial than other states. Generally speaking, we may expect particular tasks to require particular states to effectively deal with them. Therefore, within a specific task, predictions regarding the *efficacy* of specific ST-mechanisms will provide a second mode for construct validation of the patterns. With respect to this second mode a proviso has to be made concerning competence aspects that may have their own effects upon task performance apart from ST-mechanisms. An optimal experimental design would take those aspects into account thus enabling us to study the effects of state patterns *per se*.

Summarizing then, the strategy to be followed for obtaining evidence with respect to the construct validity of the patterns is two-fold. On the principle of state elicitation the patterns will be studied as dependent variables, whereas on the principle of state efficacy the patterns will be studied as independent variables in cognitive tasks especially selected.

THE SELECTION OF TASKS

The primary purpose of the tasks to be chosen is to evoke specific ST-mechanisms as distinguished by the open-systems adaptation model. Each ST-mechanism has been conceptualized to fulfil a specific control function in the interaction between person and environment. Those functions are specified with respect to the phase as well as to the level of the interaction process. The phases of the process refer to the initial situation, the transformation and the final situation as a result of transformations (cf. Hettema, 1979). In the first phase the ST-mechanisms are defined as phasic arousal mechanisms, causing specific configural changes to occur in the input of the system. The second phase contains mechanisms of effort, directed at replacement of actions initially chosen by new actions. And, finally, in the third phase tonic activation mechanisms are assumed to operate, enabling the organism to select and maintain a particular goal for a longer period of time.

What we obviously need now is a classification of tasks enabling us to select tasks connected with each of the phases as described.

A classification of the type meant here has been made by Guilford (1959) on the basis of a large number of factor analytical studies within the domain of intellectual aptitudes. Within that context Guilford has distinguished four main categories of thinking abilities, i.e. cognition, convergent thinking, divergent thinking and evaluation. The first three categories of this classification exhibit connections with the distinction into phases as has been made in the context of the open-systems adaptation model. According to Guilford, tests for *cognition* have to do with 'the possession of information, its discovery and its rediscovery or recognition' (Guilford, 1959, p. 765). Cognition tests obviously require operations on the input of the personality system, thus presumably eliciting processes of arousal. Tests for *convergent thinking* 'call for one right answer, which can be determined closely, if not exactly, from the information given' (p. 376). They require transformations that are directed at specific goals, thus presumably eliciting processes of activation. And, finally, tests for *divergent thinking* require the subject to 'go off in different directions. They require changes of direction in problem solving and also lead to a diversity of answers, where more than one answer is acceptable' (p. 381).

Thus, tests for divergent thinking require replacement of actions on the same input and will be most likely to elicit effort processes.

Within each of the three broad categories mentioned several factors have been identified and allocated by Guilford and his associates. Further specification has been obtained on the basis of additional features like test content and the type of response wanted in the tests with high loadings on the pertinent factors. We have made a selection among the factors on the basis of a careful analysis of those elements in connection with the process descriptions given in the context of the open-systems adaptation model. Within the domain of cognition the factor visual cognition was chosen; for convergent thinking the factors visualization and numerical facility were selected and for divergent thinking we took the factors figural adaptive flexibility and ideational fluency. Each of the factors was represented by a test loading high on that factor according to previous studies. Thus, for visual cognition we selected the Street Gestalt Completion Test, for visualization we took the Jigsaw Puzzles Test and for numerical facility the Adding Speed Test, for figural adaptive flexibility we selected the Gottschaldt Hidden Figures Test and for ideational fluency the Consequences Test. The battery was completed with the Water Jars Test (Luchins and Luchins, 1959) to include a test where the elicited state would presumably not coincide with the most efficacious state. Formally speaking, this test would elicit convergent thinking, but in order to meet the requirements imposed by the test the subject should manage to change his overlearned response strategy. Thus, rather than convergent thinking, divergent thinking should constitute the optimal approach. If so, the crucial difficulty of the Water Jars Test would consist of a discrepancy between elicited state and required state.

The process of selecting tests for specific ST-mechanisms is summarized in Table 1.

Table 1 The selection of tests

ST-mechanism	Guilford category	Factor	Test
Arousal	Cognition	Visual cognition	Street Gestalt Completion
Effort	Divergent thinking	Figural adaptive flexibility	Gottschaldt Hidden Figures
Effort	Divergent thinking	Ideational fluency	Consequences
Activation	Convergent thinking	Visualization	Jigsaw Puzzles
Activation	Convergent thinking	Numerical facility	Adding Speed
Activation/ Effort			Water Jars

HYPOTHESES

Elicitation of state patterns

1. The Street Gestalt Test will elicit more arousal than other states.
2. The Hidden Figures Test will elicit more effort than other states.
3. The Consequences Test will elicit more effort than other states.
4. The Jigsaw Puzzles Test will elicit more activation than other states.
5. The Adding Speed Test will elicit more activation than other states.
6. The Water Jars Test will elicit more activation than other states.

Efficacy of state patterns

Granted the confirmation of the elicitation hypotheses, the next question concerns state efficacy. In this context the levels of the behavioral system become important. All the tests used in this study are concerned with intellectual functioning, thus primarily requiring activity at the cognitive–symbolic level of the behavioral system. Depending on the domain (cognition, convergent, divergent thinking) we therefore expected reflection, uncoupling or redirection to be the crucial states. Thus the following hypotheses concerning state efficacy were put to the test:

1. In the Street Gestalt Test reflection will give better results than other states.
2. In the Hidden Figures Test uncoupling will give better results than other states.
3. In the Consequences Test uncoupling will give better results than other states.
4. In the Jigsaw Puzzles Test redirection will give better results than other states.
5. In the Adding Speed Test redirection will give better results than other states.
6. In the Water Jars Test uncoupling will give better results than other states.

METHOD

Subjects

Fifty-one students participated in the experiment. They were all volunteers who obtained dfl. 25, as a reward for participation; 38 were psychology students (16 males and 22 females), the other 13 were engineering students (12 males and one female). With respect to secondary education an additional classification was made. In the Dutch educational system two types of secondary school give access to higher studies. One of those (type A) stresses foreign languages and business administration, whereas the other (type B) puts emphasis on mathematics and sciences. Of the 38 psychology students 28 had completed A-type schools whereas 10 had come from B-type schools. The engineering students had all finished B-type schools.

Tests

Street Gestalt Completion Test

The version we used was specially designed for the present study. It consisted of 22 pictures (black on white) of familiar objects, parts of which had been deleted. The subjects were asked to indicate what each picture represented by writing their answers down on an answer sheet. They were encouraged to keep trying to find the right answer until they were sure they could not come up with it. Score was the number of correct answers given.

Hidden Figures Test

The Thurstone (1944) version of the Gottschaldt Hidden Figures Test was used. This test consists of a booklet with five pages each containing one simple geometric figure and six to eight complex figures in which the simple figure is embedded. The test contains 32 items. The subjects had to indicate the correct position of the simple figure by drawing it into the complex figure. Score was the time needed to complete the whole test. After a maximum of 20 minutes the test was stopped.

Consequences Test

In this test the question has to be answered what would happen if a familiar state of affairs is changed by a sudden event. The present version consisted of two items. The first question referred to the consequences of all plastics throughout the world suddenly melting, whereas the second question asked for the consequences of a sudden inability of all people to speak. The subjects were encouraged to write down as many different consequences as they could think of. Score was the number of different consequences mentioned for each of the two items.

Jigsaw Puzzles

This test was developed especially for this study. It consisted of three items in which larger figures drawn on a sheet of paper (a triangle, a rectangle and a pentangle) had to be filled up with a number of pieces (five, five and nine pieces respectively). Each item had a time limit of five minutes. The time needed to complete each of the figures was registered and added up to yield the score of the test.

Adding Speed Test

This test consists of a large number of simple additions of two-digit numbers. The subject was asked to work as quickly as possible without skipping any of the problems. Every 30 seconds a signal was given and the subject had to indicate the point he had arrived at. The test was continued for 12 minutes after which it was stopped. The score was the number of problems solved during the first and the last 2.5 minute period of the total test.

Water Jars Test

The test consists of 18 items, all concerned with the question how to obtain a specific amount of water with the aid of three jars, each of a particular capacity. Subjects were encouraged to look for the simplest way to solve this problem. The initial items ($N = 7$) could all be solved with the same operation, thus establishing a particular set in the subject. The second group ($N = 7$) critical items could be solved with the same procedure as the initial group, but in addition a much simpler procedure was successful as well. The last group of items ($N = 4$) were extinction items in which only the simple procedure was successful. The test had two scores: the number of short solutions in (a) the critical items, and (b) the extinction items.

Procedure

All subjects were tested individually. First, a general instruction was given concerning the tasks and the psychophysiological registration procedure. The subjects were asked to sit as quietly as possible during the experiment. Then, the electrodes and thermistors were attached in the same way as described in Chapter 9. After a 20 minutes rest period the tasks were administered in a fixed order: Street Gestalt Test, Water Jars Test, Jigsaw Puzzles Test, Hidden Figures Test, Consequences Test 1 and 2, Adding Speed Test. After finishing the last test there was a second rest period of 20 minutes.

Psychophysiological registration

During all tasks and periods of rest the subjects were continuously monitored with a Beckman polygraph on separate channels for ECG, skin conductance and finger temperature. The signals derived from 10 one-minute periods (one for each task and for the two rest periods) were used and further elaborated. They were converted to yield four different measures:

1. Mean interbeat interval (IBI).
2. T-wave amplitude (TWA).
3. Mean galvanic skin response level (GSL).
4. Mean forefinger temperature (TEMP).

The registration periods were located at the end of the two rest periods and at a fixed moment previously determined during each of the tasks.

Correction for chronicity

Before starting the main analysis to test the hypotheses of this study, the psychophysiological measures were scrutinized with respect to chronicity (Averill and Opton, 1968). For each of the four variables IBI, TWA, GSL and TEMP separately means and variances per task were computed as well as all correlations between tasks. Chronicity effects were obviously present in the means (especially TEMP and GSL) and also in the correlation matrices. Each of the four matrices showed superdiagonality, indicating some sort of time-order effect in the data. Since we are primarily interested in person × task interactions, time-order effects were considered to constitute error variance that should preferably be eliminated from the data. A major problem here is that tasks are completely confounded with order of presentation so that time-order effects could not be tracked down in any simple way. To dispose of them anyway we argued as follows. The total variance of any variable in this study may be considered to be composed of a number of different components. First there are individual differences, which, as usual, are very large in this type of data. Individual differences manifest themselves in the within-task variance as well as in the between-task correlations. Those correlations are very high, indicating strong effects of this source of variance. The next source is tasks, effecting differences between task means. The third source is time-order, manifesting itself in the difference between task means as well as the previous source. In addition to the variables mentioned there are interactions, the effects of which are less easy to track down. The crucial problem in this study was, to differentiate between person × task interactions on the one hand and person × time-order interactions on the other.

Person × task interactions can take any form since, theoretically, they will depend on the learning histories of the individuals tested. Only if the same task is administered twice can we expect to find clear indications of interaction in the form of extremely high correlations between tasks. Subjected to factor analysis the data would produce specific factors with high loadings for the same tasks. On theoretical grounds, person × time-order interactions appear less difficult to trace. They can be conceived as having their origin in general processes that are time-bound and manifest themselves differently for each individual. For instance, individuals exposed to task conditions are known to be especially activated in the beginning of the task. This may have been the case here as well, although we attempted to quiet our subjects down during the period of rest before starting. Gradually, this state of activation will disappear and perhaps be replaced by boredom. Furthermore, individuals exposed to a number of tasks with a highly repetitive (itemized) character will show habituation. Habituation curves are known to show large individual differences thus accounting for person × time-order interactions in studies like this. Another hypothesis to be considered regarding the process operating is fatigue. Again this is a general process only to be expected as a consequence of the efforts required in this type of task. Individual differences in fatiguability may provide a basis for person × time-order interactions as well. Whatever the process conception cherished it seems reasonable to expect monotonically increasing or decreasing curves to arise as a function of time. Assuming those curves to show individual differences with respect to slope, serial correlations are to be expected in addition to the correlations already present on the basis of individual differences *per se*.

The obvious technique to unravel the different types of correlation is factor analysis. Person × time-order effects should become manifest as a general factor with task loadings increasing or decreasing monotonically as a function of the order of presentation of the tasks. Once such a factor is identified, factor scores can be obtained, representing the amount of time-order effect per task per individual. Diminishing the raw scores obtained with the factor scores will yield residuals that can be considered free from time-order effects of the type mentioned.

To identify the time-order factor for each of the four variables of this study the correlation matrices were factor-analyzed with principal components to yield two factors each. Inspection of the factor patterns reveals patterns of monotonically decreasing loadings on the second factor for each of the four analyses carried out (cf. Table 2). Thus, we may conclude that person × time-order interactions have become manifest as a separate factor. We may not conclude, however, that the factor is in correct shape already. To find a criterion for factor rotation we argued that scores obtained during the two rest periods (before and after administration of the tasks) should be essentially the same, i.e. apart from being affected by time-order effects. Taking individual differences into account this means that the variances of both rest conditions should be equal after subtracting factor-scores associated with time order. Thus:

$$\sigma_{R_1}^2(1 - \alpha_{TR_1}^2) = \sigma_{R_2}^2(1 - \alpha_{TR_2}^2) \qquad 1$$

Here $\sigma_{R_1}^2$ and $\sigma_{R_2}^2$ are the variances of the raw scores obtained during the rest

Table 2 Unrotated factor loadings for tasks and rest periods derived with a two-factor solution

	IBI		TWA		GSL		TEMP	
	I	II	I	II	I	II	I	II
1. Rest 1	0.85	0.48	0.94	0.24	0.85	0.50	0.43	0.80
2. Street	0.94	0.27	0.96	0.23	0.97	0.16	0.80	0.46
3. Jars 1	0.97	0.06	0.98	0.12	0.98	0.08	0.93	0.22
4. Jars 2	0.98	0.00	0.99	0.11	0.99	0.03	0.94	0.19
5. Puzzles	0.98	−0.02	0.99	0.06	0.99	−0.03	0.96	0.00
6. HFT	0.97	−0.10	0.99	−0.06	0.99	−0.07	0.96	−0.09
7. Consequences 1	0.98	−0.10	0.99	−0.13	0.98	−0.14	0.96	−0.24
8. Consequences 2	0.97	−0.09	0.98	−0.15	0.98	−0.14	0.95	−0.26
9. Adding	0.92	−0.30	0.97	−0.20	0.97	−0.21	0.93	−0.28
10. Rest 2	0.91	−0.18	0.96	−0.21	0.96	−0.13	0.91	−0.31

periods, whereas $\alpha^2_{TR_1}$ and $\alpha^2_{TR_2}$ represent the proportions of the variance associated with time order for both rest periods.

This equality provides an unequivocal criterion for rotation. After rotation factor-scores for time-order were computed according to the component model (Rummel, 1970, p. 436) yielding exact factor scores for each individual for each task as well as for the two control conditions. All raw-scores were corrected for time-order by subtracting the corresponding time-order factors scores to yield residuals.

To test whether we have removed all time-order effects by the reduction described we computed mean residual scores per task as well as between task correlations for each of the four variables. The task means no longer vary as a function of time-order. The means for rest 1 and rest 2 always have an extreme position in the distribution of means. Those positions generally agree with theoretical expectations, with one notable exception: T-wave amplitude tends to be lower in rest as compared to task conditions. With respect to the same tasks (Water Jars 1 and 2; Consequences 1 and 2) it may be noticed that their mean values are usually close together. Regarding the correlations the general picture is that they are very high except for the two rest periods. Correlating highly with each other they show lower correlations with all tasks. The same tasks show higher correlations as compared with different tasks. And, finally, superdiagonality has disappeared altogether from the four matrices.

Data analysis

Since the results of the correction did not show important time-trends anymore, we were confident that the data were now ready for the final analyses. Per subject means and standard deviations over tasks were obtained and all scores were ipsatized. Ipsative scores for the four variables were brought together to form a pattern for each task. In sum, we obtained $51 \times 8 = 408$ patterns. Each pattern was compared with the six norm patterns derived earlier (cf. Chapter 9) and attributed to the norm pattern to which it had the smallest squared euclidean distance. The patterns with distances exceeding all critical distances as determined earlier were considered to be unclassifiable and discarded for further analysis. A total of 26 patterns (6%) had to be eliminated. The remaining patterns were used as a basis for the final analyses.

RESULTS

State patterns as dependent variables

For each task the patterns obtained were classified according to pattern type and summarized in Table 3. To test whether these frequencies depart from chance for each cell expected frequencies were computed based on the marginal totals and χ^2 was used to test whether the hypothesized states occurred more often.

From these findings the following conclusions were drawn concerning the elicitation hypotheses:

1. Hypothesis A_1 (The Street Gestalt Test eliciting arousal) is confirmed ($p < 0.01$).
2. Hypothesis A_2 (The Hidden Figures Test eliciting effort) is not confirmed.
3. Hypothesis A_3 (The Consequences Test eliciting effort) is confirmed for both of the two items ($p < 0.01$).
4. Hypothesis A_4 (The Jigsaw Puzzles Test eliciting activation) is confirmed ($p < 0.01$).
5. Hypothesis A_5 (The Adding Speed Test eliciting activation) is not confirmed (closer inspection revealed that redirection did occur more often than was to be expected on chance, so at least for one of the activation patterns the hypothesis is confirmed).
6. Hypothesis A_6 (The Water Jars Test eliciting activation) is confirmed for part (a) as well as part (b) of the test ($p < 0.01$).

Summarizing it may be stated that the data have provided impressive support to the elicitation hypotheses with only one clear exception, the results of the Hidden Figures Test.

State patterns as independent variables

To test the efficacy hypotheses all tests were scored according to the rules pointed out before. Each test was analyzed separately with analysis of variance

Table 3 Distribution of states over tasks

Test	Reflection	Exploration	Uncoupling	State Substitution	Redirection	Persistence	Σ
Street	16	9	6	0	7	3	41
Jars I	3	5	0	6	5	32	51
Jars II	3	4	0	4	6	32	49
Puzzles	4	7	3	6	12	17	49
HFT	5	22	12	3	3	3	48
Consequences I	3	17	23	6	0	1	50
Consequences II	9	13	18	5	1	3	49
Adding	5	3	10	7	17	3	45
Σ	48	80	72	37	51	94	382

in which state and type of education were factors. The state hypothesized to be effective was always contrasted with all other states. Type of education was varied to control for competence in so far as it is determined by education.

On the basis of the findings the following conclusions were drawn regarding the efficacy hypotheses:

1. Hypothesis B_1 (reflection beneficial to Street Gestalt performance) is confirmed ($p < 0.01$).
2. Hypothesis B_2 (uncoupling beneficial to Hidden Figures performance) is not confirmed.
3. Hypothesis B_3 (uncoupling beneficial to Consequence Test performance) is neither confirmed for the first item nor the second.
4. Hypothesis B_4 (redirection beneficial to Jigsaw Puzzles performance) is confirmed ($p < 0.01$).
5. Hypothesis B_5 (redirection beneficial to Adding Speed performance) is not confirmed, although there is a tendency in the direction hypothesized.
6. Hypothesis B_6 (uncoupling beneficial to Water Jars Test performance) could not be tested since the state hypothesized did neither show up in the first nor in the second part of the test.

Summarizing it may be stated that the hypotheses concerning the effects of reflection and redirection were either confirmed or showed a tendency towards confirmation. Uncoupling on the other hand did not show the results expected.

DISCUSSION

The patterns developed here have provided a sound basis to predict what patterns will be elicited by what tasks. Thus, we have corroborated earlier expectations from e.g. Lacey, Kagan, Lacey and Moss, (1963) that specific patterns of autonomic response can give results where the mass-action concept of activation has failed. The findings of this study regarding pattern elicitation have provided ample support for our claims regarding the construct validity of the patterns studied. We appeared less successful, however, in predicting state efficacy.

Only two out of five testable hypotheses were confirmed by the data. This raises the question of how adequate the efficacy criterion is with respect to construct validity studies. As we have noted before, competence as a cognitive–symbolic condition for effective performance may have played an overriding role. Transition of states at the cognitive–symbolic level can be beneficial only if symbolic elements relevant for the task are actually available. An interesting question in this respect concerns the effectivity of ST-mechanisms in the context of high versus low competence. It might well be that in low competent individuals other ST-mechanisms will be more effective than

Table 4   Norm values for uncoupling (state 7) after correction

Variable	Norm value
IBI	0.52
TWA	0.78
GSL	− 0.29
TEMP	− 0.07

the ones we have included in our hypotheses. For instance, it can be imagined that low competent individuals derive more benefit from states changing at the operational level as compared with the cognitive–symbolic level. Our analyses thus far are not fit to provide evidence *pro* or *con* this kind of speculation. Thus far we have not found any significant interaction between states and competence with respect to efficacy. An exploration of the states not studied here together with competence remains an attractive option for further study.

A completely different explanation for our failure to confirm three out of five efficacy hypotheses could be an inadequate definition of the norm patterns used. Some support for this view can be found on the basis of a further analysis of the data obtained in the Hidden Figures and Consequences Tests. After exploring those tests we have found high performers to show roughly the same patterns but those patterns deviated from the norm pattern for uncoupling (pattern 7) in the sense that IBI, GSL and TEMP had higher values. On the basis of this finding we decided to redefine pattern 7 by raising the levels of the variables mentioned. The new values of the pattern are presented in Table 4.

SUMMARY STATEMENT

For a long time it has been assumed that physiological reactions somehow reflect the psychological impact of situations upon persons, but positive results are scarce in this area. Theoretical as well as methodological problems have been forwarded to account for this state of affairs. Authors like Lacey and Pribram have advocated that the mass-action model of activation should be abandoned in favor of more complex models, emphasizing interactions between persons and situations rather than either persons or situations. In the present studies, physiological reactions are assumed to reflect tactical processes of control occurring as a consequence of frictions between person and situation.

Using films as stimuli we selected physiological variables exhibiting coherence stability. Subsequently, we managed to identify meaningful patterns presumably reflecting tactical mechanisms as defined in our model. To provide evidence on our interpretation we designed a construct validation study using cognitive tasks as the independent variable. The analysis of the data revealed that specific hypotheses concerning pattern elicitation were generally confirmed. Additional tests on the efficacy of the patterns yielded confirmation only partly. On the basis of the evidence obtained the conclusion was drawn that our first attempt to identify and test physiological patterns representing tactical mechanisms has delivered promising results. It is obvious that more research is needed to reach a more definite conclusion.

Part IV

Assessment at the sensorimotor–operational level

11

Behavioral observation: traits, situations or interactions

JOOP HETTEMA

Traditionally, naturalistic observation has been a major method to collect data on criterion behavior for test validation purposes. Behavioral observation was considered to be the main source of information concerning the 'ultimate criterion' for the validation of prediction programs containing trait measures that were assumed to cover important aspects of behavior in real life conditions. However, investigators have come to realize that criterion assessment is far from simple, so that nowadays they refer to it as the criterion problem rather than criterion analysis (cf. Wiggins, 1980). The core of the criterion problem is that behavior observed under natural conditions is very complex and that some aspects of it usually do not show much connection with others. A way out of this dilemma has been found and generally accepted by using 'intermediate criteria' rather than ultimate criteria for the purpose of test validation. Thus, for instance, a good physician is no longer defined as a good diagnostician, a good scientist, a successful healer and a good participant in community affairs, but rather as somebody obtaining his MD degree in a reasonable amount of time (example borrowed from Wiggins, 1980). This approach may solve some of the problems test makers are struggling with, but it leaves unanswered one of the major questions of personality psychology: what determines individual behavior occurring under natural conditions?

Ultimately, psychology is interested in describing and preferably explaining an individual's behavior as it occurs in normal circumstances, such as, with what other individuals he communicates, how he schedules his activities, what situations he prefers and what situations he dislikes, what are the goals he tries to accomplish, how he attempts to affect situations, how he reacts to frustration and stress. The question is, whether trait models underlying tests have something to offer here. Or, in other words, how far can models based on personality dispositions explain behavior as it occurs in naturalistic conditions. Reviews of the literature by e.g. Magnusson (1976), Mischel (1968) and Sarason, Smith and Diener (1975) have produced predominantly negative answers to this question. Since behavior in naturalistic circumstances continues to be important, especially in most applied settings, it is not surprising that a new direction of research has developed to deal with the problems more adequately. We are referring to the approach known as behavior assessment (cf. Kanfer and Saslow, 1969; Goldfried and Kent, 1972).

Investigators working with behavior assessment procedures have realized that in naturalistic observation a number of restrictions have to be taken into account. For instance, observations merely provide snapshots of behavior and it remains to be seen to what extent they provide us with information about personality as a lasting object. In addition, it is questionable if behavior observed in one situation tells us anything about behavior observed in another situation. A crucial problem in behavior assessment is to indicate precisely the effective elements in the situation where the individual's behavior is observed. Are these elements the ones assumed to be effective by the investigator or does each individual have his own way of defining the situation and determining the elements to affect his behavior?

Natural conditions are to a considerable extent devoid of experimental control, so that even within the same study one can never be sure that different subjects are confronted with the same stimuli. Replicating the original study causes the problem that the new situation is not necessarily identical with the original situation. The problems even increase if the acting subject is assumed to affect the nature of the situation on the strength of his own behavior. This latter conception (one of the assumptions of the open-systems adaptation model) leads to the suspicion that situations, even if they had been unequivocally defined initially, will develop into a direction partly determined by the acting subject.

What are the main characteristics of behavior assessment? An overview has been provided by Hartmann, Roper and Bradford (1979), pointing out that this approach emphasizes direct assessment procedures, the direct observation of behavior in natural environments. The measures used are usually of an intraindividual or idiographic character. In a concrete situation, the behavioral repertoire of an individual is crucial. Personality variables as traditionally conceived are absent or defined at a low level of abstraction. Behavior is seen as a highly specific reaction to the situation on the basis of its functional relation with the situation, whereas generalization to other situations is usually omitted.

The principles mentioned have consequences for the reliability and validity of the measures. Obviously, behavioral assessment does not assume transsituational consistency of behavior or temporal stability in a more general sense. The fact that an individual has shown aggressive behavior last week does not allow predictions to be made regarding his aggressive behavior this week. Whether or not he will demonstrate aggressive behavior will to a large extent depend upon the situations he is confronted with.

High degrees of stability are seldom found in observational studies. For example Van Lieshout (1972) studied child's social interactions using direct observations as well as global judgments by group leaders. The judgments turned out to be fairly stable over time but observations clearly fell behind in that respect. Observations were stable only if situation variables guiding behavior were stable as well.

Stability of overt behavior can be affected by several conditions. Several years ago I did a study of teacher behavior in the classroom with direct observations (Hettema, 1972a; Hettema *et al.*, 1973). Each of 103 teachers was observed during four lessons in two different classes with replication after six months. Using generalizability coefficients I found a very modest median coefficient of 0.55 for generalization over time and classes, computed for a large number of observational categories.

The type of behavioral consistency emphasized in behavior assessment clearly differs from the trait approach. According to Wiggins (1980) the trait position focuses on RR relations and assumes that 'an individual's characteristic disposition or need for trait expression is both *stable* within relatively short time periods and *generalizable* from one situation to another' (Wiggins, 1980, p. 369). The social behaviorist or situationist position on the other hand focuses on SR relationships and tends to 'view behavior observations in samples of response classes that are functionally related to environmental factors which elicit and maintain the responses in a class' (Wiggins, 1980, p. 371).

Hartmann, Roper and Bradford (1979) have designated two types of consistency that should be warranted in behavioral assessment studies. The first type is *intrasituational consistency* referring to 'functional relationships between situations and behaviors' (p. 12). Intrasituational consistency requires that different persons react in the same way to the same situation. The second type of consistency required by Hartmann, Roper and Bradford (1979) is *item homogeneity*. In the view of those authors that concept is not the same as the one used by trait theorists to refer to the compilation of different items into one composite score. Hartmann, Roper and Bradford (1979) advocate establishing composite scores at a lower level of abstraction and use only items that are very specific to a particular category of behavior to be observed. Items subsumed under the same category should exhibit a high degree of equivalence to be acceptable.

Clearly, with respect to naturalistic observation the behavior assessment approach has many virtues compared with trait theory. It focuses on the direct functional relationship between situation and behavior, it is concerned with meticulously defined categories of behavior rather than global dispositions and it offers a base for the study of behavior modification instead of mere classification of individuals in terms of traits and types. Yet, there is also room for doubts as expressed for instance by Wiggins (1980).

Although recognizing the relative neglect of situational factors by most trait theorists, Wiggins doubts whether the situation position would provide better predictions of behavior as compared with the trait position. In this connection he states:

> 'Since prediction has not been a central concern of functional analysis, there are few, if any, data available that would permit an assessment of the predictive potential of such SR relationships in terms of such conventional indices as standard error of prediction, proportion of variance explained, or number of correct decisions. Thus, although there is every reason to believe that the lawful relationships uncovered by functional analysis in the laboratory and in semicontrolled naturalistic settings may have a considerable predictive edge over conventional RR relationships, such an expectation is a matter of conviction rather than fact' (Wiggins, 1980, p. 375).

In addition, from the perspective of personality psychology the contributions of behavioral assessment will always remain limited. As an empty-organism approach it can elucidate relationships between stimuli and responses as well as the changes occurring there, without really improving our insights in personality structure or providing a basis for the explanation of individual differences in behavior. Clearly, in many respects, behavior assessment is diametrically opposed to the trait model. Interaction models, occupying an intermediate position between the two, may combine several of the virtues of either approach. The present model, the open-systems adaptation model, is a good example. Like behavior assessment, it stresses the functional links between situation and behavior. Like the trait model, it emphasizes differences between individuals dealing with the same situation. As pointed out before, in the open-systems adaptation model, consistency is conceived as coherence, referring to individual patterns of behavior that are functionally related to the situation. Strategies are the major structures establishing directional coherence, whereas tactics introduce coherent adjustments in case of disturbances.

According to the model, individual behavior will remain stable as long as situational conditions remain the same whereas situational change will establish lawful alterations in behaviour. As a consequence, the open-systems adaptation model does not claim transsituational consistency like the trait model, nor does it claim intrasituational consistency like the behavior assessment model. Instead, it predicts coherent behavior within situations as well as in repeated confrontations with the same situations.

12

Settings and schedule for the direct observation of behavior

DORIEN P. HOL

INTRODUCTION

In this chapter the development of assessment techniques will be described for the study of psychological adaptation at the sensorimotor-operational level. As Hettema has pointed out earlier (cf. Chapter 2) studies at this level should be conducted with simulation or direct representation of situations whereas behavior should be assessed with the aid of observation (cell IX of the media × modes matrix). Obviously, a number of specifications will have to be made before research can be started. Those specifications concern the setting in which the subjects are brought as well as the way in which their behaviour is registered.

The behavior to be assessed can be provisionally defined as overt behavior of individuals interacting with specific situations. Accordingly, observational settings should be designed to represent particular situations derived from the situation taxonomy. The location, the objects and the actors should satisfy the descriptions given in the taxonomy. In addition special precautions have to be taken to have the situation maintain its character while the subject behaves in its context. The subject should have an ultimate goal to be attained during the time he or she is confronted with the situation. In addition the situation should contain an aspect of friction to be able to study the tactical adjustments he or she makes. Together, these statements imply that the situation should to some extent be controlled by the investigator.

Personality and Environment: Assessment of Human Adaptation
Edited by P. J. Hettema. ©1989 John Wiley and Sons Ltd

CONTROL

With respect to the issue of control Wiggins (1980) has made a distinction into three different kinds of settings: natural settings, controlled laboratory settings, and contrived settings. With 'setting' Wiggins indicates physical characteristics of the environment as well as the presence or absence of other persons. Fiske (1971) has pointed out that a task given to the subject should be included in the setting as well. To induce the same task to all subjects provides a better basis for comparing the behaviors observed. Including task or subject of the situation we can derive five categories of settings based on the amount of control possible:

1. Direct observation in *natural* situations, in which observation of behavior occurs *unobtrusively*. An example of this type of setting may be found in the work of Barker and Wright (1951, 1955).
2. Direct observation in *natural* situations, where observers *participate* as natural partners. Examples may be found in anthropological field studies, e.g. Mead (1964).
3. *Controlled* (laboratory) situations, in which the environment, the people as well as the subject are determined by the investigator, whereas there is freedom with respect to actions. Observation occurs *secretly*. This type of setting has been used by e.g. Bales (1950).
4. *Controlled* situations, in which environment and subject are fixed, whereas the observer *structures* the course of events. An example is the structured interview.
5. *Contrived* situations, in which environment and subject are fixed, observation occurs *unobtrusively* and the activity of *stooges* is crucial. The behavior of stooges creates a special action domain for the subjects. This type of setting has been used in the past by e.g. the American Office of Strategic Services (OSS Assessment Staff, 1948).

Since we decided to create situations rather than find them, the options (1) and (2) were rejected. Since furthermore we had to be able to maintain the situation in its proper form, we decided to select the type (5) setting. That setting provides the opportunity to exert control to some crucial points, whereas the subject has every possibility to act as he likes within the boundaries set.

INSTRUCTIONS AND SCRIPTS

Control was effected in two different ways: the instruction for the subject and the script for the stooge. In his instruction the subject obtained a short explanation of the situation he was about to enter and subsequently he was asked to try and attain a specific goal. In the present context it is convenient to make a distinction with respect to the kinds of instruction a subject can obtain. He can either be asked to perform a particular task (closed instruction) or to try and reach a particular final situation (open instruction). In the first case all subjects are forced to follow more or less the same route, leaving only room for stylistic differences. In the latter case several routes are possible to reach the same final situation. Thus, in the latter case the variation of behavior is enhanced compared with the first case. As an example of a closed instruction the subject might be asked to give an oral report with the text provided to him. In an open instruction the subject might be asked to try and sell a book to somebody. The way to do it is completely left to the subject. Since we are interested in strategic differences we decided to use open instructions, only specifying the goals to be attained.

The stooges always had the role of a natural participant in the situation. In formulating the *scripts* for the stooges care was taken to grant as much freedom as possible to our subjects. The stooges' primary task was to bring in some behavioral elements that were derived from the situation's definition regarding actions. Included in the script were one or more elements of friction to be brought in at the proper moment. Thus, each subject was confronted with standardized elements of behavior making the situations comparable. Differences in treatment could occur only if a subject would behave in a way that was incompatible with the situation definition, i.e. the prototypical package. In that case the stooge had 'to keep the subject in the situation' by means of his own behavior. As the subject would act in a specific way the stooge's behavior was indicated in terms of conditional d-goals: he should move into a particular direction but the precise execution of behavior was left to his own judgment.

The spatial characteristics of the setting were derived from the taxonomy. Locations were selected and carefully furnished to include all elements that had been considered characteristic of the situation. The temporal aspects of the situation were loosely defined to allow the subject to reach his goal within the time offered.

To summarize, then, the following aspects were emphasized in the behavioral settings to represent specific situations:

1. Contrived situations with stooges.
2. Representation of spatial aspects according to the situation taxonomy.
3. Representation of actors according to the situation taxonomy.
4. Control of actions by goal prescription for the subject.
5. Control of actions by the stooge's script.
6. Provisions for undue actions of the subject in the stooge's script.

OBSERVATION

With regard to the observation of behavior in the settings described a number of specifications had to be made as well. Generally speaking, a distinction can be made with respect to the question whether or not the observer participates in the action. If he does not, he may either be bodily present in the situation, or observe the situation from a position under cover (e.g. behind a one-way screen). If observation occurs under cover, recording of sound and/or images may have definite advantages over direct observation. Especially in the case of natural or nearly natural contrived settings the presence of non-participant observers may cause undue interference with the situation even if they are under cover. Modern recording devices may diminish the effect mentioned insofar as the situation is concerned but on the other hand affect the subject's behavior.

The final choice of the type of observation will have to depend primarily on the type of behavior to be studied. The number and type of behavioral elements are crucial for the optimal way of recording and registration of behavior. The study to be reported in the next chapter was concerned with interpersonal behavior in social situations and it was decided to use a system maximally useful for that kind of behavior. Recording and categorization could be separated by using recording devices. Considerations stemming from the type of situations as well as the kind of behavior to be expected have made us choose audio-recording instead of video-recording or both audio- and video-recording.

CATEGORIES AND RULES

The categorization of behavior requires an observational schedule. That schedule should contain all categories necessary to describe the behavior by means of systematic observation. Apart from categories we need a set of rules to recognize the behavior shown and to be able to identify it as belonging to a specific category. Wiggins (1980) has made a distinction between observation schedules based on the degree to which they belong to the 'sign systems' or 'category systems'. In sign systems the behavior observed is conceived as a sample of one particular type of behavior. During a period of observation the occurrence or non-occurrence of that type of behavior is simply recorded. A category system on the other hand is meant to contain a complete set of mutually exclusive categories to represent the behavior observed. The behavior taxonomy developed by Hettema (Chapter 5) has provided the basis for the development of a category system.

As a general rule it was assumed that the primitive action categories to be represented would be restricted by the type of situations chosen, whereas the d-goal categories would all be relevant. The identification of the d-goal character of certain behaviors may cause problems because not only the action itself but also its purpose has to be identified. Special precautions had to be taken to make the category system unequivocal. Therefore for each of the cells of the behavior taxonomy examples were given to enable the observer to identify the aspects distinguished. Yet it was not possible to cover all single behaviors occurring and sometimes the observer had to rely on his general understanding of the system to be able to classify the behavior. Needless to say, this type of behavioral observation makes high demands on the training of the observers. First they will have to develop the right sense of the situation in which behavior occurs and secondly they will have to learn the gist of the categories of the system.

UNITS

Another problem that had to be solved concerned the units of behavior. Research of the process of behavioral observation has pointed out that partitioning of an ongoing stream of behavior into natural, meaningful units is led by a definite conception of what those units are. Dickman (1963) found that the degree to which purposes and motives can be attributed to behavior plays a decisive part. In that respect, d-goals as distinguished in the behavior taxonomy should give support to the identification of units. According to Newtson (1973; Newtson and Engquist, 1976) observers show a high degree of individual consistency in their choice of behavioral units, within sessions as well as over longer periods of time. A behavioral unit is assumed to be ended as soon as the behavioral sequence is interrupted, i.e. as a phenomenal characteristic of behavior is changed, as a change occurs in the information expressed in the behavior studied. A unit may also coincide with the period of time used by one person to act, e.g. the alternating turns in a dialogue. Instruction and training may serve to influence the magnitude of meaningful units, thus enhancing the agreement between observers.

In personality research a choice is usually made between molar, more global units and molecular, more tightly defined behavioral units. That choice is determined in part by the theoretical context in which research is done. The trait approach tends to work with more global units whereas the behavioral approach exhibits a preference for molecular units. Wiggins (1980, p. 325) states that 'molecular attributes can usually be defined with greater precision, can be recorded with fewer categories of alternative responses, and tend to require less inference on the part of the observers'. But, on the other hand, molecular units tend to be more specific, which can be an impediment for the interpretation. The categories used here can be located somewhere in between what is usually conceived as molar and molecular units. Definite statements are hard to make since the system used may produce very short as well as rather long units. It is governed by the principles of change of content as well as interruption in time.

OBSERVATION SCHEDULE AND PROCEDURE

The observation schedule was based on the behavior taxonomy developed earlier (Chapter 5) and contained categories defined with primitive actions and d-goals. The schedule consisted of one main schedule and subschedules for each separate situation. As mentioned before each cell of the schedule was elucidated with the aid of concrete examples. To minimize confusion the examples were taken from the situation studied and formulated in very concrete terms.

The schedules were tried out first on recordings made in a number of training sessions. Since only audiotapes were used the information obtained was restricted mainly to the things said by our subjects. Yet, a number of non-observable behaviors were observed as well, on the basis of verbal references made by the subjects regarding those behaviors. For instance, if a subject stated that he needed time to think, that behavior was categorized as MBUILD. Primitive action categories like ATTEND and INGEST were not considered appropriate to be categorized on the basis of inference of this type. PROPEL, GRASP and MOVE were omitted as well because they were not expected to occur in the situations offered. The final category system used contained 15 categories and is presented in its general form in Table 1. To provide support for the observers a fixed order of activities was practised and used:

1. Determine the range of a behavioral unit.
2. Translate the behavior observed in terms of primitive actions.
3. Identify the d-goal intended by the action.
4. Write down the code derived from the category system next to the unit identified.

Table 1   General schedule of observation

ATRANS—General
  To give or offer something, e.g. coffee, cigarettes
PTRANS—General
  To move to another position, e.g. the window, the table
PTRANS—D-SOCCONT
  To abandon the situation angrily, e.g. leave the room in protest
MBUILD—General
  Activities involving thinking with unspecified goal, e.g. reflecting or writing in the
  context of the situation
MBUILD—I-PREP
  Activities involving thinking as a preparation to other activities, e.g. making up an
  excuse, writing down an appointment
MTRANS—General
  To give information, e.g. explaining, mentioning facts or repeating statements made
  earlier
MTRANS—D-SOCCONT
  To make statements in order to acquire preponderance in the situation, e.g. making
  authoritative or critical remarks, mocking, protesting, opposing or getting angry
MTRANS—D-CONT
  To make statements in order to master the situation and have one's own way, e.g.
  arguing, pleading, negotiating, manipulating, stating personal opinions or deciding
MTRANS—D-PROX
  To make observations in order to (metaphorically) reduce the distance to other
  persons, e.g. greeting, making compliments, thanking, buttering up, inviting,
  apologizing, rousing pity, or joking
MTRANS—D-KNOW
  To ask for information or explanation
MTRANS—D-AGENCY
  To make observations in order to put others on to action, e.g. arranging, charging,
  proposing or referring
MTRANS—I-PREP
  Preparatory activities, e.g. deliberating, discussing or making 'phone calls
SPEAK-General
  To make utterances not belonging to MTRANS, e.g. laughing, sighing, making
  sounds
AWAIT—General
  To pause at moments where some activity would obviously be expected
AWAIT—D-SOCCONT
  To deliberately omit a reaction in order to intimidate others, e.g. ignoring, quit
  talking

13

An empirical study of interpersonal behavior in simulated situations

JOOP HETTEMA

and

DORIEN P. HOL

PURPOSE OF THE STUDY

Within personality psychology different paradigms are used to study overt behavior. Major points of view include the trait paradigm, the situation paradigm and the interaction paradigm. The approach advocated here is interactional: overt behavior is seen as a product of a continuous process of interaction between the person and the situation. In our view, interactions are based on stable personality characteristics as well as situation characteristics. At the ultimate level, personality traits determine individual preferences for situations as well as individual preferences for manipulation tactics to modify situations (cf. Chapter 1).

To study behavior in concrete situations, the proximate point of view becomes predominant. At a proximate level, specific connections between concrete situations and concrete behaviors are conceived as the results of the individual learning history. Behavior in real-life situations is studied here in the broader context of adaptation. Overt behavior reflects adaptation at the sensorimotor–operational level of adaptive functioning.

The open-systems adaptation model has postulated two other levels in the personality system that are involved in the regulation of overt behavior: The cognitive–symbolic level and the control level. At the cognitive–symbolic level the behavioral strategy is the major structure, at the control level behavioral tactics offer a major contribution to the regulation of overt adaptive behavior. According to the model, overt behavior will reflect the effects of both structures mentioned.

To be able to test this central hypothesis, the three levels of the personality system will have to be systematically connected and relationships will have to be specified in advance. In the measurement model used to study overt behavior, situation concepts should be connected with settings and transformation rules should be connected with behaviors to fulfil the *isomorphism* requirement stated earlier in Chapter 2.

As a corollary of the model proposed here, overt behavior should exhibit lawful relationships with the specific real-life situations in which it is observed. The relationships to be expected are of a type designated earlier as *coherence stability*. Isomorphism as well as coherence stability are structural requirements to be fulfilled, before prediction can be studied. The experiment to be reported here was meant to obtain evidence concerning both issues.

ISOMORPHISM

As we have stated earlier, isomorphism is a key condition to establish connections between levels. It pertains to situation concepts as well as to transformation rules. While developing assessment procedures at the three levels of the system we have attempted vigorously to safeguard isomorphism by meticulously defining situation elements and behavior elements. Examples are the development of a situation taxonomy and a behavior taxonomy for assessment at the cognitive–symbolic level, the development of situation films for assessment at the control level and the development of situational settings and an observational schedule for assessment at the sensorimotor–operational level. Yet, we can not be sure that our attempts have been successful. It is therefore of utmost importance to produce empirical evidence supporting our claim of isomorphism.

At the present level this statement means that we will have to show that situations simulated according to the rules developed are the same as the corresponding situations in the taxonomy (situational isomorphism). And furthermore, that the behaviors observed and categorized are the same as the transformation rules distinguished in the behavior taxonomy (behavioral isomorphism). With these statements, however, an epistemological problem is involved. We can never show that elements defined at a cognitive level are 'identical' with elements in the real world. At best, we may demonstrate that cognitively defined elements are properly applied to objects and events in the outer world. With respect to situations we would have to make it plausible that the elements observed in simulated situations are in agreement with the ones distinguished in the situation concepts. Now it could be argued that since we have taken care to represent those elements in our situational settings that question has been answered already. But there is one type of elements that we have not been able to control in detail: the actions of the subjects. Thus, one way of testing situational isomorphism would be to compare the actions of the subjects with the prototypical package of the situation.

With respect to behavioral isomorphism the question can be asked if the rules given in the observation schedule are properly applied to the behavior observed. Evidence with respect to this issue can be supplied by showing that different observers obtain the same results while using the observation schedule. Thus we decided to test interobserver agreement to answer that question.

COHERENCE STABILITY

The second major purpose of this study was to obtain evidence concerning the applicability of the open-systems adaptation model with regard to overt behavior. Only if individuals show coherent stable behavior will it be possible to study overt behavior as a function of strategies and tactics. A study in which persons and situations as well as behaviors are varied may produce evidence in the form of a specific distribution of the variance obtained over the sources mentioned and their interactions.

The present study was conducted as a comparative study in which the trait model and the situation model were tested as well as the interaction model. In addition to coherence stability, we collected evidence with respect to transsituational consistency for the trait model and intrasituational consistency for the situation model (cf. Chapter 2). Thus, as a subsidiary goal we also attempted to deliver a contribution to the debate concerning the relative explanatory power of those models with respect to overt behavior (Chapter 11).

SELECTION AND GENERAL CHARACTERISTICS OF THE SITUATIONS

To obtain evidence concerning the questions raised we decided to study interpersonal situations. Obviously the situation domain chosen should be specific to be able to study the same behavioral categories in different situations. As a consequence the primitive actions to be observed are restricted to a subset of the taxonomy. To obtain as much variation as possible in d-goals we decided to select a domain with rather complex situations allowing for many different transformations to be made. Interpersonal situations may be assumed to offer these possibilities. In addition, they possess a high degree of ecological validity for a group of student subjects. And, finally, they can be simulated rather easily, whereas response recording and observation would not cause special problems.

Six situations were selected from the taxonomy: assembly, job application, officialdom, rapprochement, report, and thought exchange. On the basis of the situation taxonomy we selected cues that are characteristic for each of the situations and included those in the situation scripts. All situations are located indoors, so we furnished six different rooms according to the scripts. Each room contained one or more tape recorders to register sound. All scripts included one or more specific actors, so we asked people to act as stooges, taking into account the person characteristics present in the scripts.

Each stooge obtained a written instruction to define his or her role and specify the activities they were supposed to show. Each stooge's role was discussed, studied and practised in a series of try-outs. In the try-outs different opponents of the stooge were played by members of the research team. The results were discussed and corrected until the stooge's performance was considered to be satisfactory.

METHOD

Subjects

From the 118 subjects having participated in the study of the strategic questionnaire (cf. Chapter 6) 33 subjects were asked to act in this study. All subjects were students of higher professional education, 18 were females and 15 males.

Procedure

The subjects were invited to come to the university in small groups of five to six and participate during one afternoon. They were given an introduction on the general purpose of the study and the things they were expected to do. They were informed of the fact that their behavior would be registered and analyzed. The only thing they had to do while playing roles was to act as naturally as possible in the situation offered. Subsequently each subject obtained his or her instruction explaining the situation and defining the goal to be attained. After some time to prepare themselves the subjects were brought to the space set up to represent the situation. From the moment they entered the room the subjects were supposed to be in that particular situation. Different subjects generally obtained the situations in a different order. At the end of the afternoon the subjects were debriefed and given the opportunity to ask questions.

Table 1 Outline of the six experimental situations

Situation	N Subjects involved	Subject's part	Stooge(s)	General issue	Subject's aim
Assembly	4–5	Member of school committee	1 Chairman 1 Secretary	Planning introduction program for new students	Get own plan accepted
Job application	1	Applicant	1 Personnel manager	Selection interview	Get the job
Officialdom	1	University student	1 University official 1 Secretary	Special arrangement for exam	Get the arrangement
Rapprochement	1	High school teacher	1 Teacher of the opposite sex	Consult on school journey	Get him/her to have a date
Report	1	University student	6 Fellow students	Give a report for fellow students	Answer questions
Thought exchange	3	University student	1 Discussion leader 1 Fellow student	Discussion on unemployment	Give own opinion

Situations

The six situations studied are specified in Table 1. The roles the subjects had to play were defined in a way to allow to play them with no great difficulties. Two situations involved more than one subject at the same time: assembly and thought exchange. In the latter case a stooge was used to play another participant of which the subjects were led to believe that he was one of them. This was done to make sure that the exchange of thought would be vivid.

Observations

The experimental sessions produced a number of audiotapes containing verbal behavior to be categorized according to the observation schedule (See Chapter 12, Table 1). To do this, six advanced psychology students were selected and trained. First they were informed of the design of the study as well as the principles governing the observation schedule. Then they were trained in pairs obtaining the same situation specific schedule. Readings of the try-outs of the stooges were the training materials.

Initially, the training was directed at obtaining agreement regarding the units to be distinguished in the behavior observed. As soon as the identification of units was done in complete agreement the training was directed at the observation schedule. Only if the observers would totally agree on the correct classification of the training materials the training was finished. Actual observation of the experimental material was done individually with two observers categorizing the behavior in each situation. Each subject obtained a score for each category of behavior in each situation. Scores were frequencies of occurrence of that type of behavior in that situation.

RESULTS

To answer the first question asked—situational isomorphism—we established summary tables over subjects per situation, for primitive action and d-goal categories separately.

From this analysis it was evident that primitive action categories showed little differentiation. No less than 90% of the responses belonged to MTRANS, whereas, in addition, only SPEAK and AWAIT had sizable numbers of responses. Comparison with the prototypical packages of the situations seems rather futile since MTRANS is ranking highly in all of them, except for officialdom. MBUILD contained only 1.5% of the responses although it is even more prominent in most prototypical packages than MTRANS. But in view of the fact that this category can only be assessed indirectly, we did not draw conclusions here regarding isomorphism of the situations offered.

Our analysis showed more differentiation in the area of d-goals. Over-all the general category contained 54% of the observations with D-CONT ranking second as it contained 21% of the observations. A surprising result was the very low rate of observations in the category I-PREP. This category is present in the prototypical package of each of the six situations but it contained only 3.5% of the observations actually made. Another striking finding was the relatively high rate of D-SOCCONT in the group situations thought exchange and assembly. D-AGENCY rates were low and this d-goal was completely absent in the group situations mentioned.

As an index of correspondence we have computed rank difference correlations(rho) between the positions of d-goals based on observational frequencies and positions in the prototypical package (cf. Appendix F-b). Correlations were positive for assembly (0.40), job application (0.49), rapprochement (0.60) and report (0.71), but slightly negative for officialdom and thought exchange (both -0.09). Regarding thought exchange we were suspicious with regard to the relatively high rate of D-SOCCONT and D-CONT, perhaps caused by our decision to include an extra stooge in the situation script. But regarding officialdom no such hypothesis is available. It may be concluded then, that for four situations isomorphism could be demonstrated, whereas for two situations we did not find evidence supporting our claims.

To study behavioral isomorphism we scrutinized interobserver agreement. Analysis of generalizability was used to answer the question of whether the effects of the main facets of this study (persons, situations and response categories) could be generalized over observers. For obvious reasons this analysis was restricted to d-goals. In view of the fact that observers were pairwise assigned to pairs of situations we did three ANOVAs instead of one. Each ANOVA was done according to a 33 (P) $\times$ 2 (S) $\times$ 7 (d-goals) $\times$ 2 (observers) completely crossed design (design XV) in which persons were treated as a random facet and the other facets fixed. The generalizability coefficients were computed according to:

$$\rho^2_{(PRS)O} = \frac{\sigma^2_P + \sigma^2_{PR} + \sigma^2_{PS} + \sigma^2_{PRS}}{\sigma^2_P + \sigma^2_{PR} + \sigma^2_{PS} + \sigma^2_{PRS} + \frac{1}{2}(\sigma^2_{PO} + \sigma^2_{PRO} + \sigma^2_{PSO} + \sigma^2_{PRSO;\ error})} \quad 1$$

The coefficients obtained were 0.973 for officialdom and assembly, 0.988 for thought exchange and report, and 0.967 for job application and rapprochement. From these results it is obvious that the observers agreed very closely on the units as well as the categories used to observe behavior. Thus, our claim of behavioral isomorphism was fully substantiated by the data.

The second major question of this study is concerned with the comparison of trait, situation and interaction models to describe the observational data obtained. This analysis was restricted to d-goals as well. To warrant optimal comparability between models we decided to use unit sample generalizability coefficients (cf. Golding, 1975) referring to the smallest samples possible.

Earlier we have indicated the objects of measurement stressed by each of the three models. For the trait model emphasizing transsituational consistency, PR is the object of measurement. Generalizability was determined separately for each set of situation pairs according to formula 7 (Chapter 2):

$$\rho^2_{(PR)S} = \frac{\sigma^2_P + \sigma^2_{PR}}{\sigma^2_P + \sigma^2_{PR} + 1/n_S(\sigma^2_{PS} + \sigma^2_{PSR;\ error})} \qquad 2$$

For the situation model stressing intrasituational consistency, SR is the object of measurement. Thus, we used formula 10 (Chapter 2) to determine generalizability:

$$\rho^2_{(SR)P} = \frac{\sigma^2_S + \sigma^2_{SR}}{\sigma^2_S + \sigma^2_{SR} + 1/n_P(\sigma^2_{PS} + \sigma^2_{PSR;\ error})} \qquad 3$$

For the interaction model emphasizing coherence stability PSR is the object of measurement. To estimate coherence stability, an odd-even split was obtained by assigning the 1st, 3rd, 5th, etc. observations to one group and the 2nd, 4th, 6th etc. observations to the other. This was done per situation for each of the two observers separately. For each set of situation pairs ANOVA was done according to a 33 (P) $\times$ 2 (S) $\times$ 7 (d-goals) $\times$ 2 (odd-even) crossed design with persons random and the other facets fixed. Generalizability coefficients were obtained according to formula 14 (Chapter 2):

$$\rho^2_{(PSR)T} = \frac{\sigma^2_P + \sigma^2_{PS} + \sigma^2_{PR} + \sigma^2_{PSR}}{\sigma^2_P + \sigma^2_{PS} + \sigma^2_{PR} + \sigma^2_{PSR} + 1/n_T(\sigma^2_{PT} + \sigma^2_{PST} + \sigma^2_{PRT} + \sigma^2_{PSRT;\ error})} \qquad 4$$

in which T refers to the odd-even facet of observation.

The results of these analyses have been represented in Table 2. These indicate that transsituational consistency is modest, the coefficients ranging from 0.35 to 0.41. Intrasituational consistency is quite substantial with unit sample coefficients ranging from 0.65 to 0.80. Coherence stability is high as

Table 2 Generalizability coefficients for different types of consistency in three sets of situations

Type of consistency	Situation pairs		
	Assembly and officialdom	Report and thought exchange	Job application and rapprochement
Transsituational	0.355	0.348	0.407
Intrasituational	0.705	0.799	0.655
Coherence stability	0.736	0.883	0.885

indicated by coefficients ranging from 0.74 to 0.89. Thus, the conclusion can be drawn that data obtained in a P × S × R observation study can be described better with a situation model than with a trait model and even better with an interaction model than with a situation model.

DISCUSSION

The conclusion drawn at the end of the previous section needs to be qualified in two respects. First, regarding the trait model it must be stated that we have not studied traits but categories of behavior defined in the context of the open-systems adaptation model. The units studied are to be conceived as samples of response classes rather than as signs of traits (cf. Wiggins, 1980). Thus, the categories used might have favored the situation model and the interaction model. Parenthetically, it must be noted that this problem could hardly be avoided and will always be an impediment in studies comparing the three models.

A second observation to be made concerns the status of the analysis done. Obviously, we have not demonstrated that assessment techniques developed in an interactional or situational context are more valid than techniques for trait assessment. In classical terminology we have performed a criterion analysis, showing that the behavior observed offers ample opportunities to be studied with the aid of an interactional model of behavior. Since this was the primary goal of the study done, we consider the results encouraging for further investigation.

A final observation concerns the impact of the situation model. It was a surprise for us to note that the situation model was powerful enough to explain two-thirds of the behavioral variance obtained. For personality theory this result does not seem to be very encouraging, especially in view of the fact that the situations offered were all taken from a rather narrowly defined domain. An explanation may be found in the instructions given to the subjects and specifying the goals to be obtained in each of the situations offered. This explanation brings us face to face with one of the enduring dilemmas of the study of personality in natural settings: the subjects have to be given enough freedom to behave in their own typical way, and, at the same time, the setting should be controlled to the extent necessary for the investigator to make comparisons and to draw conclusions. The way out of this dilemma can only be found if the investigator manages to establish an optimal balance between the requirements of ecological validity and experimental control of the observational setting.

Part V

Personality as a strategic–tactical coalition

14

Predictive validity

JOOP HETTEMA

INTRODUCTION

In the preceding part of this book procedures have been developed for the assessment of personality at different levels of functioning. In addition, evidence has been presented to support the adequacy of those procedures as measurement tools. Thus, in Part II, dealing with measurement at the cognitive–symbolic level, it was demonstrated that individual strategies can be assessed with sufficient reliability. Furthermore, within strategies, an important distinction was made between categorical preferences for situations on the one hand, and conditional preferences for actions (means) to bring about those situations, on the other. In Part III, dealing with assessment at the control level, a number of psychophysiological patterns presumably reflecting tactical ST-mechanisms were identified, and evidence was provided to support our claims concerning the construct validity of those patterns. In Part IV assessment was studied at the sensorimotor–operational level. Settings and observation schedules were developed and it was shown that overt behavior can be reliably assessed, either with an interaction model or with a situation model.

Taken together, the studies reported thus far provide a sound basis to study personality as an adaptive open system, with the capacity to transform and exploit situations, while at the same time maintaining a basic state of equilibrium with the environment. To provide evidence that the personality system as a whole functions according to the principles outlined in the open system theory connections will now be established among the three levels of the system, rather than within each of the levels separately. As has been pointed out before (Hettema, 1979), in the context of psychological adaptation personality is best conceived as a strategic–tactical coalition. Thus, to test our conception of total personality functioning, overt behavior (defined at the sensorimotor–operational level) was studied as a joint function of individual strategy (defined at the cognitive–symbolic level) and of individual tactics (defined at the control level).

STRATEGIC PREDICTION

The prediction of behavior as an adaptive phenomenon is not simply a matter of averaging general behavioral tendencies. As an adaptive being an individual will consider a number of alternative courses of action before deciding on the best way to proceed. He will pay attention to the possibilities the situation offers and make estimations of the utility of several products to be expected as a result of his endeavors. In interactionism the person is conceived as active and intentional (Endler and Magnusson, 1976b). This statement does not imply that individuals will be constantly involved in overt activities to change the world, but rather that they have a certain amount of concern with the results of their activities.

This concern will first and foremost become manifest at the cognitive–symbolic level in the shape of thought processes where different courses of action are considered and tested regarding efficiency and utility. Thought processes may serve to determine the direction of actions and also the means to reach the goals set by the individual. Earlier (Hettema, 1979) I have indicated this type of thought processes as *directed thinking* and outlined some principles guiding this type of thinking. A major criterion governing directed thinking in practical daily-life situations is maximizing the expected utility of the outcome. Outcome is defined here as a situation arising from the initial situation as a consequence of the actions of the individual. According to this criterion an individual will tend to accomplish a situation ranking highly in his personal preference order of situations.

This statement is not as simple as it seems however, as it is realized that actions are seldom restricted to reaching a situation that is just one step beyond the actual situation. In real life circumstances, directed thinking may be used to decide not only on which suit one will wear at a party or which place is most convenient for a date, but also on how to arrange one's career or how to choose one's spouse. Clearly, in most cases directed thinking involves many steps to be taken and each of those steps is concluded with a situation having its own utility in terms of the preference-order mentioned. In those cases the person will create a plan rather than a single transformation and that plan is subsequently used to control the order in which a sequence of operations is to be performed (cf. Miller, Galanter and Pribram, 1960). While establishing the plan, considerations of personal utility in terms of costs and benefits will be predominant and individuals may differ markedly in the kinds of plans they are willing to execute. In the present context these differences are largely explained on the basis of situation preferences. As long as a plan involves a sequence of preferential situations it stands a fair chance of being carried out, but as soon as non-preferential situations become inevitable the person will think twice.

To be able to predict a person's actions we obviously need a principle to decide which plan he will follow, given his personal situation preferences. In this context we have considered decision strategies like maximizing minimal gain or minimizing maximal loss (Edwards, 1954). However, taking into account the principles of situation transformation developed in Chapter 5 neither of the two appears realistic. In establishing a plan the value of all intermediate situations should be taken into account, since they are all indispensable stations on the route to the final situation wanted. To do justice to this notion we decided to choose the principle of *maximizing average expected utility*.

In a particular situation a person will consider all possible end situations as goals and select the situation with the maximal average utility for all situations to be passed to reach the end situation wanted. To determine the goal situation for an individual, given a specific initial situation, we should compare the shortest routes to all possible final situations, compute average preference values for each route, and select the route with the highest average preference value. Thus we can unequivocally determine the final situation preferred. As a result of this procedure, some individuals will frequently choose the same end situation irrespective of the starting point, but others will choose as many different situations as there are initial situations.

The approach outlined will not only provide us with goal situations but also with intermediate situations to reach the goals. Thus, some major elements of the plan structure will emerge as well. On the basis of the rules for situation transformation developed earlier (Chapter 5) we can now determine the d-goal aspects of all subsequent behaviors necessary to accomplish the transformations wanted. With respect to primitive actions we may scrutinize primitive action preferences for each initial situation and choose the most preferred primitive action fit to be combined with the delta goal selected. Thus we will obtain categories of behavior expected to be utilized by the subject to carry out his plans in a number of initial situations. Those categories can be used to predict overt behavior in observational studies. Since each person has his own preference values for situations as well as for primitive actions, we may expect each person to show an excess of transformational behavior corresponding with his plan.

TACTICAL PREDICTION

In the context of the open-systems adaptation model, behavior is conceived as a function of both strategy and tactics. The strategy will play a dominant role as long as control is maintained in the system, i.e. as long as transformations intended to be accomplished are actually brought about. But as soon as 'the world starts talking back' resistance may become manifest in the form of friction in the ongoing stream of behavior. The equilibrium between individual and environment is disturbed and the individual will react with ST-mechanisms to restore equilibrium. As we have pointed out before (Hettema, 1979) the effect of ST-mechanisms is to alter the state of any one of the elements constituting the behavior system of the individual. We have distinguished six different ST-mechanisms: reflection, exploration, uncoupling, substitution, redirection and persistence. Their specific effects are indicated in Figure 1. For the purpose of prediction it can be stated now that each ST-mechanism will cause a specific change to occur in the stream of behavior. In general terms those changes will become manifest as redistributions of the goals of behavior as well as/or the means used to obtain goals. For instance, if *reflection* occurs the conception of the initial situation will be altered to allow new goals to be intended and new means to be used. If *uncoupling* occurs, alterations will be restricted to the means aspect of behavior, whereas *redirection* will restrict alterations to the goal aspect.

In general it can be stated that tactical mechanisms will cause alterations to occur on a purely formal basis. ST-mechanisms merely indicate the kind

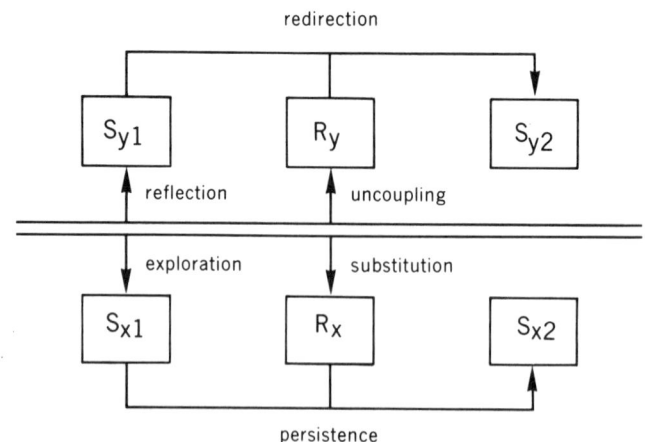

Figure 1   State transition mechanisms

of alterations to be accomplished without taking into consideration the optimality of the alterations achieved. The latter aspect is a function of the strategy rather than the tactical mechanism used. In the context of prediction this causes a problem. Normally in actual behavior the strategic and tactical aspects will be completely intertwined so that it will never be possible to predict which behavior will be demonstrated by an individual on the basis of mere tactics. Thus, tactical prediction will have to be restricted to formal aspects of behavior. In order to make predictions of this kind we will have to indicate precisely what formal bias is introduced by each of the ST-mechanisms.

To answer this question it is convenient to conceive of ST-mechanisms in terms of the levels and phases of the behavioral system at which they are active. The levels of the behavioral system are concerned with the input of the system. ST-mechanisms operative at the upper level of the system (reflection, uncoupling and redirection) act upon the *cognitive–symbolic information* derived from the strategy to alter the state of the system. ST-mechanisms at the lower level, on the other hand (exploration, substitution and persistence), are connected directly with the environment and utilize elements of the situation to alter the state of the system. As a consequence, with cognitive–symbolic ST-mechanisms behavior will be determined to a greater extent by individual strategic characteristics whereas with sensorimotor–operational ST-mechanisms behavior will be determined to a greater extent by prototypical *characteristics of the situation*. Thus, we expect individuals using sensorimotor-operational ST-mechanisms to demonstrate relatively more prototypical behavior as compared with individuals using cognitive–symbolic ST-mechanisms.

Cognitive–symbolic ST-mechanisms have the property to alter a plan structure defined before (cf. Hettema, 1979, p. 175). They function according to the principle of *replacement* of plan elements. With *reflection* the conception of the initial situation (S_{y1}) is replaced by a new conception (S_{y1}'). That new conception is related to the original conception since it has to possess validity regarding the environment (S_x) as well. This implies that no completely different behavioral elements may be included in the new situation concept. Thus, reflection will initially be restricted to concepts referring to situations with the same prototypical package as the concept used originally. In addition, all situations to be obtained with the aid of moderate transformation may be considered. Thus, for instance, the job application situation referred to earlier may be redefined by the reflecting subject as acquaintance(ship), thought exchange, interview, inquiry, inspection or test, but not as e.g. examination, instruction or conversation, the latter being radical transformation products. Likewise, the rapprochement situation may be reinterpreted as talk, flirt, meeting, or rendez-vous, but not as recreation, deliberation, or adultery.

On the basis of prototypical packages we can indicate precisely which situations may come up as a result of reflection and which situations may not.

The theory states that any product of reflection (S_{y1}') may serve as a basis for behavior, so categories of behavior to be predicted *include all behaviors strategically preferred in any situation emerging from reflection.* In our study of behavioral strategies a number of parallel situations as defined here have been included to supply predictions. Accordingly, the categories to be predicted can be obtained by determining alternative plans starting from each of the parallel situations included in that study. The rules to derive plans are the same as with strategic prediction. As a result of this method the goal situations preferred as well as the actions chosen to obtain those goals may be replaced and yield new categories of behavior to be expected.

With *uncoupling*, the procedure to obtain behavioral categories to be predicted is much simpler. As soon as friction occurs, the uncoupling subject will loosen the connection between the d-goal and the primitive action chosen initially, and turn to other primitive actions to regain control. Thus, the categories to be predicted *include all primitive actions* appearing in the *S*'s strategy in connection with the situation present.

The major function of *redirection* , the third ST-mechanism operative at the cognitive–symbolic level, is to change the goal structure of the plan. If the original situation emanating from the strategy cannot be reached, the *S* may direct his efforts to a new goal situation to restore control. That new situation may either take over the function of the original goal situation, or act as a basis to reach that situation as yet. In both cases the new situation may be defined as a derivative of the original goal situation. We have defined it as a radical transformation of the original goal appearing next in the *S*'s preference order of situations. The *d-goal aspect* distinguishing the new situation from the other defines the *behavior category expected* to appear when redirection occurs.

The second group of ST-mechanisms are the sensorimotor–operational mechanisms. Instead of changing the plan structure available, their major function is to warrant its proper execution in case of frictions. The actions occurring as a consequence of those mechanisms are complementary rather than vicarious. Actions are largely derived from the environment and selected to restore the major elements of the plan in case of disturbances. Thus, with *exploration*, the *S* will compare the actual environment with the situation concept prevailing and activate behavior to restore equilibrium. The behaviors expected to occur are prototypical and may include prototypical primitive actions as well as d-goals. All combinations of these two aspects may be expected to be emphasized if exploration is the dominant ST-mechanism. With *substitution, prototypical primitive actions* will be activated to enhance the effectivity of behavior. The major function of *persistence* is to emphasize the products of behavior, i.e. the situations intended to be accomplished. The majority of behavioral aspects to be stressed with persistence are present in the

Table 1 Behavioral aspects stressed with different ST-mechanisms

ST-mechanism	Primitive actions	Delta goals
Reflection	Actions preferred in parallel situations (S_{y1}')	Goals derived from final situations preferred in parallel situations
Uncoupling	Actions considered in S_{y1}	
Redirection		Goals derived from most preferent radical transformation of final situation
Exploration	Actions prototypical for S_{y1}	Goals prototypical for S_{y1}
Substitution	Actions prototypical for S_{y1}	
Persistence		First goal prototypical for S_{y1}

plan already, with one notable exception: the first prototypical d-goal of the initial situation. Thus, persisting subjects may be expected to show more behavior characterized with that goal aspect.

To summarize this section, the behavioral categories expected to be emphasized as a function of each of the ST-mechanisms are presented in Table 1. From this table it becomes clear that, depending on the particular mechanism, either the primitive action·aspect or the d-goal aspect or both aspects are specified. With the rules given in Table 1 it is possible to specify exactly for each person in each situation which categories of behavior are expected to be emphasized and which categories are not.

THE PREDICTION MODEL

Some basic features of the prediction model have been outlined in Chapter 2. After completing the development of assessment procedures at different levels of the personality system, it is now possible to explain the prediction model in more detail. To do this we shall start from the classical approach to the study of prediction. Wiggins (1980) has defined the classical prediction paradigm in terms of six basic steps to be taken in studies designed to establish predictive validity. In sequential order the six steps are:

1. Criterion analysis.
2. Selection of instruments.
3. Development of a predictor battery.
4. Combination of data.
5. Cross validation.
6. Application of the predictor battery.

In the course of this book some of the steps have been taken already. Criterion analysis (1) has been described in detail in Part IV. The situations offered there will act as criterion situations, and the observation schedule will serve to establish criterion behavior. The instruments selected (2) are the SRS-questionnaire to establish individual strategies and the situation film technique to establish tactical mechanisms. Instead of developing a predictor battery (3) for all subjects, specific predictions will be made for each subject and for each situation separately. Predictions will be based on individual strategies and individual tactics. Two of the steps (4 and 5) are necessary only in the absence of a theory specifying predictor-criterion relations in advance, as is usually the case in classical validity studies. Combination of data (4) is customarily done empirically using e.g. multiple regression techniques, but our theory contains specific rules for data combination (cf. Hettema, 1979) so we can do without these techniques. For the same reason we can dispense with cross validation (5) altogether.

A final question to be answered concerns the test statistic to be used. The classical approach, assuming a linear additive prediction model, often makes use of correlation coefficients to represent validity. The current model, however, is interactive and cannot use correlations to demonstrate validity. The model is meant to specify individual behavioral preferences based on strategy and tactics given a particular situation. Thus, predictions are situation specific, i.e. they do not generalize to other situations.

Within a particular situation an individual will prefer specific categories of behavior and will reject other categories. A proper test of the model will therefore always have to focus upon *intraindividual behavior distributions*. The model does not preclude the situation to have general effects upon behavior as well, irrespective of individual preferences. Thus, the obvious way to test the model is to compare individual behavior distributions with more general behavior distributions that are prototypical for the situation studied. Predictions may be considered successful to the extent that individual deviations from the prototypical distribution are correctly predicted. This implies that the model can be tested separately for each person × situation combination studied. A person's behavior may be predicted correctly in one situation but not in another situation. Alternatively, in a specific situation one person's behavior may be properly predicted, whereas the model fails with regard to another person. An advantage of this prediction model is that it allows for the study of individual predictability, focusing upon the results of one individual over different situations. It is also possible to focus upon one situation and draw conclusions on situational ambiguity based on the results obtained with different subjects. Detailed feedback on both issues will eventually allow for specific improvements to be made for the prediction system as a whole.

THE PREDICTION OF OVERT BEHAVIOR BASED ON STRATEGY AND TACTICS

Method

Subjects and procedure

First 118 subjects, students of higher professional education, completed a strategic SRS-questionnaire containing 17 different situations (for an overview see Appendix F). The subjects indicated rank order preferences for the behavioral options offered. The scoring procedure is explained in detail in Chapter 6. As a result for each subject we obtained preference values per situation for primitive actions and for d-goals.

Four months after completing the data collection on strategies, 56 subjects randomly selected from the total group were asked to participate again and were confronted with situation films to establish tactical states. As a buffer the film 'Lesson' was shown first. Subsequently, each subject saw six experimental films in a fixed order of presentation:

1. Job application.
2. Thought exchange.
3. Report.
4. Rapprochement.
5. Assembly.
6. Officialdom.

The films have been described in Chapter 8 and details of the procedure have been given in Chapter 9 to which the reader is referred. During the films recordings were made of heart beat, galvanic skin response and finger temperature. For each subject two separate minutes of the records per film were analyzed to yield measures of heart interbeat intervals (IBI), T-wave amplitude (TWA), galvanic skin response level (GSL) and finger temperature (TEMP), according to the procedures described in Chapters 9 and 10.

Three months after the film experiment 33 subjects, selected at random from the previous group, acted as subjects in the role-playing study reported in Chapter 13. In that study the subjects acted in six situations, identical with the experimental film situations mentioned above. Role-playing behavior was observed and analyzed with the procedures described in Chapters 12 and 13. For the final analysis, one subject had to be dropped because of incomplete physiological data. The remaining group of 32 subjects was used to study predictive validity. It contained 17 females and 15 males.

Results

Preliminary analyses

1. *The assessment of tactical states*

   For the 56 subjects of the film study, the physiological data were scrutinized with respect to time-related trends. As we have pointed out before (Chapter 10) those trends are to be considered as a source of error variance from the point of view of state measurement and should preferably be removed. For each of the four physiological measures IBI, TWA, GSL and TEMP correlations were obtained among 12 records (two for each film) and chronologically arranged.

   Each of the four matrices clearly demonstrated superdiagonality, indicating individual time trends. The four matrices were subjected to factor analysis (principal components) to yield two factors each. The loadings for unrotated factors are given in Table 2. Since in the present study no records have been made during rest conditions the rotation procedure developed in Chapter 10 could not be used. Thus, factor scores for time-order were computed according to the component model on the basis of unrotated Factor II loadings. Raw scores were corrected for time-order by subtracting factor scores. Subsequently all scores were ipsatized and put into patterns containing scores for IBI, TWA, GSL and TEMP. A total number of 56 (Ss) × 6 (films) × 2 (replications) = 672 patterns were compared with the six standard patterns, obtained in Chapter 9 and corrected in Chapter 10. Each pattern was allocated to the standard pattern with the smallest squared euclidean distance.

   The results indicated that the six states were distributed rather evenly with

Table 2 Unrotated factor loadings of films, derived with a two-factor solution

	IBI		TWA		GSL		TEMP	
	I	II	I	II	I	II	I	II
1. Job application 1	0.97	0.11	0.98	0.15	0.88	0.44	0.77	0.60
2. Job application 2	0.96	0.13	0.98	0.16	0.89	0.41	0.80	0.56
3. Thought exchange 1	0.96	0.16	0.99	0.14	0.96	0.24	0.87	0.47
4. Thought exchange 2	0.97	0.12	0.99	0.15	0.96	0.18	0.89	0.40
5. Report 1	0.97	0.09	0.99	0.06	0.97	0.04	0.96	−0.16
6. Report 2	0.97	0.08	0.99	0.01	0.99	−0.05	0.94	−0.08
7. Rapprochement 1	0.98	0.06	0.99	−0.05	0.99	−0.04	0.96	−0.15
8. Rapprochement 2	0.96	0.08	0.99	−0.08	0.96	−0.10	0.96	−0.19
9. Assembly 1	0.94	−0.04	0.99	−0.11	0.97	−0.17	0.95	−0.26
10. Assembly 2	0.97	−0.11	0.97	−0.13	0.96	−0.23	0.91	−0.13
11. Officialdom 1	0.93	−0.33	0.98	−0.15	0.93	−0.33	0.94	−0.27
12. Officialdom 2	0.91	−0.37	0.98	−0.15	0.91	−0.35	0.92	−0.27

exploration and uncoupling occurring most frequently (19% each) and reflection and redirection least frequently (14% each). A comparison of states as a function of moments within films revealed that exploration and uncoupling predominated in the first replication whereas substitution and redirection tended to occur more frequently in the second replication. For reasons explained before (Chapter 9) the second replication was considered to offer the best representation of the states wanted, so those states were used in the remainder of this study.

2. The behavioral categories predicted

For each subject we identified the behavior categories, expected to become dominant in the six situations. Strategic as well as tactical information was used to indicate the categories.

First the procedure described in the section on strategic prediction was applied to the data obtained with the SRS-questionnaire. As a result for each subject we obtained preference values for 17 different situation types. Each of those types was considered as a possible final situation to be accomplished as a result of each of the six initial situations offered in the observation study. All routes from initial to final situations were determined and for each route the average preference values were computed. The highest average values were taken to indicate the routes preferentially chosen. Thus for each subject we obtained six final situation types, one for each of the six initial situations. Applying the rules for situation transformation we obtained the d-goal aspects of the behavior necessary to reach the final situation. The d-goals were combined with preferred primitive actions to yield categories of behavior. Those categories acted as predictors of overt behavior for each situation offered based on strategy.

Subsequently the categories obtained were completed with behaviors predicted on the basis of tactics. The rules for obtaining those categories are given in the section on tactical prediction and summarized in Table 1. As a result, for each subject we had a complete set of behavioral categories predicted to become dominant in each of the six situations.

On the criterion side we obtained frequencies of overt behavior in different categories according to the procedure described in Chapter 13. For comparability per subject and per situation frequencies were converted to percentages. The median percentage for each category of behavior was assumed to give the base rate value for that category in that situation. To test validity the categories predicted per subject and per situation were singled out among the observation data and scrutinized to establish whether the individual percentage was above, at, or below the group median. Above median scores were treated as hits, scores at the median as ties, and below the median as misses.

FINAL ANALYSES

For each situation the numbers of hits, ties and misses were determined and brought together in Table 3. This table reveals that in each situation the number of hits exceeded the number of misses. The over-all hit rate was 122.5/192 or 63.8%, a result well beyond the level to be expected on chance ($\chi^2 = 14.1$; $p < 0.01$).

In Table 4 the data have been arranged according to subjects. The frequency distribution of hit rates per subject is close to normal. Finally, hit rates were scrutinized as a function of tactics on the basis of Table 5. In this Table the results per state are gathered across situations as well as subjects. It shows that most tactical states have been about equally effective. Only exploration (0.79) and uncoupling (0.52) show clear deviations from the grand mean. As a whole, we may conclude that predictions based on strategy and tactics are better than chance and that the hits are distributed evenly across situations, persons and tactical states.

Table 3   Hit rates as a function of the situation

Situation	Validity			% hits
	+	0	–	
Officialdom	22	—	10	0.69
Thought exchange	19	1	12	0.61
Job application	19	—	13	0.59
Report	21	—	11	0.66
Assembly	23	—	9	0.72
Rapprochement	18	—	14	0.56
Total	122	1	69	0.64

Table 4   Distribution of hit rates per subject

N hits	Frequencies
6	3
5	7
4	$9\frac{1}{2}$
3	$7\frac{1}{2}$
2	4
1	1
0	0

Table 5 Hit rates as a function of tactical states

Situation	Validity			
	+	0	–	% hits
Reflection	17	—	9	0.65
Exploration	22	—	6	0.79
Uncoupling	17	—	16	0.52
Substitution	27	—	15	0.64
Redirection	22	1	13	0.63
Persistence	17	—	10	0.63
Total	122	1	69	0.64

DISCUSSION

With this study we have been able to show that it is possible to predict overt behavior using individual strategy and individual tactics as predictors. The results obtained are clearly better than chance, but, on the other hand, the relationship found is not very strong. It should be kept in mind however, that the major objective of this study was not to develop a test for selection or classification, but to provide evidence concerning personality functioning in the context of the open-systems adaptation model. To do this we have used an experimental design testing individual distributions of behavior against average distributions obtained from a sample of subjects. The sample contained students all participating in the same type of higher education and, presumably, with a comparable social cultural background. Thus, especially strategies as products of social learning, could be expected to be similar as well. Homogeneity was further enhanced by the procedure used in the role playing study (cf. Chapter 13). Nevertheless, our predictions have obtained support in different states as well as in different situations.

A general conclusion that can be drawn from the results is that it is possible to predict overt behavior with a prediction system stressing differential reactions for the same individuals in different situations. Thus, the results support one of the basic contentions of interactionism stating that neither the situation as such nor the organism in itself but, instead, a continuous process of interaction between the two underlies behavior (Endler and Magnusson, 1976b).

In the past, interactionists have not been unequivocally successful in their attempts to support this central claim. Using SR questionnaires as major tools, positive results as well as negative results have been found. For instance, Mellstrom, Zuckerman and Cicala (1978) predicted anxiety in subjects exposed to anxiety-provoking situations and obtained better results with situation specific as opposed to general measures of anxiety. On the other hand Knudson and Golding (1974) obtained better results with traditional trait inventories compared with SR inventories in the prediction of interpersonal behavior. More recently Van Heck (1981) failed to find any substantial correspondence between SR anxiety questionnaire data and criterion measures of anxiety.

Our approach in which self-reports and physiological reactions have a different status may offer a solution for these problems. In the context of the open-systems adaptation model, strategy and tactics are conceived as two separate systems, each making its own contribution to overt behavior. The choice of goals and means is primarily a function of the individual's strategy, whereas the adjustments made while behavior is executed are largely dictated by tactics. Together, strategy and tactics act as a powerful alliance for the individual to come to terms with the environment. The relative contribution of strategy and tactics in specific situations remains an issue to be studied more thoroughly than has been possible in the present study. Meanwhile, the evidence obtained has shown the strategic–tactical approach to be basically fruitful, so that proceeding along the way chosen appears to be indicated.

15
Towards a two-process conception of human adaptation

JOOP HETTEMA

INTRODUCTION

This final chapter will be restricted to the main conclusions of the investigations presented, while the various results have been discussed in detail in the preceding chapters. First of all the personality system that has emerged from our studies, will be summarized. Attention will be paid to a major theme discussed in the introductory chapter of this book: the outflows of our proximate studies with respect to ultimate or distal personality. The main question concerns the nature of personality to be conceived as an ultimate given apart from the concrete context in which it operates. Our findings with overt behavior will be discussed and conclusions will be drawn that are directly relevant for the person–situation debate, presented earlier.

Subsequently, the attention will be directed at the connections of the system with current issues in personality psychology, notably emotions, cognition and intelligence.

Finally, some new perspectives will be given for the study of personality in applied settings such as organizations, clinics and educational institutions.

THE OPEN-SYSTEMS CONCEPTION AND PERSONALITY AT THE ULTIMATE LEVEL

The study of adaptive behavior in daily-life situations has met with many problems, theoretically as well as methodologically. Rather than trying to

Personality and Environment: Assessment of Human Adaptation
Edited by P. J. Hettema. ©1989 John Wiley and Sons Ltd

explain overt behavior directly on the basis of some personality model, we have chosen a strategy in which proximal person–situation connections are scrutinized first. Obviously, this can only be done in the context of a theory, conceptualizing the person–situation interface in detail. The open-systems adaptation model is meant to provide that context. Our studies have shown that the model is fruitful, yielding operationalizations of the basic concepts as well as evidence regarding the processes involved. Our studies have opened up several new perspectives with respect to person–situation interactions, and, as a consequence, our initial conception of personality structure (cf. Hettema, 1979) is expanded, crystallized and partly modified.

The open system as an important metaphor to describe human behavior has been advocated a long time ago by Von Bertallanffy (1952). In personality psychology Gordon Allport (1961) was the first to point out several major aspects of open systems, as, e.g. the interchange between matter and energy, homeostasis, increasing order over time, and, last but not least, transaction with the environment. Later developments in general systems theory have yielded a more concise summary of the properties of open systems. Using mathematical isomorphism, Rapoport (1972) defined an open system as a set of non-homogeneous differential equations. Two major properties can be derived from this conception: equifinality and dynamic equilibrium.

The notions of equifinality and dynamic equilibrium have played a major part in the present conception of adaptation (cf. Hettema, 1979; Chapter 1 this volume). Together they provide a basis for the definition of control, that is the capacity to modify or transform the environment while at the same time maintaining a state of equilibrium with the environment (cf. Hettema, 1979, p. 121). Transformation is based structurally on the strategic subsystem of personality, whereas dynamic equilibrium is based on the tactical subsystem.

Strategies are deliberate and goal-directed. They reflect individual intentions to exploit, or to modify and transform situations into a specific direction. Our studies have shown that the goals set by a person in a specific situation are consistent with a general preference order of situations existing for that individual. Strategies are internally coherent and tend to impose a specific direction upon the situation, relatively independent of starting positions (cf. Chapter 6). Clearly, then, strategies can be conceived to fulfil the major function of equifinality in the personality system.

Tactics are spontaneous reactions to disequilibrium. Activated by discrepancies existing between cognitions and situational events, they tend to eliminate discrepancies by transforming either cognitions or situational elements. While functioning on the principles of feedback and/or feedforward, tactics have the capacity to maintain a state of dynamic equilibrium between the personality system and its environment. Our studies have provided evidence that tactics can be studied with the aid of autonomous reactions to situations represented with films (cf. Chapter 9). Tactical states are coherent stable, so that individuals will tend to use the same tactics throughout the same situation. We could demonstrate that different tactical states are elicited by specific tasks, thus providing evidence with respect to their functioning (cf. Chapter 10).

As a consequence of this conceptualization, a two-process conception of human adaptation is developed here, postulating two different aspects in every behavior observed. Overt behavior is always governed by control, but the system involved is not always clear. Behavior will be regulated now by strategic options, now by tactical reactions, whereas for an outside observer it remains obscure which system is involved. For instance, a critical remark may be interpreted as a deliberate attempt to insult somebody else, but it may as well be seen as a spontaneous outflow of the tactical system to restore one's own equilibrium. In the present conception, overt behavior is essentially ambiguous, and, in itself, overt behavior is often insufficient to provide the proper interpretation.

The methodology developed here offers a basis to scrutinize overt behavior in more detail and, notably, to discriminate clearly between strategic and tactical aspects. In the example given, the person may be strategically inclined to create situations enhancing his power and social control. But, on the other hand, he may as well be perfectly satisfied with the situation actually prevailing using tactics merely to maintain his equilibrium. Only a profound knowledge of strategic and tactical tendencies in that situation may provide the answer.

Can we make more general statements about personality surpassing individual adaptation to specific situations? In the introductory chapter of this book we have argued that personality should be studied in close connection with situations. Accordingly, the research program presented has dealt with concrete person–situation encounters, in no instance drawing conclusions beyond the paradigm chosen. While doing so, we have worked in the context of a *proximate model of personality*, emphasizing restricted conditions and momentary states. The behaviors scrutinized represent immediate transactions between persons and topical situations. But what can we say about personality *per se*, apart from the concrete environments in which observations are made? Or, in other words, what *ultimate conception* of personality is postulated at the basis of adaptation observed in specific situations?

To answer that question we will have to look for evidence in the major structures of personality: the strategic and tactical systems. Within those structures it is especially the stable, lasting elements that deserve attention. While studying strategies, we have found evidence that specific aspects are valid across the concrete situations offered. Individuals exhibited general preferences for situations, implying that persons may be characterized on the basis of their individual preference orders for the types of situations occurring in daily life.

What can be said about enduring personality characteristics determining situational preferences? A promising approach seems to be to look for connections with temperament variables. In the introductory chapter we have argued that the balance between situations and the typical style of behaving of the person is the major basis for 'goodness of fit'. Individuals will prefer situations allowing them to 'be themselves' rather than situations forcing them to act differently. In the work of Thomas and Chess (1985) a connection is postulated with temperament, defining congenial situations as well as aversive situations. Evidence in favor of this hypothesis has been obtained in a recent study by Van Heck, Hettema and Leidelmeijer (1990). In another recent study, Przymusinski and Strelau (1986) found relationships between risk taking strategies and temperament variables. Risk takers and risk avoiders could be discriminated on the basis of variables like strength of excitation, mobility, vigor, and impulsivity. The authors interpreted their results as referring to differences in need for stimulation.

In our conceptual framework, temperament is primarily concerned with control (cf. Hettema, 1979; Chapters 1 and 7, this volume). It should be noted however, that neither strategies nor tactics are determined completely by temperament. In strategies, temperament is particularly involved in situational preferences, leaving aside the question how preferred situations are attained. As we pointed out earlier, the behavioral means used to attain situations are obtained primarily by social learning. In tactics, on the other hand, temperament is especially involved in preferences for ST- and disruption-mechanisms without taking into consideration the conditions (situations) in which those mechanisms are called upon. The conditions eliciting specific ST- and disruption mechanisms are assumed to be established on the basis of conditioning. Thus, at a more proximate level, in tactics as well as in strategies, learning processes are assumed to play a major part: temperament as an ultimate given is covered with the effects of social learning and conditioning.

This view also has consequences for the relationship between temperament and behavior. As a proximate given, behavior is a function of the person as well as the situation. To predict behavior, the relationship existing between the person and the situation is essential. This relationship is determined by temperament merely in an indirect way, i.e. via strategy and tactics.

The common temperamental background of strategy and tactics would raise the suspicion of a causal relationship existing between the two. In our conception, the preference for tactical mechanisms as an innate given deserves priority in this relationship. If it is true that persons have definite preferences for specific tactical mechanisms, they will tend to prefer situations in which those mechanisms provide control. This notion could provide a theoretical basis for the existence of situation preferences. Those preferences might then be conceived as a derivative of tactical preferences combined with specific experiences with situations. For instance, persons with an innate preference for reflection as an ST-mechanism would prefer scholastic situations in which reflection provides control. Or, individuals with an innate preference for persistence would prefer sports and other situations in which persistence provides control. A major hypothesis then, emanating from this line of reasoning is that strategic preferences for specific situations are a function of tactical preferences providing control in the situations preferred. The methodology, developed in the studies reported here, provides a basis to study this question. If confirmation could be obtained, a more direct link might be established between ultimate personality variables, i.e. temperament, and proximate behavior.

THE PERSON–SITUATION DEBATE REVISITED

Human behavior in natural conditions is extremely complex. To reduce complexity, psychologists have emphasized different aspects of overt behavior as, for instance, developmental, interpersonal, perception and performance, learning aspects, and the like. Personality psychology is primarily interested in the individual point of view, stressing consistent individual ways to behave in different conditions. However, consistency in a more general sense appears hard to be obtained. Neither internal consistency nor transsituational consistency are usually warranted in studies of overt behavior in natural conditions (cf. Block, 1977; Fiske, 1966; Hettema, 1972a, 1981; Hettema *et al.*, 1973; Mischel, 1968; Van Lieshout, 1972). The only type of consistency obtained frequently in the study of overt behavior is stability, i.e. persons exhibit stability in their ways of reacting to the same situation at different moments in time (cf. Epstein, 1979, 1980; Chapter 13 this volume). In our interpretation, stability primarily reflects stable person × situation interactions, rather than individual differences or effects of the situation *per se.*

Now classical studies of the person–situation type have revealed that considerable portions of the behavioral variance is due to different interaction components rather than the main effects of the persons observed (cf. Chapter 1). During the years following those findings, interactionists have attempted to obtain better estimates of the magnitude of the variance components involved.

More recently, however, students of person–situation interactions tend to shift emphasis from so-called mechanistic interactions to dynamic interactions, from the interdependence of determinants of behavior to the reciprocal interaction between behavior and situational events (cf. Endler, 1982, pp. 230–231). The crucial problem with dynamic interactions is to create 'a dynamic, process-oriented model which examines the effects of persons on situations and vice versa...' (Endler and Edwards, 1986). No doubt, such a model requires fundamental reflection on a multitude of possible relations connecting person and situation as well as the complex processes occurring in persons dealing with situations. Magnusson (1976, 1980) has given a first impetus to reflection on this issue by dealing with dynamic person–situation interactions at two levels of analysis: between- or across-situations interactions versus within-situation interactions. Between-situation interactions refer to the selections individuals make with respect to the situations they participate in, while at the same time rejecting other situations. According to Magnusson (1980, p. 23) 'The result of this process of selection of situations that one encounters is that each individual appears in a restricted set of situations and these types of situations are a function of and have relevance for the person concerned'. Within-situation interactions, on the other hand, are defined within the context of a situation in which the individual finds him- or herself. According to Magnusson, within a situation: 'At any moment the individual selects, interprets, and treats the situational information and transforms it into behavior, which in the next stage of the process becomes an important part of the situation information for the individual' (Magnusson, 1980, p. 24).

The two types of interaction proposed by Magnusson provide an explanation for the lack of consistency found in studies of overt behavior. If between-situation interactions occur with some regularity, transsituational consistency of behavior will seldom be found. And, furthermore, within-situation interactions will have the effect of disturbing the internal consistency of overt behavior. Can we substantiate this important line of reasoning on the basis of the studies reported here?

Our findings may throw new light upon dynamic interactions as conceived by Endler, Magnusson and others. First of all, in our study of individual strategies we found individuals to use categorical preferences for situations, i.e., tendencies to approach some situations and to avoid other situations, irrespective of their present position. In our behavior observation study we found a predominance of coherence stability rather than transsituational consistencies or intrasituational consistencies with respect to the goal aspect of behavior. Taking into account the different starting positions induced by the situations offered, this finding may be interpreted as a directional bias in individual behavior, based on a preference for particular situations. These results support Magnusson's conception of between-situation interactions since they provide a basis for individuals to direct behavior at obtaining specific types of situations and to avoid others.

Within-situation interactions on the other hand, reflect transactions occurring between individual and situation. According to the present position, those transactions are controlled by tactical mechanisms, i.e. autonomous processes activated by discrepancies taking place between cognitions and situational events. Their function is to restore equilibrium by transforming either cognitive elements or situational events. As our study on predictive validity has shown, the effect of tactical mechanisms is to enhance variability in specific aspects of behavior, thus introducing behaviors different from those resulting directly from the strategy.

Strategy and tactics are different in many respects. Yet, they share one feature, i.e. to enhance the situation-specific nature of individual behavior. Therefore, together they may offer a framework to explain person–situation interactions rather than merely establishing interactions.

In my view, any explanation of person–situation interactions should be based on an explicit conception of the relationship between person and situation, between personality and environment. We cannot just conceive of those as two independent determinants of behavior, or sources of behavioral variation. Personality and environment are seen here as the major determinants of the adaptive process. The role they play in that process is explained in the open-systems adaptation model: while the person is governed by the tendency to control the situation, so is the situation governed by norms making only some forms of control effective and others ineffective. To obtain and maintain control, the person has several means at his disposal, ranging from intentional strategic options to autonomous mechanisms preserving equilibrium.

Clearly, this conception of person–situation relations has consequences for the person–situation debate. First of all, I reject the idea of the person versus the situation as some kind of contest including a winner and a loser. Not the dominance of one over the other, but the agreement between the two is the major issue. Agreement between person and situation is the very core of human adaptation. The original question of the person–situation debate was: which of the two is the main determinant of behavior, the person or the situation? The answer is unequivocal: both are. But this does not preclude that conditions can be specified favoring either the person or the situation.

For instance, Olweus (1977) pointed out that the *homogeneity/heterogeneity* of the samples of persons, situations and behaviors studied can have considerable effects on the outcomes with regard to the issue. Mischel (1973) has stated that the variance for the person facet will be diminished if the situations studied are highly structured. In this connection he introduced the notion of *situational power versus weakness*, implying that the choice of powerful situations will reduce the effects of individual differences. Mischel's argument rests on his cognitive social learning approach, suggesting that uniform cognitions produce uniform behaviors. A closely related view is expressed by Magnusson (1974).

From an adaptation point of view, the question 'when do individual differences make a difference' is not to be answered that easily. In this context, situational power refers to the norms imposed by the situation. How persons cope with powerful norms remains to be seen. The notion of situational power seems important as a condition to be taken into account while studying person–situation interactions in the context of adaptation. For that reason we have studied this concept in more detail than was done before (cf. Hettema, Van Heck, Appels and Van Zon, 1986). While developing and comparing several different indices of situational power we found that at least two more or less independent aspects are involved: cognitive situational power and behavioral situational power. While Mischel (1973) obviously referred to the first notion we are more interested in the second one. Behavioral situational power includes behavioral norms and goals as well as behavioral consequences. Clearly, those aspects are of major importance for adaptation.

Both aspects of homogeneity and power may be combined to study the impact of situations in person–situation research. On the person side, the open-systems adaptation model has suggested strategy and tactics as the major structures to be taken into account. Combining situation and person aspects in one schedule we obtain the picture presented in Table 1. In this table on the situation side, strong and weak refer to the power of situations to regulate behavior, i.e. the amount of strictness of situations to admit behaviors that are non-prototypical. Within each, a further distinction is made referring to homogeneity. Homogeneous sets contain only situations that are proto- typically identical, whereas heterogeneous sets contain situations that are prototypically dissimilar. On the person side, preference for situations is the first strategic issue to be taken into account: according to the model preferred situations will be preserved, non-preferred situations will be modified or transformed. Success or failure of transformation will be largely a function of situational power: strong situations will resist transformation, whereas weak situations will allow transformation to occur. Especially in strong situations the tactical system of personality will become involved in the regulation of behavior. Within strong situations, ST-mechanisms may have the effect to restore equilibrium; if not, according to the open-systems adaptation model, disruptive mechanisms will take over to minimize loss of control.

What are the effects of the different types of activity postulated here? First of all, preferred situations will elicit prototypical behavior to preserve their original form. If the different situations involved are prototypically equiv- alent, in every situation every subject is expected to show the same behavior. So, behavior will vary neither as a function of persons, nor as a function of situations. If the situations are prototypically different, all persons will behave according to the situations' prototypical packages, thus favoring the *situation- model*.

Transformational behavior will be effective especially in weak situations. Behavior is governed by individual strategies, yielding the same behavior for a person in prototypically equivalent situation. So in this case the *person-model* will be favored. In non-equivalent situation, persons will diverge, thus supporting the person × situation model.

Tactical adjustments will be elicited especially in powerful situations. If all situations are equivalent, the same state transition mechanism will be activated in a person in all situations, but among persons there will be differences. Since strategies will differ accordingly, we expect the person-model to be supported

Table 1 Models expected to be confirmed as a function of situation characteristics and adaptive personality systems

		Situations		
	Strong		Weak	
	Equivalent	Non-equivalent	Equivalent	Non-equivalent
Strategy				
Situation Preference	Invariance	S-model	Invariance	S-model
Situation Transformation	—	—	P-model	P × S-model
Tactics / *Persons*				
State transition	P-model	P × S-model and S-model	—	—
Disruption	P-model	P × S-model and P-model	—	—

in this condition. In non-equivalent situations, tactics as well as strategies may yield different results for the same person, although ST-mechanisms may exhibit some transsituational consistency. Accordingly, the person × situation model will be supported here.

Yet, one further observation should be made here with respect to the effect of different ST-mechanisms. In our conception as explained in Chapter 14, the type of consistency to be expected from tactics differs according to the specific tactical mechanism used. Cognitive symbolic states will tend to magnify coherence, whereas sensorimotor–operational states will enhance intra-situational consistency. So, in addition to the interaction model, some support may be expected for the situation-model.

Finally, if ST-mechanisms fail, disruption will occur. In equivalent powerful situations the same mechanisms may be expected to become effective in a person, but individuals will differ in their use of disruption mechanisms. Thus, the person-model may be expected to find support in this condition. In non-equivalent situations, the person–situation model will be supported, whereas the person-model may benefit from generalization of disruption across situations.

Summarizing, all three basic models may find support from an adaptation point of view, but the distribution across conditions varies. Contrary to Mischel's views at this point, I expect support for the *individual differences paradigm in strong situations as well as weak situations.* But, while in weak situations the predominantly cognitive strategic system is the basis for stable individual differences, in strong situations it is especially the biology-based tactical system that is responsible. My expectations regarding the effect of homogeneity/heterogeneity of situations are to a great extent parallel to earlier views: equivalence furthers individual differences, whereas non-equivalence boosts the impact of the interaction and situation models.

Summarizing then, from the present point of view, each model may find support, although not every outcome is equally likely. Most person–situation studies will include strong as well as weak situations, while situations will usually be dissimilar. In that case, according to Table 1, we may expect the person–situation and situation models to be confirmed predominantly, at the expense of the person model. In that respect our observation study (cf. Chapter 13) may well be typical for the results to be obtained in this area. It should be kept in mind, however, that the theoretical model on which predictions are based is interactionistic rather than either personalistic or situationistic.

INTELLIGENCE, EMOTIONS AND ADAPTATION

The theoretical framework presented here is broadly defined and comprehensive to encompass the divergent aspects of human adaptation. Thus, by nature, it is connected with several current paradigms directed at the study of specific aspects of adaptation. To illustrate the scope of the adaptation point of view two major aspects are singled out here: intelligence and emotions.

At first sight, it is tempting to connect intelligence with the strategic system and emotions with the tactical system. Strategies are primarily concerned with transformations. The strategic system, while specifying behavioral goals and means, includes choices among alternatives on the basis of costs and benefits for the individual. The major processes involved have been summarized earlier (Hettema, 1979) as directed thinking, an obvious aspect of intelligence. Yet, in our conception, intelligence does not coincide with strategy.

Intelligence primarily refers to outcomes, to performance in task situations, to be defined at the sensorimotor level rather than the cognitive–symbolic level of the system. Thus, intelligent behavior is the result of control processes as well as of cognitive–symbolic processes. Intelligence is a specific aspect of the total adaptation of the individual rather than mere cognition (cf. Hettema and Snow, in preparation). With this statement we join the classical theorists of intelligence who emphasized the adaptive function of intelligent behavior.

Most prior definitions of intelligence emphasize adaptive functioning, or more specifically, adaptation to changing circumstances in the service of perseverance toward an accepted goal (Snow, 1986). Binet (1909) has defined intelligence as 'the tendency to take and maintain a definite direction; the capacity to make adaptations for the purpose of attaining a desired end; and the power of auto-criticism' (Terman, 1916, p. 45).

Freeman (1955) defined intelligence as '... adjustment or adaptation of the individual to his total environment, or to limited aspects thereof ... the capacity to reorganize one's behavior patterns so as to act more effectively and more appropriately in novel situations' (pp. 60–61).

In daily life, intelligence becomes manifest in judgement, good sense, practical sense, initiative, comprehension and reasoning (cf. Binet and Simon, 1909, pp. 42–43).

Intelligence research in the early psychometric tradition has emphasized the general dispositional nature of intelligence discriminating between individuals. More recent models have stressed the hierarchical structure of intelligence, with general intelligence as the dominant factor and content-defined specific factors occupying a lower position (cf. Cattell, 1971; Horn, 1976) Currently, much attention is paid to component-process models of intelligence, emphasizing the serial nature of processes involved in solving cognitive tasks (Sternberg, 1978). This approach assumes problem solvers to use fixed strategies, specifying a number of steps to be taken consecutively in order to arrive at the correct solution. However, as task complexity is increased, the model appears to be too simple. Individuals then tend to shift strategies, changing component processes like encoding, rule construction and evaluation (Kyllonen, Woltz and Lohman, 1981).

To account for strategy shifting, other processes are required regulating the organization of the components involved. Hettema and Snow (in preparation) have forwarded the idea that separate control processes at the interface between the inner and outer environments should be postulated. The major function of these processes is to restore the balance between cognitions and external events. Obviously, the tactical mechanisms proposed here, are fit to perform that function. Accordingly, intelligent behavior is attributed neither to a single disposition, nor to cognitive strategies alone, but is seen to involve strategic as well as tactical processes. The results obtained in our study with cognitive tests (Chapter 10) offer empirical evidence to support this statement. In the conception of intelligence advocated here, strategic considerations are always involved, whereas the emergence of tactics is primarily a function of increasing complexity. The study of intelligence in complex daily-life situations, i.e. practical intelligence (Sternberg and Wagner, 1986), may be improved considerably by taking tactical mechanisms into consideration.

If the picture with regard to intelligence is complex, emotions seem even more problematic. After having dealt with emotions for a long time as fundamentally antagonistic to rationality, mainstream psychology has gradually adopted a new point of view regarding emotions. Instead of stressing the disorganizing and maladaptive aspects of emotion, in recent years there is a growing tendency to study its organizing and functional aspects (cf. Kleinginna and Kleinginna, 1981). Modern theories of emotion tend to agree that emotions are fundamentally adaptive in nature and play a major role in establishing goal-directed behavior in multifarious situations (cf. e.g. Izard, 1971; Leventhal, 1984; Plutchik, 1980; Scherer, 1984; Tomkins, 1980). The development described has created a new problem for theoretical psychology, however, because, if not antagonistic, how should the relationship between emotion and cognition be conceived? This question has given rise to the so-called emotion-cognition debate, reflecting a fundamental disagreement between leading theorists on the issue mentioned. In this debate, Zajonc (1980; Zajonc, Pietromonaco and Bargh, 1982) has taken the position that cognition and emotion are partially independent systems, whereas Lazarus (1982; Lazarus, Coyne and Folkman, 1982) emphasizes the intimate connection between the two.

In a recent attempt to explain both positions more clearly Hettema and Van Heck (1987) have analyzed a number of emotion theories in detail, including the work of Zajonc and of Lazarus. The major difference between the two appeared paradigmatic. Whereas Lazarus studies emotions within the cognitive paradigm, Zajonc uses the behavioral paradigm as a context.

Obviously, the paradigm used as a context to study emotions has repercussions for the status of emotions as a system. The cognitive paradigm, for instance, primarily conceives of emotions as a result of appraisals. The consequences of emotions are labelings, attributions, or reappraisals, i.e. cognitions again. Emotions are thus given the status of links or intermediaries between subsequent cognitions. Hence, the emotional system is treated as a subsystem of the cognitive system, with input as well as output defined by the latter system.

The behavior paradigm views emotions as a consequence of exposure to specific sensory stimulation. Emotions have the capacity to lend extra power and intensity to overt behavior. The emotional system is thus conceived as a subsystem of the sensorimotor system with input as well as output defined by that system.

According to the present position, both the cognitive and the sensorimotor aspects are indispensible. They should be combined in a so-called interactive-systems conception (cf. Hettema and Van Heck, 1987). The interactive-systems conception views the emotional system essentially as a relay system, connecting elements of the cognitive system with elements of the sensorimotor system. The system is activated by disruptive or interruptive events, causing a discrepancy to occur between the states of the elements of the two systems mentioned. Emotions have the capacity to alter the state of any of the two systems to dissolve the discrepancy and reestablish convergence. The interactive-systems conception of emotions is represented in the work of e.g. Scheier and Carver (1982) with emphasis on hierarchical control, of Scherer (1984) stressing component processes, and of Hettema (1979) emphasizing reciprocity of the control processes involved.

In my conception, emotions can only be understood in the context of both the cognitive and the sensorimotor systems. Those systems are conceived as parallel systems in the execution of behavior. The cognitive system is assumed to represent as well as to direct overt events. It therefore contains representational elements (concepts) as well as transformational elements (rules). The emotional system is conceived as an intermediary between the cognitive and sensorimotor systems and shares elements with both systems. The major functions of emotions are regulation and control. Emotions are activated by discrepancies occurring between the cognitive and sensorimotor systems. They serve to eliminate discrepancies by changing the state of either cognitive elements or sensorimotor elements.

Earlier I have postulated two types of emotional process: one process affecting the sensorimotor system (expression–exploration) and one affecting the cognitive system (reflection–appraisal)(Hettema, 1979, 1986, 1988b). In that conception the situation is assumed to be the pivotal issue, connecting cognition and emotion. The representational elements of the cognitive system also have the capacity to act as monitoring elements of the emotional system. As elements of the cognitive system, situation concepts can act as starting points as well as results of cognitive transformations, for instance, in processes of directed thinking. As elements of the emotional system, situation concepts are the basis for evaluation of environmental events.

Obviously, the nature of emotions should be treated in more detail than appeared possible here. Special attention should be paid to their position with respect to the cognitive system. The nature of the emotional system as a central subsystem of behavior, including presumably many couplings with other systems, will always be an impediment while studying those questions. Therefore empirical scrutiny will have to be guided by theory, however fallible the latter may be as yet.

Concluding this section, it can be stated that our contributions to the fields of intelligence and emotions have followed the same lines. In the context of adaptation, intelligence as well as emotions involve all three levels of the personality system, although the emphasis is different. Intelligence is focused at the cognitive–symbolic level, whereas the control and sensorimotor levels are important conditions as well. Emotions are focused at the control level of the personality system, but cognitive–symbolic as well as sensorimotor data are involved as well.

PERSPECTIVES FOR APPLIED RESEARCH

The studies reported in this book are concerned with the adaptation of individuals to everyday situations. To open up this field several new developments appeared necessary: conceptually, methodologically as well as empirically. The open-systems adaptation model served to conceptualize the interface between the person and the situation. Taxonomies of situations and behaviors were established to conceptualize key elements of adaptation. Situations were presented verbally and pictorially as well as via simulation. Behavior was studied using self-reports, physiological reactions and naturalistic observation. Relations within and between the several measures were established empirically to test the underlying model.

Object and scope of the research program have obviously raised expectancies concerning practical applications of our results. The question to be answered in this final section is: What is the major gain for applied purposes of the research reported here?

For practical purposes our endeavors have opened up several possibilities with regard to personality assessment as well as treatment. An attractive feature of the procedures developed is that they allow for very specific assessment instruments to be constructed. For instance, if an investigator is interested in individual behavior in specific settings as e.g. a school, a company or even household, he may derive situations from the taxonomy created by Van Heck. Based on an ecological analysis of the pertinent setting he may wish to represent all relevant situations, or select a subset for special purposes. As regards behavior to be recorded the investigator can select among the many categories offered in the response taxonomy. Assessment can be directed at divergent issues as, for instance, leadership, teaching, negotiating or partnership. All selections made of situations as well as behaviors refer to a well-established frame of reference in which prototypical packages are known and the effects of specific transformations can be inferred.

With regard to modes three different types of data may be analyzed. Researchers interested in questions concerning competence and directionality of behavior may prefer the SRS-technique. Others more concerned with transactional and control aspects can develop films and use physiological measures. A third possibility is to use an observation technique for the study of overt behavior *in situ*.

Several types of questions may be studied on the basis of the open-systems adaptation model and the methodology developed here. Four major types can be derived immediately from the model. Research may be directed at questions concerning either ecological analysis, behavior analysis, the adaptation process, or products of adaptation. Each type of research has obtained attention in studies done in our laboratory. They will be briefly described to illustrate the scope of the present approach.

First of all, a precise and systematic description may be obtained of the conditions to which adaptation is wanted. *Ecological analysis* may yield situation descriptions that can either be studied in their own right or as stimulus material for the study of adaptive processes. For instance, in educational psychology, much effort has been invested in the conceptualization of the classroom. The present approach opens up the possibility to conceptualize the classroom as an educational context and situations occurring there.

In an early study (Hettema, 1972a; Hettema *et al.*, 1973) I observed teacher behavior during class, mapping out the goals and means used by teachers to convey knowledge. In the current context this information would be designated as pertaining to the teacher's strategy. As a consequence of teacher strategies, specific situations will be created in the classroom, that may either enhance or inhibit performance. Teachers may direct the learning process by imposing norms and structure, or support the process by stimulation and acceptance. Not only the teacher will use strategies but also the learner. The present methodology allows to obtain a picture of learner strategies as a function of the situations created by the teacher. Discrepancies occurring between both types of strategy may provide a basis to improve the learning process by adjusting teacher and/or learner strategies.

The open-systems adaptation model including its methodology can also be applied to yield an explicit description of specific behaviors reflecting adaptation. *Behavior analysis* in the present context comes down to defining strategic or tactical elements in an ongoing stream of behavior. An example of this approach can be found in a recent study by Verhulst (1987), directed at the phenomenon of resistance during psychotherapy. In the classical conception, resistance has been treated either as an outflow of the client's personality (psychoanalysis) or as a function of the therapist's behavior (behavior therapy). Verhulst (1987) started from the assumption that both the client and his environment are involved in resistance. A thorough analysis of clients' behaviors revealed that resistance becomes manifest in two types of behavior: quarreling and evasion. On the therapist side, the occurrence of resistance was particularly enhanced by asking questions.

In Verhulst's interpretation of these results, the client feels threatened by the questions asked, because he anticipates loss of control. Accordingly, resistance is conceived as an adaptive reaction of the client to retain his equilibrium. As we have pointed out earlier, many tactical reactions can perform the function of retaining equilibrium, including ST-mechanisms maximizing control, or disruption mechanisms minimizing non-control. Verhulst's study explains why very different reactions can all refer to resistance. This study has also created clarity with respect to environmental conditions eliciting resistance during psychotherapy.

A third major perspective, presenting itself here, is to study *adaptive processes* by directly confronting individuals with concrete situations. Due to our multilevel approach, adaptive processes may be scrutinized in the realm of strategies, tactics or overt behavior. Examples of each may elucidate this approach.

A study by Adank and Van Bekkum (1985) was especially concerned with strategies in problem situations. These authors developed an SRS-questionnaire containing 15 problematic situations (private, public or health problems). Not only did they ask what the subject would do in a situation, but also to what extent he would ask others to support him with respect to each behavior mentioned. The results of this study showed that, as a strategy, seeking support is preferred more in public and health situations than in private situations. The primary purpose of seeking support is to increase knowledge (D-KNOW), rather than to attain other goals. Summarizing, this study showed that in problematic situations, strategies depend on the nature of the situation as well as the goals to be achieved.

Adaptive processes may also be studied in the realm of tactics. An elaborate study by Vingerhoets (1985) was especially concerned with reactions to life event stress. In stress situations, tactics may either be directed at short-term adaptation maximizing control, or at long-term adaptation minimizing non-control. In Vingerhoets' study a connection was postulated between those two reactions on the one hand and problem-directed coping versus emotion-directed coping (cf. Folkman and Lazarus, 1980) on the other. To study coping, Vingerhoets used films representing specific stressful life events, as, e.g. death of a relative, divorce, loss of a job and surgical operation. The subjects were especially recruited among victims of one of the events presented. As dependent variables several electrophysiological and biochemical reactions were measured. The results of this investigation did not show significant interactions between groups of subjects and films. However, coping styles were clearly related with base levels of ACTH, growth hormone, catecholamines and testosterone. These results may indicate a general tendency in individuals to react to stressful life events either with short- or long-term adaptation. This general tendency would have its basis in specific patterns of psychobiological functioning.

Finally, adaptive processes may be studied directly with the aid of observations of overt behavior in real life conditions. This opportunity is especially worthwhile if information is needed concerning the adaptation of individuals that are hard to be tested otherwise. An example are mentally retardates. In a recent publication (Hettema and Bunt, 1988) we have developed a design for the study of adaptation of mentally retardates in institutions. In the program outlined, standard settings will be identified in specific institutions to act as situations in which individuals can be observed. The observation schedule will be based on the behavior taxonomy described earlier, extended with special non-verbal categories that seem to be relevant with these subjects. Observations will be obtained repeatedly in the same situations over a larger period of time. The design provides the opportunity to scrutinize several types of consistency and coherence in individual behavior, allowing conclusions to be drawn on the nature and development of the adaptive process in this particular group.

In addition to the types of research mentioned, a fourth approach is directed at the *products of adaptation*, including personality change. According to the open-systems adaptation model, as a consequence of specific types of education, training or experience, specific products are to be expected, henceforth determining individual behavior. Several designs can be used to study products of adaptation, for instance experimental designs or group comparisons. Both have been used in attempts to study adaptation in our program. The study of Begeer (1984) described earlier, was directed at strategy change as a function of training. Using a pretest–posttest design with controls, an SRS-questionnaire was administered twice, before and after a training program aimed at the improvement of leadership. The results of this study revealed that strategies had changed, notably with respect to d-goals. The tendency to obtain social control was diminished, whereas proximity was enhanced.

In a final study to be mentioned here, Dooremalen (1984) studied the effect of experience upon strategies in social workers. He administered an SRS-questionnaire based on professional counselling situations to groups of student social workers and professionals. Using a group comparison design, Dooremalen obtained significant differences between the two groups with respect to the d-goals preferred. Whereas the students had a preference for D-KNOW, the professionals predominantly indicated to prefer D-PROX as a d-goal.

Both studies by Begeer (1984) and Dooremalen (1984) indicate changes in the goal structure of strategies as a consequence of training or experience.

They also found situation specific effects that have not been treated in detail here. In sum then, it can be stated that the adaptation paradigm has opened up the perspective to fruitfully study the precise effects of divergent treatments, ranging from training to experience and from education to psychotherapy.

Resuming my initial query concerning the major gain of this research regarding applied questions I can state the following. We have developed new opportunities to study behavior in everyday conditions, inside as well as outside the laboratory. Person and situation can be studied in one comprehensive design, analyzing the person with respect to behavioral choices and the situation with respect to behavioral opportunities. Depending on the questions asked, research can be focused on strategies, tactics or both. Behavioral coherence is a major guideline to be taken into account in most studies done in this context. Several types of study readily present themselves, the most important of which are: projects concerned with situational conditions, behavioral analysis, process analysis and the analysis of treatment effects. Each type of study requires a thorough reflection of the major aspects of persons and situations determining behavior, before research can be started. It is hoped and expected that the outcomes will justify the effort invested.

CONCLUDING COMMENT

Traditionally, personality has been studied from different points of view, including the behavioral, trait and cognitive perspectives. None of these was obviously wrong, but each approach has shown severe limitations as soon as daily life conditions were taken into account. The crisis in personality psychology not only revealed several shortcomings of the classical approaches, but also indicated the direction into which innovative efforts should move. Personality psychology should widen its scope and, notably, pay more attention to the context in which people live their lives. The search for an integrative understanding of individuals in complex environments should be encouraged and supported. Our work is meant to be an answer to this challenge. The final product provides a first map of the relevant terrain, which we hope will act as a guide for further extensions and integrations.

The biosocial framework acting as a background for studying personality here, has introduced more complexity than is usually met in this area. Its choice can only be justified by the recognition that personality is a very complex object, showing phenotypically different behavior as a function of several specific conditions. After dealing with those complexities in detail, we were able to preserve the integrity of personality by showing stability and coherence in the behavior of individuals. We also obtained evidence for the existence of complex patterns of interaction within individuals as well as between individuals and their environment. Those interactions have revealed some fascinating views of personality in daily life conditions, including relations with several major central processes, directing and guiding behavior.

Further exploration of these areas along the lines developed here is an attractive option for future research. It is to be expected that modification of the theory and development of new theory will be necessary to cover the field. Meanwhile, we hope and expect that the open-systems adaptation model provides a sufficiently firm foundation on which to build.

References

Abramson, L. Y., Seligman, M. E. P., and Teasdale, J. D. (1978). Learned helplessness in humans; Critique and reformulation. *Journal of Abnormal Psychology*, **87**, 49–74.

Adank, C., and Van Bekkum, J. (1985). *Help. Een onderzoek naar probleemoplossend en hulpvragen gedrag* [Help. A study of problem-solving and help-seeking behavior]. Unpublished MA Thesis, Department of Psychology, Tilburg University, The Netherlands.

Alker, H. A. (1972). Is personality situationally specific or intrapsychically consistent? *Journal of Personality*, **40**, 1–16.

Allport, G. W. (1937). *Personality: A psychological interpretation*. Holt, New York.

Allport, G. W. (1961). *Pattern and growth in personality*. Holt, Rinehart & Winston, London.

Allport, G. W. (1966). Traits revisited. *American Psychologist*, **21**, 1–10.

Alston, W. P. (1975). Traits, consistency, and conceptual alternatives for personality theory. *Journal for the Theory of Social Behaviour*, **5**, 17–48.

Amelang, M., and Borkenau, P. (1982). *In search of persons with traits; Intraindividual variability, moderator scales, and differential predictability*. Unpublished manuscript, Department of Psychology, University of Heidelberg, FRG.

Andreasen, N. A. (1984). *The broken brain: The biological revolution in psychiatry*. Harper & Row, New York.

Angyal, A. (1941). *Foundations for a science of personality*. Commonwealth Fund, New York.

Argyle, M. (1976). Personality and social behaviour, in Harré, R. (Ed.), *Personality*. Basil Blackwell, Oxford, pp. 145–188.

Argyle, M. (1977). Predictive and generative rules models of P × S interaction, in Magnusson, D., and Endler, N. S. (Eds.), *Personality at the crossroads: Current issues in interactional psychology*. Erlbaum, Hillsdale, NJ, pp. 353–370.

Argyle, M. (1980). *The structure of action*. Basil Blackwell, Oxford.

Averill, J. R. (1981). A bare-bones theory of personality. *Contemporary Psychology*, **26**, 4, 285–286.

Averill, J. R., and Opton, E. M., Jr. (1968). Psychophysiological assessment; Rationale and problems, in McReynolds, P. (Ed.), *Advances in psychological assessment*. Science and Behavior Books, Palo Alto, CA, Vol. 1, pp. 265–288.

Bales, R. F. (1950). *Interaction process analysis*. Addison–Wesley, Reading, MA.

Bandura, A. (1969). *Principles of behavior modification*. Holt, New York.

Bandura, A. (1986). *Social foundations of thought and action. A social cognitive theory*. Prentice-Hall, Englewood Cliffs, NJ.

Barker, R. G. (1963). On the nature of the environment. *Journal of Social Issues*, **19**, 17–38.

Barker, R. G. (1968). *Ecological psychology: Concepts and methods for studying the environment of human behavior*. Stanford University Press, Stanford, CA.

Barker, R. G., and Wright, H. F. (1951). *One boy's day*. Harper, New York.

Barker, R. G., and Wright, H. F. (1955). *Midwest and its children: The psychological ecology of an American town*. Row-Peterson, Evanston, IL.

Begeer, W. (1984). *De meting en beïnvloeding van de strategieën van leiders in een onderneming* [The measurement and changement of strategies of leaders in concerns]. Unpublished MA Thesis, Department of Psychology, Tilburg University, The Netherlands.

Bem, D. J., and Allen, A. (1974). On predicting some of the people some of the time: The search for cross-situational consistencies in behavior. *Psychological Review*, **81**, 506–520.

Berlyne, D. E. (1960). *Conflict, arousal and curiosity*. McGraw-Hill, New York.

Berlyne, D. E. (1965). *Structure and direction in thinking*. Wiley, New York.

Binet, A. (1909). *Les idées modernes sur les enfants* [Modern ideas concerning children]. Flammarion, Paris.

Binet, A., and Simon, Th. (1909). L'intelligence des imbéciles [The intelligence of imbeciles]. *L'Année Psychologique*, **15**, 1–147.

Block, J. (1977). Advancing the psychology of personality, paradigmatic shift or improving the quality of research, in Magnusson, D., and Endler, N. S. (Eds.), *Personality at the crossroads: Current issues in interactional psychology*. Erlbaum, Hillsdale, NJ, pp. 37–63.

Block, J., and Block, J. H. (1981). Studying situational dimensions: A grand perspective and some limited empiricism, in Magnusson, D. (Ed.), *Toward a psychology of situations: An interactional perspective*. Elrbaum, Hillsdale, NJ, pp. 85–102.

Block, J., Weiss, D. S., and Thorne, A. (1979). How relevant is a semantic similarity interpretation of personality ratings? *Journal of Personality and Social Psychology*, **37**, 1055–1074.

Bonarius, H. (1981). Persoon en situatie: De adaptatie-theorie van P. J. Hettema [Person and situation:. The adaptation theory of P. J. Hettema], *De Psycholoog*, **16(3)**, 125–141.

Bowlby, J. (1969). *Attachment and loss. I. Attachment*. Basic Books, New York.

Brennan, R. L. (1978). *Generalizability analyses: Principles and procedures*, A.C.T. Technical Bulletin, Iowa City, Iowa (revised edition).

Bronfenbrenner, U. (1977). Toward an experimental ecology of human development. *American Psychologist*, **32**, 513–531.

Brunswik, E. (1943). Organismic achievement and environment probability. *Psychological Review*, **50**, 255–272.

Brunswik, E. (1956). *Perception and the representative design of psychological experiments*. University of California Press, Berkeley, CA.

Buss, A. H., and Plomin, R. (1975). *A temperament theory of personality development*. Wiley, New York.

Buss, D. M. (1982). A new theory, a new era. *Journal of Personality Assessment*, **46(1)**, 98–100.

Buss, D. M. (1985). Human mate selection. *American Scientist*, **73**, 47–51.

Buss, D. M., and Craik, K. H. (1980). The frequency concept of disposition: Dominance and prototypically dominant acts. *Journal of Personality*, **48**, 379–392.

Buss, D. M., and Craik, K. H. (1981). The act frequency analysis of interpersonal dispositions: Aloofness, gregariousness, dominance and submissiveness. *Journal of Personality*, **49**, 175–192.

Buss, D. M., and Craik, K. H. (1983). The dispositional analysis of everyday conduct. *Journal of Personality*, **51(3)**, 393–412.

Buss, D. M., Gomes, M., Higgins, D. J., and Lauterbach, K. (1987). Tactics of manipulation. *Journal of Personality and Social Psychology*, **52**, 1219–1229.

Campbell, D. T., and Fiske, D. W. (1959). Convergent and discriminant validation by the multitrait-multimethod matrix. *Psychological Bulletin*, **16**, 81–105.

Cantor, N. (1981). Perceptions in situations: Situation prototypes and person–situation prototypes, in Magnusson, D. (Ed.), *Toward a psychology of situations: An interactional perspective*. Erlbaum. Hillsdale, NJ, pp. 229–244.

Cantor, N., and Kihlstrom, J. F. (1987). *Personality and social intelligence*. Prentice-Hall, Englewood Cliffs, NJ.

Cantor, N., Mischel, W., and Schwartz, J. C. (1982a). A prototype analysis of psychological situations. *Cognitive Psychology*, **14**, 45–77.

Cantor, N., Mischel, W., and Schwartz, J. C. (1982b). Social knowledge: Structure, content, use, and abuse, in Hastorf, A. H., and Isen, A. M. (Eds.), *Cognitive social psychology*. Elsevier/North-Holland, New York, pp. 33–72.

Carruthers, M., and Taggart, P. (1973). Vagontonicity of violence: Biochemical and cardiac responses to violent films and television programs. *British Medical Journal*, **3**, 384–389.

Cattell, R. B. (1965). *Scientific analysis of personality*. Penguin Books, Harmondsworth.

Cattell. R. B. (1966). *The scientific analysis of personality*. Aldine, Chicago.

Cattell, R. B. (1971). *Abilities: their structure, growth and action*. Houghton-Mifflin, Boston, MA.

Cattell, R. B., and Birkett, H. (1980). The known personality structures found aligned between first order T-data and second order Q-data factors, with new evidence on the inhibitory control, independence, and regression traits. *Personality and Individual Differences*, **1**, 229–238.

Cheek, J. M. (1982). Aggregation, moderator variables, and the validity of personality tests: A peer-rating study. *Journal of Personality and Social Psychology*, **43**, 1254–1269.

Clustan (1978). Package of cluster analysis programs. *User manual* by D. Wishart. Edinburgh University, Edinburgh.

Coombs, C. H. (1964). *A theory of data*. Wiley, New York.

Coutu, W. (1949). *Emergent human nature*. Knopf, New York.

Coyne, J. C. (1976). Depression and the response of others. *Journal of Abnormal Psychology*, **85**, 186–193.

Craik, K. H. (1970). Environmental psychology, in Craik, K. H., Kleinmuntz, B., Rosnow, R. L., Rosenthal, R., Cheine, J. A., and Walters, R. L. *New directions in psychology*, Holt, New York, Vol. 4, pp. 1–22.

Craik, K. H. (1971). The assessment of places, in McReynolds, P. (Ed.), *Advances in psychological assessment*. Science and Behavior Books, Palo Alto, CA, Vol. 2, pp. 40–62.

Craik, K. H. (1973). Environmental psychology. *Annual Review of Psychology*, **24**, 403–422.

Craik, K. H. (1986). Personality research methods: an historical perspective. *Journal of Personality,* **54**, 18–51.

Cronbach, L. J., Gleser, G. C., Nanda, H., and Rajaratnam, N. (1972). *The dependability of behavior measurements: theory of generalizability for scores and profiles.* Wiley, New York.

Cunningham, M. R. (1986). Measuring the physical in physical atractiveness: quasi experiments on the sociobiology of female facial beauty. *Journal of Personality and Social Psychology,* **50**, 925–935.

Davis, M. H., Hull, J. G., Young, R. D., and Warren, G. G. (1987). Emotional reactions to dramatic film stimuli: The influence of cognitive and emotional empathy. *Journal of Personality and Social Psychology,* **52**, 126–133.

De Bonis, M. (1977). Assessing interactions between trait anxiety and stressful situations with special emphasis on the coherence of response modes, in Magnusson, D., and Endler, N. S. (Eds.), *Personality at the crossroads. Current issues in interactional psychology.* Erlbaum, Hillsdale, NJ, pp. 207–211.

DeFries, J. C., and Plomin, R. (1978). Behavior genetics. *Annual Review of Psychology,* **29**, 473–515.

Dicken, C. (1963). Good impression, social desirability and acquiescence as suppressor variables. *Educational and Psychological Measurement,* **23**, 699–720.

Dickman, H. R. (1963). The perception of behavioral units, in Barker, R. G. (Ed.), *The stream of behavior.* Appleton-Century-Crofts, New York, pp. 23–41.

Dion, K. K. (1972). Physical attractiveness and evaluations in children's transgression. *Journal of Personality and Social Psychology,* **24**, 207–213.

Dollard, J., and Miller, N. E. (1950). *Personality and psychotherapy: An analysis in terms of learning, thinking and culture.* McGraw-Hill, New York.

Dooremalen, J. C. J. (1984). *Hulpverleningsstrategieën bij maatschappelijke werkers: Op weg naar een taxonomie* [Counselling strategies in social workers: Towards a taxonomy]. Unpublished MA Thesis, Department of Psychology, Tilburg University, The Netherlands.

Duffy, E. (1972), Activation, in Greenfield, N. S., and Sternbach, R. A. (Eds.), *Handbook of psychophysiology.* Holt, New York, pp. 577–622.

Eckes, T., and Six, B. (1984). Prototypenforschung: Ein integrativer Ansatz zur Analyse der alltagssprachlichen Kategorisierung von Objekten, Personen und Situationen [Prototype research: An integrative attempt towards the analysis of everyday categorising of objects, persons, and situations]. *Zeitschrift für Sozial Psychologie,* **15**, 2–17.

Edelberg, R. (1972). Electrical activity of the skin: its measurement and uses in psychophysiology, in Greenfield, N. S., and Sternbach, R. A. (Eds.), *Handbook of psychophysiology,* Holt, New York, pp. 367–418.

Edwards, W. (1954). The theory of decision making. *Psychological Bulletin,* **51**, 380–418.

Ekehammar, B. (1974). Interactionism in personality from a historical perspective. *Psychological Bulletin,* **81**, 1026–1048.

Elliott, R. (1972). The significance of heart rate for behavior. A critique of the Laceys' hypothesis. *Journal of Personality and Social Psychology,* **22**, 389–409.

Endert, E. (1979). Determination of noradrenaline and adrenaline in plasma by a radioenzymatic assay using high pressure liquid chromatography for the separation of the radiochemical products. *Clinica Chimica Acta,* **96**, 233–239.

Endler, N. S. (1982). Interactionism comes of age, in Zanna, M. P., Higgins, E. T., and Herman, C. P. (Eds.), *Consistency in social behavior: The Ontario Symposium.* Erlbaum, Hillsdale, NJ, Vol. 2, pp. 209–249.

Endler, N. S., and Edwards, J. M. (1986). Interactionism in personality in the twentieth century. *Journal of Personality and Individual Differences*, **7**, 379–384.

Endler, N. S., and Magnusson, D. (1976a). *Interactional psychology and personality*. Hemisphere, Washington, DC.

Endler, N. S., and Magnusson, D. (1976b). Personality and person by situation interactions, in Endler, N. S., and Magnusson, D. (Eds.), *Interactional psychology and personality*. Hemisphere, Washington, DC pp. 1–25.

Endler, N. S., Hunt, J. M., and Rosenstein, A. J. (1962). An S-R inventory of anxiousness. *Psychological Monographs*, **76**, (17).

Epstein, S. (1977). Traits are alive and well, in Magnusson, D., and Endler, N. S. (Eds.), *Personality at the crossroads: Current issues in interactional psychology*. Erlbaum, Hillsdale, NJ, pp. 83–98.

Epstein, S. (1979). The stability of behavior. I. On predicting most of the people much of the time. *Journal of Personality and Social Psychology*, **37**, 1097–1126.

Epstein, S. (1980). The stability of behavior. II. Implications for psychological research. *American Psychologist*, **35**, 790–806.

Epstein, S. (1983). The stability of a confusion: a reply to Mischel and Peake. *Psychological Review*, **90(2)**, 179–184.

Epstein, S., and O'Brien, E. J. (1985). The person–situation debate in historical and current perspective. *Psychological Bulletin*, **98**, 513–537.

Eysenck, H. J. (1967). *The biological basis of personality* (3rd edition). Methuen, London.

Eysenck, H. J. (1970). *The structure of human personality* (3rd edition). Methuen, London.

Eysenck, H. J., and Rachman, S. (1965). *Causes and cures of neurosis*. Routledge and Kegan Paul, London.

Farber, I. E. (1964). A framework for the study of personality as a behavioral science, in Worchel, P., and Byrne, D. (Eds.), *Personality change*. Wiley, New York, pp. 3–37.

Feij, J. A. (1984). The psychophysiological and neurochemical bases of sensation seeking, in Bonarius, H., Van Heck, G. L., and Smid, N. (Eds.), *Personality psychology in Europe: Theoretical and empirical developments*. Swets & Zeitlinger, Lisse, Vol. 1, pp. 317–326.

Feij, J. A., and Kuiper, C. M. (1984). *Handleiding ATL. Adolescenten Temperament Lijst* [Manual of the Temperament Test for Adolescents]. Swets and Zeitlinger, Lisse.

Fiske, D. W. (1966). Some hypotheses concerning test adequacy. *Educational and Psychological Merasurement*, **26**, 69–88.

Fiske, D. W. (1971). *Measuring the concepts of personality*. Aldine, Chicago, IL.

Fiske, D. W. (1978). *Strategies for personality research*. Jossey-Bass, San Francisco, CA.

Flanagan, J. C. (1949). A new approach to evaluating personnel. *Personnel*, **26**, 35–42.

Folkman, S., and Lazarus, R. S. (1980). An analysis of coping in a middle-aged community sample. *Journal of Health and Social Behavior*, **21**, 219–239.

Forgas, J. (1978). Social episodes and social structures in an academic setting: The social environment of an intact group. *Journal of Experimental Social Psychology*, **32**, 191–209.

Forgas, J. P., Bower, G. H., and Krantz, S. E. (1984). The influence of mood on perceptions of social interactions. *Journal of Experimental Social Psychology*, **20**, 497–513.

Frederiksen, N. (1972). Towards a taxonomy of situations. *American Psychologist*, **27**, 114–123.

Frederiksen, N., and Melville, S. D. (1954). Differential predictability in the use of test scores. *Educational and Psychological Measurement*, **14**, 647–656.

Freeman, F. S. (1955). *Theory and practice of psychological testing* (Revised edition). Holt, New York.

Furnham, A. (1981). Personality and activity preference. *British Journal of Social and Clinical Psychology*, **20**, 57–68.

Furnham, A., and Jaspars, J. (1983). The evidence for interactionism in psychology. *Personality and Individual Differences*, **4**, 627–644.

Gara, M. A., and Rosenberg, S. (1981). Linguistic factors in implicit personality theory. *Journal of Personality and Social Psychology*, **41**, 450–457.

Gescheider, G. A. (1976). *Psychophysiology, method and theory*. Erlbaum, Hillsdale, NJ.

Ghiselli, E. E. (1960). The prediction of predictability. *Educational and Psychological Measurement*, **20**, 3–8.

Gleser, G. C., Cronbach, L. J., and Rajaratnam, N. (1965). Generalizability of scores influenced by multiple sources of variance. *Psychometrika*, **30**, 395–418.

Goldberg, L. R., Rorer, L. G., and Greene, M. M. (1970). The usefulness of 'stylistic' scales as potential suppressor or moderator variables in predictions from the CPI. *Oregon Research Institute Research Bulletin*, **10(3)**.

Goldfried, R., M., and Kent, R. N. (1972). Traditional versus behavioral personality assessment: A comparison of methodological and theoretical assumptions; *Psychological Bulletin*, **77**, 409–420.

Golding, S. L. (1975). Flies in the ointment: methodological problems in the analysis of the percentage of variance due to persons and situations. *Psychological Bulletin*, **82**, 278–288.

Goldman, W., and Lewis, P. (1977). Beautiful is good: evidence that the physically attractive are more socially skilled. *Journal of Experimental Social Psychology*, **13**, 125–130.

Goldsmith, H. H. (1983). Genetic influences on personality from infancy to adulthood. *Child Development*, **54**, 331–355.

Gorynska, E., and Strelau, J. (1979). Basic traits of temporal characteristics of behavior and their measurement by an inventory technique. *Polish Psychological Bulletin*, **10**, 199–207.

Gotlib, I. H., and Robinson, L. A. (1982). Responses to depressed individuals: discrepancies between self-report and observer-rated behavior. *Journal of Abnormal Psychology*, **91**, 231–240.

Grossman, P. (1983). Respiration, stress and cardiovascular function. *Psychophysiology*, **20(3)**, 284–300.

Guilford, J. P. (1959). *Personality*. McGraw-Hill, New York.

Guilford, J. P., and Fruchter, B. (1978). *Fundamental statistics in psychology and education*. (6th edition). McGraw-Hill, New York.

Guilford, J. P., and Zimmerman, W. S. (1956). Fourteen dimensions of temperament. *Psychological Monographs*, **70**, (417).

Gulliksen, H. (1950). *Theory of mental tests*. Wiley, New York.

Gunn, C. G., Wolf, S., Block, R. T., and Person, R. J. (1972). Psychophysiology of the cardiovascular system, in Greenfield, N. S., and Sternbach, R. A. (Eds.), *Handbook of psychophysiology*. Holt, New York, pp. 457–489.

Günther, G. (1982). Book review of Hettema, P. J. *Personality and adaptation*. *Zeitschrift für Psychologie*, **1982**, 189.

Guyton, A. C. (1976). *Textbook of medical physiology.* (5th edition). Saunders, Philadelphia.

Hahn, W. W. (1973). Attention and heart rate: A critical appraisal of the hypothesis of Lacey and Lacey. *Psychological Bulletin,* **79,** 59–70.

Hare, R. D. (1975). Psychophysiological studies of psychopathy, in Fowles, D. C. (Ed.), *Clinical applications of psychophysiology.* Columbia University Press, New York.

Harré, R., and Secord, P. F. (1972). *The explanation of social behavior.* Erlbaum, Totowa, NJ.

Hartmann, D. P., Roper, B. L., and Bradford, D. C. (1979). Some relationships between behavioral and traditional assessment. *Journal of Behavioral Assessment,* **1,** 3–23.

Heslegrave, R. J., and Furedy, J. J. (1979). Sensitivities of Hr and T-wave amplitude for detecting cognitive and anticipatory stress. *Physiology and Behavior,* **22,** 17–23.

Hettema, P. J. (1966). *Stijlkenmerken in de waarneming* [Style characteristics in perception]. Swets & Zeitlinger, Amsterdam.

Hettema, P. J. (1967). Trekken, processen en persoonlijkheidstests [Traits, processes, and personality tests]. *Nederlands Tijdschrift voor de Psychologie,* **22,** 618–641.

Hettema, P. J. (1968). Cognitive abilities as process variables. *Journal of Personality and Social Psychology,* **10,** 461–471.

Hettema, P. J. (1972a). *Doceerstijlen* [Teaching styles]. Internal Report, NIVOR, Nijmegen, The Netherlands.

Hettema, P. J. (1972b). *Verschillen tussen mensen* [Differences between people]. Inaugural Lecture, Tilburg University, The Netherlands.

Hettema, P. J. (1979). *Personality and adaptation.* North-Holland, Amsterdam.

Hettema, P. J. (1981). Persoonlijkheid en sociaal gedrag [Personality and social behavior], in Jaspars, J. M. F., and Van Der Vlist, R. (Eds.), *Sociale psychologie in Nederland I. Het individu* [Social Psychology in the Netherlands I. The individual]. Van Loghum Slaterus, Deventer, pp. 235–260.

Hettema, P. J. (1982a). Ontwikkelingen in de interactionistische persoonlijkheidspsychologie [Developments in interactionistic personality psychology]. *De Psycholoog,* **17,** 157–166.

Hettema, P. J. (1982b). Situatie-specifieke persoonlijkheidsdiagnostiek [Situation-specific diagnostics of personality], in Soudijn, K. A. (Ed.), *Psychologisch onderzoek in perspectief* [*Psychological research in perspective*]. Tilburg University, The Netherlands.

Hettema, P. J. (1984). The prediction of interpersonal behavior in specific situations, in Bonarius, H., Van Heck, G. L., and Smid, N. (Eds.), *Personality psychology in Europe: Theoretical and empirical developments.* Swets & Zeitlinger, Lisse, Vol. 1, pp. 165–177.

Hettema, P. J. (1986). *Emotions and adaptation. An open-systems perspective.* Paper presented at the International Conference on Stress and Emotion. Visegrad, Hungary.

Hettema, P. J. (1988a). *Method specificity in person-environment interactions.* Paper presented at the IVth European Conference on Personality in Stockholm.

Hettema, P. J. (1988b). *Intelligence and emotions.* Paper presented at the XXIVth International Congress of Psychology in Sydney.

Hettema, P. J., and Bunt, A. A. (1988). Adaptatie van zwakzinnigen in inrichtingen [Adaptation of mentally retardates in institutions] *Gedrag en Gezondheid,* **16(2),** 95–98.

Hettema, P. J., and Snow, R. E. Intelligence, adaptation, and personality (in preparation).

Hettema, P. J., and Van Heck, G. L. (1987). Emotion-cognition interactions in personality. *Communication and Cognition*, **20**, 141–170.

Hettema, P. J., Van Heck, G. L., Appels, M. T., and Van Zon, I. (1986). The assessment of sutuational power, in Angleitner, A., Furnham, A., and Van Heck, G. L., *Personality psychology in Europe: Current trends and controversies*. Swets & Zeitlinger, Lisse, Vol. 2, pp. 85–99.

Hettema, P. J., Verhoeven, A. F. M., and Woolthuis, A. J. G. (1973). Een analyse van het doceergedrag met het oog op de afstemming van docent en leerling [An analysis of teaching behavior for teacher-student matching], in Van Kemenade, J. A. (Ed.), *Bijdragen uit de onderwijswetenschappen* [Contributions from educational sciences]. Samson, Alphen aan de Rijn, pp. 125–242.

Hoefert, H. W. (1982). Ansätze zu einer kompetenzspezifischen Situationstaxonomie [Towards a competence-specific taxonomy of situations], in Hoefert, H. W. (Ed.), *Person und Situation. Interaktionspsychologische Untersuchungen* [Person and situation. Interactionist studies] Hogrefe, Göttingen, pp. 85–106.

Hogan, R. (1982). A socioanalytic theory of personality. *Nebraska Symposium on Motivation*, 1981. University of Nebraska Press, Lincoln, NE, pp. 55–89.

Hogan, R., De Soto, C. B., and Solano, C. (1977). Traits, tests, and personality research. *American Psychologist*, **32**, 255–264.

Hol, Th. P. (1990). *The prediction of person × situation interactions: A model comparison*, Doctoral dissertation, Tilburg University, The Netherlands.

Horn, J. L. (1976). Human abilities: A review of research and theory in the early 1970s. *Annual Review of Psychology*, **27**, 437–485.

Houts, A. C., Cook, T. D., and Shadish, W. R. Jr. (1986). The person-situation debate: A critical multiplist perspective. *Journal of Personality*, **54(1)**, 52–105.

Hunt, J. McV. (1965). Traditional personality theory in the light of recent evidence. *American Scientist*, **53**, 80–96.

Izard, C. E. (1971). *The face of emotion*. Appleton-Century-Crofts, New York.

Johnson, S. C. (1967). Hierarchical clustering schemes. *Psychometrika*, **32**, 241–254.

Jones, E. E., and Nisbett, R. E. (1972). The actor and the observer: Divergent perceptions of the causes of behavior, in Jones, E. E., Kanouse, D. E., Kelley, H. H., Nisbett, R. E., Valins, S., and Weinen, B. (Eds.), *Attribution: Perceiving the causes of behavior*. General Learning Press, Morristown, NJ. pp. 79–94.

Kanfer, F. H., and Saslow, G. (1969). Behavioral diagnosis, in Franks, C. M. (Ed.), *Behavior therapy: Appraisal and status*. McGraw-Hill, New York, pp. 417–444.

Katz, J. J. (1972). *Semantic theory*. Harper-Row, New York.

Kelly, G. A. (1955). *The psychology of personal constructs*. Norton, New York, Vols. 1 and 2.

Kenrick, D. T. (1987). Gender, genes, and the social environment: A biosocial interactionist perspective, in Shaver, P. C., and Hendrick, C. (Eds.), *Review of Personality and Social Psychology*, Sage, Newbury Park, CA, Vol. 7, pp. 14–43.

Kenrick, D. T., and Braver, S. L. (1982). Personality: idiographic and nomothetic! A rejoinder. *Psychological Review*, **89**, 182–186.

Kenrick, D. T., and Dantchik, A. (1983). Interactionism, idiographics, and the social psychological invasion of personality. *Journal of Personality*, **51**, 286–307.

Kenrick, D. T., Dantchik, A., and MacFarlane, S. (1983). Personality, environment, and criminal behavior: an evolutionary perspective, in Laufer, W. S., and Day, J. M. (Eds.), *Personality theory, moral development, and criminal behavior*. D. C. Heath, Lexington, MA, pp. 217–241.

Kenrick, D. T., and Funder, D. C. (1988). Profiting from controversy: lessons from the person-situation debate. *American Psychologist*, **43(1)**, 23–34.

Kenrick, D. T., Montello, D. R., and MacFarlane, S. (1985). Personality: social learning, social cognition, or sociobiology? in Hogan, R., and Jones, W. H. (Eds.), *Perspectives in personality*. JAI Press Inc, Greenwich, CO, Vol. 1, pp. 201–234.

Kenrick, D. T., and Stringfield, D. O. (1980). Personality traits and the eye of the beholder: crossing some traditional philosophical boundaries in the search for consistency in all of the people. *Psychological Review*, **87**, 88–104.

Kjellberg, A., and Magnusson, E. (1979). Physiological response patterns during 'intake' and 'rejection' tasks. *Biological Psychology*, **9**, 63–76.

Kleinginna, P. R., and Kleinginna, A. M. (1981)). A categorical list of emotion definitions, with suggestions for a consensual definition. *Motivation and Emotion*, **5**, 345–379.

Kluckhohn, C., and Kelly, W. H. (1945). The concept of culture, in Linton R. (Ed.), *The science of man in the world crisis*, Columbia University Press, New York, pp. 78–105.

Knudson, R. M., and Golding, S. L. (1974). Comparative validity of traditional versus S–R format inventories of interpersonal behavior. *Journal of Research in Personality*, **8**, 111–127.

Kogan, N., and Wallach, M. A. (1964). *Risk taking: A study in cognition and personality*, Holt, New York.

Krause, M. S. (1970). Use of social situations for research purposes. *American Psychologist*, **25**, 748–753.

Kulcsár, Z., Kutor, L., and Arató, M. (1984). Sensation seeking, its biochemical correlates, and its relation to vestibulo-ocular functions, in Bonarius, H., Van Heck, G. L., and Smid, N. (Eds.), *Personality psychology in Europe: Theoretical and empirical developments*. Swets and Zeitlinger, Lisse, Vol. 1, pp. 327–346.

Kyllonen, P. C., Woltz, D. J., and Lohman, D. F. (1981). Models of strategy and strategy-shifting in spatial visualization performance. *Technical Report Nr. 154-376 ONR. No. 17.*

Lacey, J. I. (1959). Psychophysiological approaches to the evaluation of psychotherapeutic process and outcome, in Rubinstein, E. A., and Parloff, M. B. (Eds.), *Research in psychotherapy*. American Psychological Association, Washington, DC, pp. 160–208.

Lacey, J. I. (1967). Somatic response patterning and stress: Some revisions of activation theory, in Appley, M. H., and Turnbull, R. (Eds.), *Psychological stress*. Appleton-Century-Crofts, New York, pp. 14–37.

Lacey, J. I., Kagan, J., Lacey, B. C., and Moss, H. A. (1963). The visceral level: Situational determinants and behavioral correlates of autonomic response patterns, in Knapp, P. H., (Ed.), *Expression of the emotions in man*. International Universities Press, New York, pp. 161–196.

Lamiell, J. T. (1981). Toward an idiothetic psychology of personality. *American Psychologist*, **36**, 276–289.

Lang, P. J., Rice, D. G., and Sternbach, R. A. (1972). The psychophysiology of emotions, in Greenfield, N. J., and R. A. Sternbach, (Eds.), *Handbook of psychophysiology*. Holt, New York, pp. 623–643.

Lantermann, E. D. (1980). *Interaktionen. Person, Situation und Handlung* [Interactions. Person, situation and action]. Urban & Schwarzenberg, München.

Lazarus, R. (1982). Thoughts on the relations between emotion and cognition. *American Psychologist*, **37**, 1019–1024.

Lazarus, R. S., Coyne, J. C., and Folkman, S. (1982). Cognition, emotion and motivation: the doctoring of Humpty-Dumpty, in Neufeld, J. (Ed.), *Psychological stress and psychopathology*. McGraw-Hill, New York, pp. 218–239.

Lazarus, R. S., Speisman, J. C., Mordkoff, A. M., and Davison, L. A. (1962). A laboratory study of psychological stress produced by a motion picture film. *Psychological Monographs*, **76(34)**, 1–35 (Whole No. 553).

Leventhal, H. (1984). A perceptual-motor theory of emotion, in Scherer, K. R., and Ekman, P. (Eds,), *Approaches to emotion*. Erlbaum, Hillsdale, NJ, pp. 271–291.

Levi, L. (1972). *Stress and distress in response to psychosocial stimuli*. Pergamon, New York.

Lewin, K. (1935). *A dynamic theory of personality*. Mc-Graw-Hill, New York.

Lingoes, J. C., and Roskam, E. E. (1973). A mathematical and empirical analysis of two multidimensional scaling algorithms. *Psychometrika, Monograph Supplement*, **38**, 1–93.

Little, B. R. (1983). Personal projects. A rational and method for investigation. *Environment and Behavior*, **15**, 272–309.

Loehlin, J. C. (1982). Are personality traits differentially heritable? *Behavior Genetics*, **12**, 417–428.

Loehlin, J. C., and Nichols, R. C. (1976). *Heredity, environment and personality*. University of Texas Press, Austin, TE.

Lord, F. M., and Novick, M. R. (1968). *Statistical theory of mental tests*. Addison-Wesley, Reading, MA.

Lott, D. F. (1979). A possible role for generally adaptive features in mate selection and sexual stimulation. *Psychological Reports*, **45**, 539–546.

Luchins, A. S., and Luchins, E. H. (1959). *Rigidity of behavior: A variational approach to the effect of Einstellung*. University of Oregon Books, Eugene, OR.

Magnusson, D. (1971). An analysis of situational dimensions. *Perceptual and Motor Skills*, **32**, 851–867.

Magnusson, D. (1974). The individual in the situation: some studies on individuals' perception of situations. *Studia Psychologica*, **16**, 124–132.

Magnusson, D. (1976). The person and the situation in an interactional model of behavior. *Scandinavian Journal of Psychology*, **17**, 253–271.

Magnusson, D. (1978). On the psychological situation. *Reports from the Department of Psychology. The University of Stockholm*. Number 544.

Magnusson, D. (1980). Personality in an interactional paradigm of research. *Zeitschrift für differentielle und diagnostische Psychologie*, **1**, 17–34.

Magnusson, D. (1981). Wanted: a psychology of situations, in Magnusson, D. (Ed.), *Toward a psychology of situations: An interactional perspective*. Erlbaum, Hillsdale, NJ, pp. 9–32.

Magnusson, D., and Ekehammar, B. (1975). Anxiety profiles based on both situational and response factors. *Multivariate Behavior Research*, **10**, 27–43.

Magnusson, D., and Ekehammar, B. (1978). Similar situations—similar behaviors? A study of the intraindividual congruence between situation perception and situation reactions. *Journal of Research in Personality*, **12**, 41–48.

Magnusson, D., and Endler, N. S. (Eds.), (1977). *Personality at the crossroads: Current issues in interactional psychology*. Erlbaum, Hillsdale, NJ.

Magnusson, D., and Stattin, H. (1978). *How unique and stable are individual cross-situational patterns of behavior*? Reports from the Department of Psychology, University of Stockholm, No. 534.

Mason, J. W. (1972). Organization of psychoendocrine mechanisms: a review and reconsideration of research, in Greenfield, N. S., and Sternbach, R. A. (Eds.), *Handbook of psychophysiology*. Holt, New York, pp. 3–91.

Matyas, T., A., and King, M. G. (1976). Stable T-wave effects during improvement of heart rate control with biofeedback, *Physiological Behavior*, **16**, 15–20.

Mead, M. (1964). *Anthropology, a human science. Selected papers, 1939–1960.* Van Nostrand, Princeton, NJ.

Mednick, S. A., Gabrielli, W. F., and Hutchings, B. (1984). Genetic influences in criminal convictions: Evidence from an adoption cohort. *Science*, **224**, 891–894.

Meehl, P. E., and Hathaway, S. R. (1946). The K factor as a suppressor variable in the MMPI. *Journal of Applied Psychology*, **30**, 525–564.

Mellstrom, M. Jr., Zuckerman, M., and Cicala, G. A. (1978). General versus specific traits in the assessment of anxiety. *Journal of Consulting and Clinical Psychology*, **46**, 423–431.

Miller, G. A., and McNeill, D. (1969). Psycholinguistics, in Lindzey, G., and Aronson, E., (Eds.), *Handbook of Social Psychology*. Addison-Wesley, Cambridge, MA, Vol. 3, pp. 666–794.

Miller, G. A., Galanter, E., and Pribram, K. H. (1960). *Plans and the structure of behavior*. Holt, New York.

Miller, N. E. (1948). Theory and experiment relating psychoanalytic displacement to stimulus response generalization. *Journal of Abnormal and Social Psychology*, **43**, 155–178.

Minissa, (1977). Program by the *MDS (X) Series of multidimensional scaling programs*. University of Edinburgh, Edinburgh.

Mischel, W. (1968). *Personality and Assessment*. Wiley, New York.

Mischel, W. (1973). Toward a cognitive social learning reconceptualization of personality. *Psychological Review*, **80**, 252–283.

Mischel, W. (1977a). The interaction of person and situation, in Magnusson, D., and Endler, N. S., (Eds.), *Personality at the crossroads: Current issues in interactional psychology*. Erlbaum, Hillsdale, NJ, pp. 333–352.

Mischel, W. (1977b). On the future of personality measurement. *American Psychologist*, **32**, 246–254.

Mischel, W., Jeffery, K. M., and Patterson, C. J. (1974). The layman's use of trait and behavioral information to predict behavior. *Journal of Research in Personality*, **8**, 231–242.

Mischel, W., and Peak, P. K. (1982). Beyond *déjà vu* in the search for cross-situational consistency. *Psychological Review*, **89**, 730–755.

Mitchell, J. H., and Shapiro, A. P. (1954). The relationship of adrenaline and T-wave changes in the anxiety state. *American Heart Journal*, **48**, 323–330.

Moos, R. H. (1976). *The human context. Environmental determinants of behavior*. Wiley, New York.

Murray, H. A. (1938). *Explorations in personality*. Oxford University Press, New York.

Myrtek, M. (1984). *Constitutional psychophysiology*. Academic Press, London.

Nebylitsyn, V. D. (1972). *Fundamental properties of the human nervous system*. Plenum, New York.

Newtson, D. (1973). Attribution and the unit of perception of ongoing behavior. *Journal of Personality and Social Psychology*, **28**, 28–38.

Newtson, D., and Engquist, G. (1976). The perceptual organization of ongoing behavior. *Journal of Experimental Social Psychology*, **12**, 436–450.

Olweus, D. (1977). A critical analysis of the 'modern' interactionist position, in Magnusson, D., and Endler, N. S. (Eds.), *Personality at the crossroads: Current issues in interactional psychology*. Erlbaum, Hillsdale, NJ, pp. 221–233.

OSS Assessment Staff (1948). *Assessment of men*. Holt, Rinehart & Winston, New York.

Ozer, D. J. (1986). *Consistency in personality: a methodological framework*. Springer, Berlin.

Patterson, G. R., and Cobb, J. A. (1973). Stimulus control for classes of noxious behaviors, in Knudson, J. F. (Ed.), *The control of aggression: implications from basic research*. Aldine, Chicago, IL.

Pavlov, I. P. (1950). *Selected Works*, Gibbons, J. (Ed.) Foreign Languages Publishing House, Moscow.

Pavlov, I. P. (1951). *Collected works*. Akademiya Nauk USSR, Moscow.

Pennebaker, J. W., and Epstein, D. (1983). Implicit psychophysiology: Effects of common beliefs and idiosyncratic physiological responses on symptom reporting. *Journal of Personality*, **51**, 478–496.

Pervin, L. A. (1968). Performance and satisfaction as a function of individual-environment fit. *Psychological Bulletin*, **59**, 56–58.

Pervin, L. A. (1977). The representative design of person–situation research, in Magnusson, D., and Endler, N. S. (Eds.), *Personality at the crossroads: current issues in interactional psychology*. Erlbaum, Hillsdale, NJ, pp. 371–384.

Pervin, L. A. (1978). Definitions, measurements and classifications of stimuli, situations and environments. *Human Ecology*, **6**, 71–105.

Petersen, D. R. (1965). Scope and generality of verbally defined personality factors. *Psychological Review*, **72**, 48–59.

Plomin, R. (1986). Behavior genetic methods. *Journal of Personality*, **54**, 226–261.

Plomin, R., DeFries, J. C., and Loehlin, J. C. (1977). Genotype-environment interaction and correlation in the analysis of human behavior. *Psychological Bulletin*, **84**, 309–322.

Promin, R., DeFries, J. C., and McClearn, G. E. (1980). *Behavior genetics. A primer*, Freeman, San Francisco, CA.

Plutchik, R. (1980). A general psychoevolutionary theory of emotion, in Plutchik, R., and Kellerman, H. (Eds.), *Emotion, theory, research and experience. Vol. I: Theories of emotion*. Academic Press, New York, pp. 3–33.

Postman, L., and Tolman, E. C. (1959). Brunswik's probabilistic functionalism, in Koch, S. S. (Ed.), *Psychology: A study of a science*. McGraw-Hill, New York, Vol. 1, pp. 502–564.

Pratt, J. J., Wiegman, T., and Lappöhna, R. E. (1975). Estimation of plasma testosterone without extraction and chromatography. *Clinica Chimica Acta*, **59**, 337–346.

Pribram, K. H. (1971). *Languages of the brain: experimental paradoxes and principles in neurophysiology*. Prentice Hall, Englewood Cliffs, NJ.

Pribram, K. H., and McGuiness, D. (1975). Arousal, activation and effort in the control of attention. *Psychological Review*, **82**, 116–149.

Price, R. H. (1981). Risky situations, in Magnusson, D. (Ed.), *Toward a psychology of situations: An interactional perspective*. Erlbaum, Hillsdale, NJ, pp. 103–112.

Przymusinski, R., and Strelau, J. (1986). Temperamental traits and strategies of decision-making in gambling, in Angleitner, A., Furnham, A., and Van Heck, G. L. (Eds.), *Personality psychology in Europe. Current trends and controversies*. Swets & Zeitlinger, Lisse, Vol. 2, pp. 225–236.

Punch, J. C., King, M. G., and Matyas, T. A. (1976). ECG T-wave amplitude, muscle tension, and heart rate concomitants of conditional suppression, *Physiological Psychology*, **4**, 294–302.

Rapoport, A. (1972). The use of mathematical isomorphism in general systems theory, in Klir, G. J. (Ed.), *Trends in general systems theory*. Holt, New York.

Raush, H. L., Barry, W. A., Hertel, R. K., and Swain, M. A. (1974). *Communication conflict and marriage*. Jossey-Bass, San Francisco, CA.

Rosch, E. (1978). Principles of categorization, in Rosch, E., and Lloyd, B. B. (Eds.), *Cognition and categorization*. Erlbaum, Hillsdale, NJ, pp. 27–48.

Rosch, E., Mervis, C., Gray, W., Johnson, D., and Boyes-Braem, P. (1976). Basic objects in natural categories. *Cognitive Psychology*, **8**, 382–439.

Rosenberg, S., and Jones, R. A. (1972). A method for investigating and representing a person's implicit theory of personality: Theodore Dreiser's view of people. *Journal of Personality and Social Psychology*, **22**, 372–386.

Rotter, J. B. (1954). *Social learning and clinical psychology*. Prentice-Hall, New York.

Rubinstein, S. L. (1946). *Fundamentals of psychology* (2nd edition). Institute Filosofii Akademii NAUK, USSR, Moscow.

Rummel, R. J. (1979) *Applied factor analysis*. Northwestern University Press, Evanston, IL.

Rushton, J. P., Jackson, D. N., and Paunonen, S. V. (1981). Personality: nomothetic or idiographic? A response to Kenrick and Stringfield. *Psychological Review*, **88**, 582–589.

Rushton, J. P., Fulker, D. W., Neal, M. C., Nias, D. K. B., and Eysenck, H. J. (1986). Altruism and aggression: the heritability of individual differences. *Journal of Personality and Social Psychology*, **50**, 1192–1198.

Sanders, A. F. (1963). *The selective process in the functional visual field*. Van Gorcum, Assen.

Sarason, I. G. (1977). The growth of interactional psychology, in Magnusson, D., and Endler, N. S. (eds.), *Personality at the crossroads: Current issues in interactional psychology*. Erlbaum, Hillsdale, NJ, pp. 261–272.

Sarason, I. G., Smith, R. E., and Diener, E. (1975). Personality research: components of variance attributable to the person and the situation. *Journal of Personality and Social Psychology*, **32**, 199–204.

Schachter, S., and Latané, B. (1964)., Crime, cognition, and the autonomic nervous systems, in Levine, D. (Ed.), *Nebraska Symposium on Motivation*, University of Nebraska Press, Lincoln, NE, Vol. 12, pp. 221–273.

Schank, R. C. (1973). Identification of conceptualizations underlying natural language, in Schank, R. C., and Colby, K. M. (Eds.), *Computer models of thought and language*. Freeman, San Francisco, CA, pp. 187–247.

Schank, R. C., and Abelson, R. (1977). *Scripts, plans, goals and understanding: An inquiry into human knowledge structures*, Erlbaum, Hillsdale, NJ.

Scheier, M. F., and Carver, C. S. (1982). Cognition, affect, and self-regulation, in Clark, M. S., and Fiske, S. T. (Eds.), *Affect and cognition. The seventeenth Carnegy Symposium on Cognition*, Erlbaum, Hillsdale, NJ, pp. 157–183.

Scherer, K. R. (1982). Emotion as a process: function, origin and regulation. *Social Science Information*, **21**, 55–570.

Scherer, K. R. (1984). On the nature and function of emotion: a component process approach, in Scherer, K. R., and Ekman, P. (Eds), *Approaches to emotion*. Erlbaum, Hillsdale, NJ, pp. 293–317.

Schmale, A. H. (1970). Adaptive role of depression in health and disease, in Scott, J. P., and Senay, E. C. (Eds.), *Separation and depression*. American Association for the Advancement of Science Publication, Washington, DC.

Secord, P. F. (1977). Social psychology in search of a paradigm. *Personality and Social Psychology Bulletin*, **3**, 41–50.

Seligman, M. E. P. (1975)). *Helplessness: On depression, development, and death*. W. H. Freeman, San Francisco, CA.

Selye, H. (1976). *Stress in health and disease*. Butterworth, Boston.

Shepard, R. N. (1966). Metric structures in ordinal data. *Journal of Mathematical Psychology*, **3**, 287–315.

Shotter, J. (1980). Action, joint action and intentionality, in Brenner, M. (Ed.), *The structure of action*. Basil Blackwell, Oxford, pp. 28–65.

Shweder, R. A., and D'Andrade, R. (1979). Accurate reflection or systematic distortion? A reply to Block, Weiss, and Thorne. *Journal of Personality and Social Psychology*, **37**, 1075–1084.

Simonov, P. V., Frolov, M. V., and Sviridov, E.P. (1975). Characteristics of the electrocardiogram under physical and emotional stress in man. *Aviation, Space and Environmental Medicine*, **46**, 141–143.

Smirnov, A., Leontev, A., Rubinstein, S., and Teplov, B. (Eds.) (1966). *Psychologia* [Psychology]. Warszawa: Panstwowe Wydawnictwo Naukowe.

Snow, R. E. (1986). On intelligence, in Sternberg, R. J., and Detterman, D. K. (Eds.), *What is intelligence? Contemporary viewpoints on its nature and definition*. Ablex, Norwood, NJ, pp. 133–139.

Snyder, M., and Ickes, W. (1985). Personality and social behavior, in Lindzey, G., and Aronson, E. (Eds.), *Handbook of social psychology* (3rd edition), Addison-Wesley, Reading, MA, Vol. II, pp. 883–948.

Snyder, M., Tanke, E. D., and Berscheid, E. (1977). Social perception and interpersonal behavior: On the self-fulfilling nature of social stereotypes. *Journal of Personality and Social Psychology*, **35**, 656–666.

Sokal, R. R., and Sneath, P. H. A. (1963). *Principles of numerical taxonomy*. Freeman, San Francisco, CA.

Stagner, R. (1976). Traits are relevant: Theoretical analysis and empirical evidence, in Endler, N. S., and Magnusson, D. (Eds.), *Interactional psychology and personality* Hemisphere, Washington, DC, pp. 109–124.

Sternberg, R. J. (1978). Isolating the components of intelligence. *Intelligence*, **2** 117–128.

Sternberg, R. J., and Wagner, R. K. (Eds.) (1986). *Practical intelligence. Nature and origins of competence in the everyday world*. Cambridge University Press, Cambridge.

Stokols, D. (1978). Environmental psychology. *Annual Review of Psychology*, **29**, 253–295.

Strack, S., and Coyne, J. C. (1983). Social conformation of dysphoria: shared and private reactions to depression. *Journal of Personality and Social Psychology*, **44**, 798–806.

Strelau, J. (1972). A diagnosis of temperament by non-experimental techniques. *Polish Psychological Bulletin*, **3**, 97–105.

Strelau, J. (1983). *Temperament—personality—activity*. Academic Press, New York.

Strelau, J. (1984). Temperament and personality, in Bonarius, H., Van Heck, G. L., and Smid, N. (Eds.), *Personality Psychology in Europe: theoretical and empirical developments*. Swets and Zeitlinger, Lisse, Vol. 1, pp. 303–315.

Strelau, J. (1985). Temperament and personality: Pavlov and beyond, in Strelau, J., Farley, F. H., and Gale, A. (Eds.), *The biological bases of personality and behavior* Hemisphere, Washington, DC, Vol. 1, pp. 25–43.

Strelau, J. (1988). *The diagnosis of temperament/personality based on inventories and experimental procedures: Sources of divergencies*. Paper presented at the XXIVth International Congress of Psychology, Sydney, Australia.

Symons, D. (1979). *The evolution of human sexuality*. Oxford University Press, New York.

Teplov, B. M. (1964). Problems in the study of general types of higher nervous activity in man and animals, in Gray, J. A. (Ed.), *Pavlov's typology*. Pergamon, Oxford, pp. 3–15.

Terman, L. M. (1916). *The measurement of intelligence*. Houghton-Mifflin, Boston, MA.

Terry, P. G. (1953). Autonomic balance and temperament. *Journal of Comparative and Physiological Psychology*, **46**, 454–460.

Thomas, A., and Chess, S. (1985). The behavioral study of temperament, in Strelau, J., Farley, F. H., and Gale A. (Eds.), *The biological bases of personality and behavior* Hemisphere, Washington, DC, Vol. 1, pp. 213–225.

Thomas, W. I., and Znaniecki, F. (1927). *The Polish peasant in Europe and America*. (2nd edition) Alfred A. Knopf, New York, Vols. I and II.

Thurstone, L. L. (1944). *A factorial study of perception*. University of Chicago Press, Chicago.

Tomkins, S. S. (1980). Affect as amplification: some modifications in theory, in Plutchik, R, and Kellerman, H. (Eds.), *Emotion, theory, research and experience. Vol. 1: Theories of emotion*. Academic Press, New York, pp. 141–164.

Van Heck, G. L. (1981). *Anxiety: The profile of a trait*. Unpublished doctoral dissertation, Tilburg University, The Netherlands.

Van Heck, G. L. (1984). The construction of a general taxonomy of situations, in Bonarius, H., Van Heck, G. L., and Smid, N. (Eds.), *Personality psychology in Europe: Theoretical and empirical developments*. Swets and Zeitlinger, Lisse, Vol. 1, pp. 149–164.

Van Heck, G. L., Hettema, P. J., and Leidelmeijer, C. M. (1990). Temperament, act preferences, and situation preferences. *Nederlands Tÿdschrift voor de Psychologie*.

Van Heck, G. L., and Welvaart, A. W. (1984). Individuele versus algemene situatietaxonomieën [Individual vs. general taxonomies of situations]. *Gedrag. Tijdschrift voor Psychologie*, **12**, 15–29.

Van Lieshout, C. F. M. (1972). *Het vaststellen van stabiliteit in de sociale interacties van kleuters* [The determination of stability in social interactions of toddlers]. Unpublished doctoral dissertation. Catholic University of Nijmegen, The Netherlands.

Verhulst, J. C. R. M. (1987). *Weerstand tijdens psychotherapie* [Resistance during psychotherapy]. Tilburg University Press, Tilburg.

Vingerhoets, A. J. J. M. (1985). *Psychosocial stress: An experimental approach*. Swets and Zeitlinger, Lisse.

Volkart, E. H. (Ed.). (1951). *Social behavior and personality. Contributions of W. I. Thomas to theory and social research*. Greenwood Press, Westport, CO.

Von Bertalanffy, L. (1952). Theoretical models in biology and psychology, in Krech, D., and Klein, G. S. (Eds.), *Theoretical models and personality theory*. Duke University Press, Durham, NC.

Wallace, J. (1966). An abilities conception of personality: Some implications for personality measurement. *American Psychologist*, **21**, 132–138.

Wallace, J. (1967). What units shall we employ? Allport's question revisited. *Journal of Consulting Psychology*, **31**, 56–64.

Wicker, A. W. (1979). Ecological psychology. Some recent and perspective developments. *American Psychologist*, **34**, 755–765.

Wiggins, J. S. (1980). *Personality and prediction: Principles of personality assessment*. Addison-Wesley, Reading, MA.

Wilson, E. (1978). The nature of human nature. *New Scientist*, **5**, 20–22.

Winer, B. J. (1971). *Statistical principles in experimental design* (2nd edition). McGraw-Hill, New York.

Wings, J. J. (1979). *Respons-taxonomie* [A taxonomy of responses]. Unpublished MA Thesis, Department of Psychology, Tilburg University, The Netherlands.

Wittgenstein, L. (1968). *Philosophical investigations* (English edition). Basil Blackwell, Oxford.

Zajonc, R. B. (1980). Feeling and thinking: Preferences need no inferences. *American Psychologist,* **35**, 151–175.

Zajonc, R. B., Pietromonaco, P., and Bargh, J. (1982). Independence and interaction of affect and cognition, in Clark, M., and Fiske, S. T. (Eds.), *Affect and cognition. The Seventeenth Annual Carnegie Symposium on Cognition.* Erlbaum, Hillsdale, NJ, pp. 211–227.

Zuckerman, M. (1979). *Sensation seeking: beyond the optimal level of arousal.* Erlbaum, Hillsdale, NJ.

Zuckerman, M. (1980). Sensation seeking and its biological correlates. *Psychological Bulletin,* **88**, 187–214.

Zuckerman, M., Koestner, R., DeBoy, T., Garcia, T., Maresca, B. C., and Sartoris, J. M. (1988). To predict some of the people some of the time: A reexamination of the moderator variable approach in personality theory. *Journal of Personality and Social Psychology,* **54**, 1006–1020.

Appendices

Appendix A: list of situation concepts

abortion
accident
accusation
acquaintance (ship)
address/speech
admission (hospital)
adultery
air-crash
alarm
ambush
appointment
arrest
arrival
assault
assembly
assistance
atrocity
attack
auction
autopsy
bad luck
bankruptcy
battle
being a hostage
birthday party
blackmail
bombardment
boycott
breakfast
bribery
burglary
campaign

capitulation
carnival
catastrophe
celebration
childbirth
collection
collision
company
concert
conflict
confrontation
congress
consecration
conspiracy
contest
control
cooperation
coup d'état
courtship
cremation
criticism
crowding
dancing-party
deceit
declaration of love
defense
deliberation
demonstration
deportation
desecration (graves)
dinner
disaster

discharge
discussion
display of power
dispute
disturbance of domestic peace
diversion
divine service
divorce
drill
drinking-bout
duel
dying-bed
elections
emigration
espionage
evacuation
examination
exchange of thoughts
execution
exhibition
expectation
experiment
expropriation
failure
fair
famine
farewell
feast
fight
fire
flight
flirt
fornication
funeral
gala night
gambling
game
gathering/assemblage
gossip
guard
happening
homage
hold-up
holiday
house arrest
housekeeping
house-moving
house to house visit
hypnosis
ill-treatment
imprisonment

inauguration
inquiry
inspection
instruction
interference/disturbance
intermission
interrogation
interruption
interview
intimidation
intrigue
job
job application
jubilee
judgment
kidnapping
lawsuit
lecture
lesson
loss
lynching
manslaughter
making love
manipulation
marauding
market
match
meal
meeting/encounter
misunderstanding
mobbing
mobilization
motor tour
mutiny
murder
negotiation
night-duty
nursing
obscenity
observation
obstruction
occupation (of a place)
offer of marriage
officialdom
official inquiry
operation
ordination
orgy
outrage
overwork
panic

passage
pause
performance
persecution
phone call
physical violence
pilgrimage
plea
plundering
pop-concert
pregnancy
procession
protest
provocation
punishment
quarrel
queue
quiz
race
raid
rape
rapprochement/advances
reception
recreation
rehabilitation
rehearsal
rejoining
religious ceremony
rendez-vous
report
reprisal
resistance
retreat
retreat (for meditation)
reunion
revolt
rivalry
round-up
rowdyism
sabotage
sacrilege

sale (public)
seduction
seizure
separation
shipwreck
show
siege
slaughter
small intimate party
smuggling
strike
study
talk/conversation
teasing
tea-table gossip
terror
test
theft
therapy
thrashing
torture
traffic
traffic accident
training
transport
travel
travel by plane
treason
turbulence
turning night into day
uproar
victory
visit
voyage of discovery
walk
wander
wedding
welcome
work
wrong track

Appendix B: clusters of cues

Code	Clusters of cues
C01	working circumstances, promotion
C02	problems within the family, ignorance, misfortune, religion, (full) employment, housing problems, measures by public authorities
C03	adventure
C04	makes a profit, advertising
C05	get a new job
C06	commemoration
C07	start a new relationship, sexuality, diversion
C08	sanitary measures, nature-protection, developmental aid
C09	space travel
C10	technical trouble
C11	lottery
C12	struggle for power, politics, mismanagement, war, power
C13	offence, treason
L01	at home, living room, bedroom
L02	at the door
L03	sex club
L04	vestibule
L05	castle
L06	monastery
L07	houses, apartment-buildings
L08	shop, bank, post-office, station
L09	public house, restaurant, club-room, dance-hall/discotheque, hotel, cinema, theater, holiday cottage, camping-ground, hall, holiday-resort, canteen
L10	stadium/arena, swimming pool
L11	garage, town hall, office
L12	room for treatment/therapy, employment bureau
L13	library, museum
L14	hospital, church, industrial building, school, shelter, institution, street, square, city, village, district, abroad, The Netherlands, barracks, government building, police office, law-court, prison

(Continued)

Appendix B (continued)

Code	Clusters of cues
L15	highway, airport, harbour, frontier
L16	cell
L17	cemetery, crematorium
L18	forest, beach, park, island, mountain district, farm
L19	garden, grass-land
L20	in the air
L21	sea, river, lake, canal
L22	bridge, dike
L23	storehouse
L24	elevator
L25	crossroad, parking space
L26	underground shelter
L27	bathroom, kitchen
L28	desert

Code	Clusters of cues
CL01	rain, storm, snow, ice, thunder-storm, sun, coldness, heat, exposed place, overgrowth
CL02	traffic-signals
CL03	fog, stench, flood
CL04	fence, wall
CL05	remoteness, (on) unfamiliar ground, dark, noise, bustle, disorder, music, sound-box, tape recorder, in a row, in a circle
CL06	entertainments on a fair, buffet
CL07	pulpit, platform
CL08	divisions/sections/departments, desk
CL09	ticket-window/office-window, assembly-line
CL10	market-stalls, shop-window
CL11	altar
CL12	grave
CL13	table, chair, bench, bed
CL14	cupboard
CL15	fireplace
CL16	door, window, wardrobe, stairs
CL17	mirror
CL18	cubicle
CL19	clouds
CL20	worn (out)
CL21	rack

Code	Clusters of cues
P01	boss, workman, colleague
P02	business-man, politician, journalist, official, board-member, scientist, member of the jury
P03	soldier, police, judge/lawyer, guard, public authorities, group of activists, adversary
P04	nurse, doctor, helper, patient, clergyman, aged person, neighbors
P05	human being, man, woman, friend, acquaintance, spouse, parents, brother, sister, members of the family, child, foreigner, youth

Appendix B (continued)

Code	Clusters of cues
P06	member of a gang, spy
P07	prisoner, criminal, witness, the accused, fugitive, resistance group
P08	artist, teacher, pupil
P09	sportsman, trainer, crew
P10	office employees, notary
P11	farmer, fireman
P12	applicant
P13	supporter, referee
P14	waiter, driver, shopkeeper, seller, tourist
P15	hairdresser, counter-clerk, mechanic, household help, cook
P16	wanderer
P17	whore
P18	personnel of an undertaker's business
P19	baby
CP01	being wounded, having pain, being a victim, being seized by panic
CP02	uniformed, military service
CP03	being dismissed, being poor, being addicted
CP04	being homeless, hunger
CP05	being disabled
CP06	being innocent
CP07	being a loser
CP08	having a driving licence
CP09	dressed in warm clothes, being sleepy
CP10	being insured
CP11	being drunk, being impudent, losing one's temper
CP12	hilarity
CP13	being tired, being hard at work, being in a hurry, having difficulty in breathing, in a perspiration
CP14	showing discipline, having much experience, many persons
CP15	having been away for a long time, being far away from home
CP16	being friendly, know each other
CP17	being sick, being alone, being absent
CP18	being married, courtship
CP19	being pregnant
CP20	being naked
CP21	dressed in white, dressed in black
CP22	having finished one's studies
CP23	having failed in an examination
CP24	being a member of, being elected
CP25	being a volunteer
CP26	being disguised
CP27	working-clothes
CP28	wet
CP29	being lost
CP30	being unconscious

(Continued)

Appendix B (continued)

Code	Clusters of cues
CP31	evening wear
CP32	flush
CP33	fashionable
CP34	being rich
CP35	formal, being neatly dressed
CP36	long-haired
CP37	belonging to the nobility
CP38	having one's birthday
A01	surrender, comply, persuade, plead, deny
A02	push, remove
A03	send away
A04	abandon, separate, make a mistake, be frightened, lose
A05	lock, look back
A06	reassure, comfort, reconcile, apologize, approach, sigh
A07	record, predict
A08	prepare, exert oneself, help, assemble, have a look at, seek, be silent, discover, address, talk, listen, ask, inform, consult (with), advise, agree upon, make a proposal, take a vote, answer, pay, wait, smoke, drink
A09	assert, discuss, protest, criticize, judge, investigate, work, control, negotiate, instruct, call up, phone, write
A10	close
A11	travel, transport, ride, collect, distribute
A12	clean up, clear away, operate (a machine or an apparatus), take delivery of (the goods)
A13	die, bury
A14	awake
A15	pray, sacrifice
A16	kneel
A17	cure, save, take care of
A18	operate
A19	hitch-hike
A20	loan, look for work
A21	park (e.g., motor-cars), hire
A22	buy, sell
A23	expose for sale
A24	guess
A25	approve, offer, reward, encourage, perform on the stage
A26	enter, eat, visit, greet, shake hands, thank, serve
A27	give, embrace, seize, touch
A28	read, stay at home
A29	walk, leave, come home, call for a person, take along with one, meet, go out of the house
A30	ring (the bell), sit
A31	study, teach
A32	bike
A33	engaged in sport activities, exercise

Appendix B (continued)

Code	Clusters of cues
A34	camp, swim
A35	repair, build
A36	extinguish (a fire)
A37	sail, fly
A38	pack
A39	climb
A40	deliver
A41	save up (e.g., money)
A42	manufacture
A43	step in, step out, dress, stand, open
A44	bring, carry
A45	pick up
A46	jump, push
A47	creep
A48	lay
A49	undress
A50	take a bath
A51	go to sleep, rest, awake
A52	give birth to
A53	marry
A54	sexual intercourse
A55	declaration of love, make love
A56	laugh, joke, compliment a person, stand (drinks)
A57	celebrate, go out, dance, play games
A58	make music, sing
A59	cook
A60	decorate
A61	honour
A62	applaud
A63	dig
A64	unearth
A65	swallow
A66	cut
A67	force, require, ignore, refuse, quarrel, fight, call names, trouble (about), shout, disturb, stop a person, warn, offer resistance, instigate, ridicule, challenge, accuse, punish, forbid, curse
A68	break into (a house), overpower, collide with, hurt, destroy, threaten, deceive, snatch away something from a person, pursue, hide, arrest
A69	beat, kick
A70	lure
A71	use drugs, inject
A72	escape, liberate, guard
A73	throw, run, fall down
A74	demolish, hunt
A75	make a fire
A76	summon

(Continued)

Appendix B (continued)

Code	Clusters of cues
A77	strike
A78	occupy (e.g., a town, a building), take prisoner
A79	throw a bomb
A80	kill, shoot, rope
Ob01	car, train, boat, plane, bicycle, moped
Ob02	medicine, limb, animal
Ob03	telephone, story, motion-picture, photo, television, newspaper, rules of the game
Ob04	drugs, liquor, money, law, signal, damage
Ob05	art-object, monument
Ob06	clothes, food, book, letter, clock, paper, writing-materials
Ob07	form, announcement, document
Ob08	coffin
Ob09	corpse, stretcher
Ob10	narcosis, hypodermic syringe
Ob11	weapon, barricade
Ob12	tank
Ob13	banner
Ob14	instrument of punishment
Ob15	cage
Ob16	machine, apparatus, tool, materials
Ob17	measuring-instrument
Ob18	map, luggage
Ob19	trace/foot-marks, telescope
Ob20	rails
Ob21	stone, metal
Ob22	rope, fire, water, ground
Ob23	flag
Ob24	smoking materials, matches, bottle, key, lock
Ob25	perfume
Ob26	curtain, lamp, candle
Ob27	lavatory
Ob28	cloth
Ob29	wood
Ob30	tent
Ob31	sports goods
Ob32	merchandise
Ob33	cost price
Ob34	seal
Ob35	cash-desk, counter
Ob36	detergent
Ob37	crockery, cutlery
Ob38	plant
Ob39	decoration, gramophone-record, musical instrument, flowers, presents
Ob40	toys
Ob41	sweets

Appendix B (continued)

Code	Clusters of cues
Ob42	cane
Ob43	coach/carriage
Ob44	stage-properties
T01	in former days, sometimes
T02	regularly, often, in the morning, in the afternoon, summer, winter, short duration, long duration, during the week, every day, every week, every year, every month
T03	with a one year duration
T04	always
T05	in the evening, during the night, all night long
T06	suddenly, quickly
T07	in the week-end, feast-days, holidays, the end of the year
T08	the whole year, slowly
T09	duration of 15 minutes, duration of 30 minutes, duration of one hour
T10	duration of a few hours, duration of one day
T11	duration of a few days, duration of a week, duration of a few weeks, duration of one month, duration of a few months

Notes: C = Context; L = Location; CL = Characteristics of location; P = Persons; CP = Characteristics of persons; A = Actions; Ob = Objects; T = Temporal features.

Appendix C: clusters of situations arranged in terms of factor loadings

Clusters of situations	Factors									
	1	2	3	4	5	6	7	8	9	10
Blackmail, bribery, murder, sabotage, terror, interrogation, assault, ambush, defense	92									
Panic, intimidation, fight, outrage, disaster, atrocity, ill-treatment, display of power	91									
Attack, retreat, flight, treason, wrong track, boycott, resistance, imprisonment, torture, persecution, turbulence	90									
revolt, conspiracy, obstruction, espionage	88									
Accusation, uproar, interference/disturbance, alarm, teasing, quarrel	87									
Rowdyism, physical violence, thrashing	83							33		
Mobilization, coup d'état, capitulation, execution, house arrest	81					32				
Manslaughter, raid, round up, deportation, kidnapping	80					34				
Punishment	80									

(Continued)

Appendix C (continued)

Clusters of situations	1	2	3	4	Factors 5	6	7	8	9	10
Criticism, conflict	80	33								
Arrest	77									
Duel, protest, demonstration, provocation, lawsuit, confrontation	76	38								
Lynching, slaughter	75									
Plundering	75									
Being a hostage, mutiny, siege, battle, bombardment, campaign	71					33	36			
Interruption, disturbance of domestic peace, burglary	71									
Marauding, smuggling, hold-up, expropriation, theft, hunting	64				33					40
Sacrilege	64						−34			
Reprisal, dispute, rivalry	60	53								
Intrigue, deciet, manipulation	51	44								
Seizure, loss, bad luck, famine, assistance	45									
Traffic accident, accident	41				39	33				
Lecture, test, job application, examination, interview		79								
Appointment, talk/conversation, judgment		75	36							
Inspection, inquiry, job		75								
Instruction		70								
Work, overwork		69								
Plea, report	30	68		37						
Discussion, mobbing, cooperation, assembly, occupation (possession and control of a place)	48	66								
Negotiation, discharge		64								40
Training, deliberation, observation, therapy, exchange of thoughts		61	50				31			
Study		58								
Congress, lesson		58					32			
Officialdom	37	57								
Strike	48	51								
Failure, misunderstanding	44	49								
Control, guard	47	47								
Phone call		47	34		30					
Elections	31	47		31						

Appendix C (continued)

Clusters of situations					Factors					
	1	2	3	4	5	6	7	8	9	10
Experiment		46						31		
Quiz		46		34						
Collection		46								
Official inquiry		44								
Rehearsal		37								
Victory		36								
Pregnancy			81							
Dying-bed			74							
Seduction, declaration of love, making love, adultery, rape			71					46		
Divorce			70							
Abortion			68							
Childbirth			66							
Offer of marriage			66							
Gossip, rejoining			66							
Wedding			65	43						
Courtship, flirt, carnival			61					42		
Small intimate party			57	37						
Meeting/encounter, welcome, rendez-vous, rapprochement/advances, travel, visit, emigration		34	56	45	39					
Acquaintance(ship)		40	55							
Expectation		36	50							
House to house visit			47						30	
Rehabilitation			38						33	
Reception, dancing-party, inauguration				83						
Dinner, jubilee, reunion				82						
Consecration, company, happening, celebration, procession, ordination				75						
Gala night, birthday party				74						
Feast, homage			38	73						
Concert, pop-concert				62						
Address/speech, gathering/assemblage		51		57						
Diversion, show, performance				49				35		
Game, recreation				40	31	−30	38			
Tea-table gossip				39						
Intermission			32	37						

(Continued)

Appendix C (continued)

Clusters of situations	Factors									
	1	2	3	4	5	6	7	8	9	10
Motor tour, travel by plane, holiday, transport, wander, passage, voyage of discovery					76					
Farewell, arrival, walk					60					
Traffic, queue					57					
Pilgrimage, retreat (for meditation)					53	30				
Shipwreck, catastrophe					52	41				
Evacuation					48					
Collision, air-crash, fire					45	42				
Pause					31					
Funeral, cremation, religious ceremony, divine service						75				
Autopsy						73				
Desecration of graves						58				
Crowding						− 30				
Contest, match				32			56			
Race							54			
Drill							45			
Fornication, obscenity			36				71			
Orgy, drinking-bout, turning night into day			37	54			56			
Night-duty							47			
Hypnosis						36	43			
Gambling							34			
Housekeeping			36					55		
Admission (into hospital), nursing, operation						41	31	43		
Breakfast, meal								38		
Bankruptcy	40	33								51
Market, auction, fair										50
Sale (public), exhibition		45								48
House-moving									31	36
Separation										− 28

Notes: Decimal points omitted. The 10 factors explained respectively 27.5, 21.4, 8.9, 7.7, 5.8, 4.9, 3.6, 3.3, 2.7, and 2.4 % of the variance.

APPENDIX D1:   dendrogram of 25 situations (see Chapter 4, Table 1) based on actions

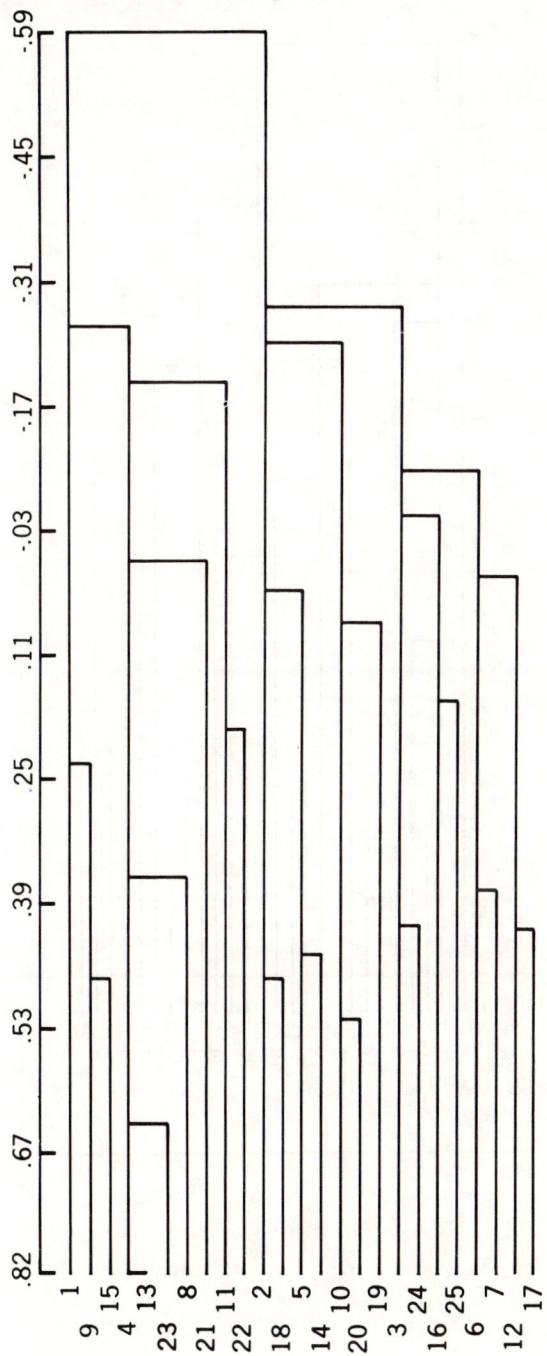

APPENDIX D2: dendrogram of 25 situations (see Chapter 4, Table 1) based on persons and person characteristics

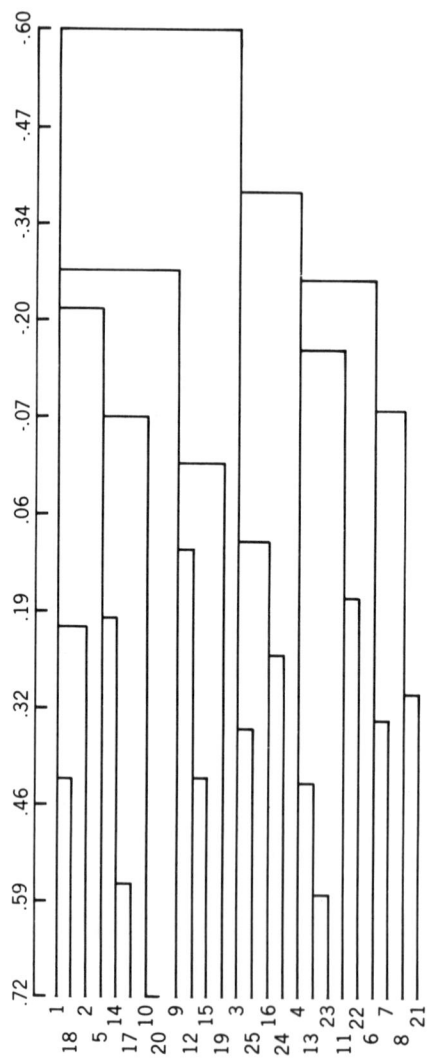

APPENDIX D3: dendrogram of 25 situations (see Chapter 3, Table 1) based on locations and location characteristics

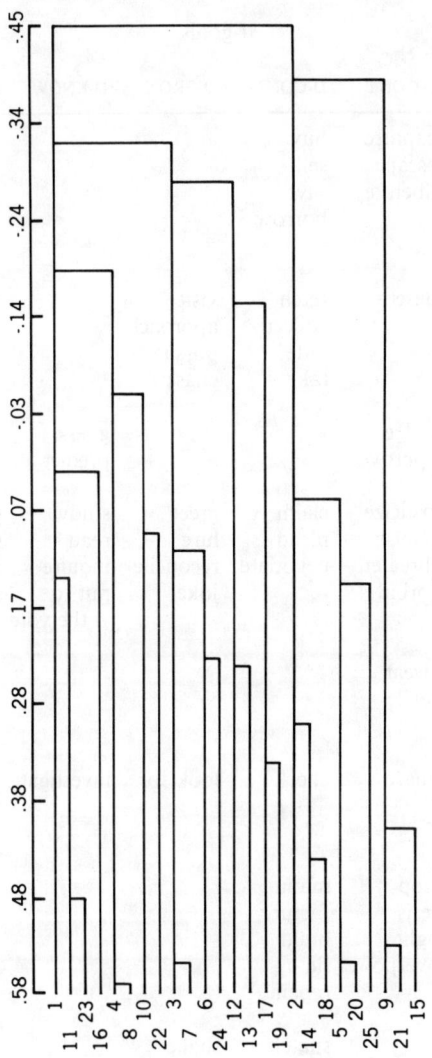

APPENDIX E: verbs classified according to primitive actions and d-goals

Primitive Actions:	GENERAL	D-SOC-CONT	D-CONT	D-PROX	D-KNOW	D-AGENCY	I-PREP
ATRANS	give offer regale	capture escape liberate	buy sell save borrow				
PTRANS	leave carry bring walk	desert	fetch collect hide take	visit approach pursue chase			
MBUILD	think write	judge approve			guess predict		prepare
MTRANS	talk inform answer address	criticize punish threaten forbid	claim plead negotiate	greet lure reconcile joke	study read inquire put to the vote	propose summon charge send away	deliberate discuss telephone
SPEAK	sigh laugh shout	swear revile					
ATTEND	listen watch look back	guard	check	look for	investigate		
PROPEL	strain push work strike	stop resist fight overpower	manu-facture build tie up repair				
GRASP	seize		snatch pick up take hold	shake hands touch embrace			
MOVE	jump sport dance swim			pet make love			

Appendix E (continued)

Primitive Actions:	GENERAL	D-SOC-CONT	D-CONT	D-PROX	D-KNOW	D-AGENCY	I-PREP
			d-goals				
INGEST	eat drink swallow smoke						
AWAIT	rest lie sit stand	go on strike ignore				wait for	

APPENDIX F: rank-order of primitive actions (F-a) and d-goals (F-b) in the prototypical package

| Situations | F-a Primitive actions | | | | | | | | | F-b d-goals | | | | | |
	ATRANS	PTRANS	MBUILD	MTRANS	SPEAK	ATTEND	PROPEL	GRASP	AWAIT	D-SOCCONT	D-CONT	D-PROX	D-KNOW	D-AGENCY	I-PREP
Accusation	8	$1\frac{1}{2}$	9	5	$1\frac{1}{2}$	4	7	6	3	1	2	6	4	3	5
Interference	8	4	9	5	7	6	$1\frac{1}{2}$	3	$1\frac{1}{2}$	1	2	4	5	3	6
Quarrel	7	6	8	$2\frac{1}{2}$	1	9	4	$2\frac{1}{2}$	5	1	2	5	6	4	3
Criticism	8	9	$6\frac{1}{2}$	3	2	4	5	6	1	1	$2\frac{1}{2}$	6	$2\frac{1}{2}$	4	5
Conflict	7	8	9	3	2	6	5	4	1	1	2	6	5	4	3
Intrigue	$6\frac{1}{2}$	2	9	1	5	$6\frac{1}{2}$	3	8	4	$1\frac{1}{2}$	$1\frac{1}{2}$	$4\frac{1}{2}$	6	$4\frac{1}{2}$	3
Deceit	6	$7\frac{1}{2}$	4	1	4	9	2	$7\frac{1}{2}$	4	5	1	3	4	6	2
Manipulation	7	8	4	1	5	6	3	9	2	2	1	6	5	4	3
Lecture	5	7	$1\frac{1}{2}$	3	$1\frac{1}{2}$	$8\frac{1}{2}$	$8\frac{1}{2}$	6	4	$4\frac{1}{2}$	2	6	1	$4\frac{1}{2}$	3
Job application	8	$4\frac{1}{2}$	1	2	9	3	6	$4\frac{1}{2}$	7	6	3	5	2	4	1
Examination	9	8	1	2	7	3	5	4	6	3	3	6	1	5	3
Interview	8	7	1	3	5	6	4	9	2	6	4	4	2	4	1
Appointment	5	7	4	2	$8\frac{1}{2}$	1	6	$8\frac{1}{2}$	3	4	3	6	5	2	1
Talk	$5\frac{1}{2}$	7	2	1	3	10	$5\frac{1}{2}$	8	4	4	3	2	5	6	1

Judgment	7	8½	2	1	3	5½	5½	8½	4	2½	2½	6	2½	5	2½
Plea	6	9	4	1½	5	7½	1½	7½	3	3	1	5	4	6	2
Report	8	4	1	2	9	3	6	5	7	6	3	5	1	4	2
Discussion	5	9	2	1	3	6½	6½	8	4	4	2	6	3	5	1
Cooperation	4	8	2	1	8	6	5	8	3	5½	3½	2	3½	5½	1
Assembly	9	5½	1	3	8	4	7	5½	2	5	2	3½	3½	6	1
Negotiation	6	7	2	1	5	8	9	4	3	5½	1½	5½	3	4	1½
Discharge	9	8	6	2	1	7	5	4	3	1	2	5½	5½	3	4
Deliberation	4	6	2	1	9	5	8	7	3	5½	2	5½	4	3	1
Observation	4	6½	2	4	8½	1	4	8½	6½	5	3	3	1	6	3
Thought exchange	6	8	2	1	9	3½	3½	5	7	6	4	3	2	5	1
Officialdom	9	3	1½	4	8	1½	6	5	7	5	2	6	3	4	1
Failure	6½	9	1½	6½	4½	1½	8	4½	3	2	5½	5½	1	3	4
Misunderstanding	4	5	1½	3	7	8	6	9	1½	1	3	4	6	5	2
Meeting	4	5	3	1	9	2	7	6	8	6	4	2½	2½	5	1
Rendez-vous	4	1	3	2	7	8	5	9	6	6	4½	2	4½	3	1
Rapprochement	6½	4	1	2	9	5	6½	3	8	6	5	1	4	3	2
Address	5	6	4	1	3	7	9	8	2	4	1	6	4	4	2
Gathering	7	4	3	1½	6	8	5	9	1½	4	1	6	2½	5	2½

Author index

Subject index

Page numbers in **bold** refer to definitions.